More Praise for *Readers at Risk*

"Jack Umstatter shares a treasure trove of practical and vigorous activities that spark the interest level of all readers . . . a golden opportunity to capture the wonder, foster critical thinking, and realize results for all students. Teachers will embrace the chance to teach meaningful and purposeful lessons that engage students. It's an invitation to learn!"—Linda Lippman, Ed.D., director of human resources, Islip Union Free School District, New York

"*Readers at Risk* contains activities that will aid both the student with limited reading ability as well as the reluctant reader, particularly as they develop strategies for comprehending nonfiction. The across-the-curriculum passages and related activities are excellent."—Tom Hall, principal, Bromfield High School, Harvard, Massachusetts

Jossey-Bass Teacher

Jossey-Bass Teacher provides K–12 teachers with essential knowledge and tools to create a positive and lifelong impact on student learning. Trusted and experienced educational mentors offer practical classroom-tested and theory-based teaching resources for improving teaching practice in a broad range of grade levels and subject areas. From one educator to another, we want to be your first source to make every day your best day in teaching. *Jossey-Bass Teacher* resources serve two types of informational needs—essential knowledge and essential tools.

Essential knowledge resources provide the foundation, strategies, and methods from which teachers may design curriculum and instruction to challenge and excite their students. Connecting theory to practice, essential knowledge books rely on a solid research base and time-tested methods, offering the best ideas and guidance from many of the most experienced and well-respected experts in the field.

Essential tools save teachers time and effort by offering proven, ready-to-use materials for in-class use. Our publications include activities, assessments, exercises, instruments, games, ready reference, and more. They enhance an entire course of study, a weekly lesson, or a daily plan. These essential tools provide insightful, practical, and comprehensive materials on topics that matter most to K–12 teachers.

Readers *at* Risk

160 Activities to Develop Language Arts Skills in the Inclusive Classroom

JACK UMSTATTER

JOSSEY-BASS
A Wiley Imprint
www.josseybass.com

Published by Jossey-Bass
A Wiley Imprint
989 Market Street, San Francisco, CA 94103-1741   www.josseybass.com

ISBN-13: 9780787975494
ISBN: 0-7879-7549-4

Printed in the United States of America

FIRST EDITION
PB Printing   10 9 8 7 6 5 4 3 2 1

ABOUT THIS RESOURCE

Mark Twain once said, "The man who does not read good books has no advantage over the man who cannot read them." Twain, an intelligent, articulate, well-read man, could easily say and live these words, for reading was an enjoyable activity for him. Good books and the thoughts found within them were his constant companions. Unfortunately, for many of today's students, comprehending good books and the beauty of their ideas and characters is nearly impossible. Simply stated, they just do not find reading enjoyable. Instead, reading is often an arduous and unrewarding task, one that many poor readers try to avoid at all costs. Many have nearly given up trying to read because they have been so unsuccessful at it. The reading problems of these reluctant readers include vocabulary, word recognition, interpretation, sequence, details, and a host of other obstacles.

The politician, essayist, and writer Joseph Addison remarked, "Reading is to the mind what exercise is to the body." In other words, reading is a necessity. Today's job market requires that your students be better educated than any other group of students before them. Students who lack the essential reading skills will fall dramatically behind those who can read well. How do we start to change the course of their reading experiences—and perhaps the course of their academic, social, and financial lives?

Let us start with words, the foundation of reading. "Building Words," the first of the seven sections in *Readers at Risk,* will help students recognize and identify words better through the thirty-two activities that cover prefixes, roots, suffixes, spelling, and analogies.

The seventeen activities in the second section, "Making Sense with Words," are intended to expand students' knowledge and recognition of words, as well as their meanings and usage. Activities feature idioms, connotations, word origins, homophones, paraphrasing, and other vocabulary expanders.

Section Three, "Becoming a Better Reader," contains twenty-three exercises to inspire greater reading confidence. Here readers will focus on detecting the key words in a sentence, recognizing a sentence's tone, and appreciating the various strategies writers use to interest readers from the start. This section also features several cloze reading, sequence, and cause-and-effect activities.

The fourth section, "Reading Comprehension in Math and Science Classes," contains twenty-eight activities. Starting with terms used in math class, the section also presents other math-related activities such as algebra, computation, and probability. The main focus of this section is on science reading comprehension. Cloze reading activities on crocodiles, bats, salamanders, and sharks are sure to interest and excite students. Ghosts, vampires, phobias, snakes, rain forests, and caving are other featured topics that your students will enjoy. Nature's wonders are discussed in activities focused on global warming, tornadoes, the eruption of Krakatoa, and the Tunguska event.

Section Five, "Reading Comprehension in Social Studies Classes," will help students understand more about comparisons between Presidents Lincoln and Kennedy, civil disobedience, Lincoln's Gettysburg Address, the Black Death, and the Tower of London. Two-part activities on aviator Amelia Earhart and the Roman gladiators and a three-part activity on John F. Kennedy's 1961 inaugural address give students practice in understanding both historical stories and primary documents—key components of success in social studies courses.

Biographies, controversial social issues, business predicaments, and stories about fun activities account for many of the twenty-three activities in Section Six, "Reading Comprehension in Biography and Current Affairs." When reading about Superman, Harry Houdini, Barry Bonds, Jackie Robinson, Muhammad Ali, or Lance Armstrong, students will become more proficient at looking for details, understanding an author's purpose, and interpreting meaning, all in an enjoyable way. Articles about hip-hop, skateboarding, fashions, and video games are sure to pique their interests.

The concluding section, "Reading Comprehension in Language Arts Classes," features twenty-one activities focused on topics ranging from terms used in English and fine arts classes to a story about Harry Potter's creator, J. K. Rowling. Students will also read about Romeo and Juliet, Frankenstein, and Macbeth. These, plus an advice column and the works of several poets, will help students expand their literary knowledge, interpret works of literature, and detect details more astutely and confidently.

Each of the 160 ready-to-use activities provides students with the skills to become more proficient readers. Numerous activities include a self-check component, which might be a riddle, a hidden quotation, or a mathematical sum. The many crossword puzzles and magic squares provide interesting strategies to enhance the students' reading experiences. All these activities provide students with reading across the curriculum on topics that really interest them. As their skills and reading abilities improve, students will enjoy reading more and approach reading more confidently. And since each activity is ready-to-use and comes with its own answer key, you will save yourself much time, a commodity in short supply in the hectic life of today's educator.

More than a century ago, the writer Martin Farquhar Tupper said, "A good book is the best of friends, the same today and for ever." The activities and skills found in *Readers at Risk* will provide your students with the means to make many best friends. I am certain that these newfound relationships will be both rewarding and long-lasting.

Jack Umstatter

ABOUT THE AUTHOR

Jack Umstatter has taught English at both the junior and senior high school levels since 1972. He has also taught education at Dowling College in Oakdale, New York, for fourteen years and writing and literature at Suffolk County Community College for three years. He currently teaches English in the Cold Spring Harbor School District on Long Island, New York.

Jack graduated from Manhattan College with a bachelor's degree in English and completed his master's degree in English at the State University of New York at Stony Brook. He earned his educational administration degree at Long Island University.

Jack has been named Teacher of the Year several times, was elected to *Who's Who Among America's Teachers,* and is listed in *Contemporary Authors.* He has taught all levels of secondary English classes, including honors and Advanced Placement classes. As coach of the high school's academic team, the Brainstormers, he led the team in capturing the Long Island and New York State championships. His teams have also competed in the Questions Unlimited National Academic Championships in New Orleans and Los Angeles.

Jack's other publications include *201 Ready-to-Use Word Games for the English Classroom* (1994), *Brain Games!* (1996), *Hooked on English!* (1997), the six-volume *Writing Skills Curriculum Library* (1999), *Grammar Grabbers!* (2000), *English Brainstormers!* (2002), and *Words, Words, Words* (2003), all published by Jossey-Bass.

ACKNOWLEDGMENTS

My special thanks go to my wife, Chris, for her constant involvement and assistance throughout the writing of this book. You helped make this a memorable project.

Thanks once again to Dr. Steve Thompson, my editor, for his knowledge, enthusiasm, confidence, and care throughout this and other projects. You are always so supportive (and busy)!

Thanks to my publisher, Paul Foster, and the other Jossey-Bass staff members who provide these wonderful writing opportunities.

Thanks to the industrious Jossey-Bass team of production editor Joanne Clapp Fullagar and copyeditor Bruce Emmer for their guidance throughout the revision process.

Thanks to Diane Turso, the terrific proofreader, whose eyes catch what no other person's eyes can detect!

Many of the reading comprehension articles used in the text are from Wikipedia, the Free Encyclopedia, at en.wikipedia.org.

Certain definitions are from *Webster's New World Dictionary* (Third College Edition), published by Prentice Hall.

CONTENTS

Section Three   Becoming a Better Reader

Section Four   Reading Comprehension in Math and Science Classes

Section Five   Reading Comprehension in Social Studies Classes

Section Six   Reading Comprehension in Biography and Current Affairs

Section Seven   Reading Comprehension in Language Arts Classes

Section One

BUILDING WORDS

The thirty-two activities in Section One focus on word recognition and word construction. Students will rely on sight recognition in Activities 1 and 2. They will work on anticipating words in context in Activity 3. Students will spell words in Activities 4, 5, 6, and 9. They will construct words in Activities 7, 8, and 32. Activities 10, 11, and 12 allow students to anticipate cause and effect and other relationships, the last two through analogies. Prefixes, a major part of word recognition and word development, are featured in four consecutive activities (13 through 16) that list the prefixes alphabetically. The next thirteen activities do the same with roots. Activities 30 and 31 deal with suffixes.

The activities feature magic squares, matching columns, word finds, crossword puzzles, and other stimulating and enriching formats. The answer keys often contain self-check methods to give students immediate feedback and added confidence as they work their way through the exercises.

1 HOW QUICK ARE YOU?

It is time for a race. Let us see how fast and accurate you are in recognizing words that are exactly alike. In each row, underline or circle the word that is the same as the word in parentheses. Wait until your teacher gives you the signal to start. Record the time it took you to complete the exercise. Then check your answers and note how many were correct. Good luck!

1. (fool)	A. foot	B. fool	C. foal	D. fowl
2. (spine)	A. spine	B. spike	C. spoke	D. swine
3. (love)	A. live	B. level	C. glove	D. love
4. (shove)	A. shore	B. shone	C. short	D. shove
5. (missing)	A. milling	B. mussing	C. missing	D. mending
6. (water)	A. waiter	B. waster	C. water	D. waters
7. (gone)	A. gone	B. gold	C. goner	D. groan
8. (raven)	A. craven	B. raven	C. rayon	D. raved
9. (last)	A. least	B. lost	C. last	D. list
10. (whine)	A. white	B. whine	C. while	D. whist
11. (grease)	A. grease	B. greasy	C. great	D. greater
12. (lower)	A. lawyer	B. flower	C. allowed	D. lower
13. (sum)	A. mum	B. some	C. summa	D. sum
14. (least)	A. last	B. lease	C. least	D. feast
15. (first)	A. fist	B. fast	C. first	D. frisk
16. (smile)	A. smile	B. smiley	C. small	D. stile
17. (slam)	A. slat	B. slam	C. slams	D. spam
18. (wait)	A. weir	B. wail	C. waiter	D. wait
19. (grown)	A. gown	B. crown	C. grown	D. growth
20. (slipper)	A. slipped	B. slipper	C. flipper	D. slapper
21. (break)	A. bread	B. beak	C. bleak	D. break
22. (show)	A. show	B. shot	C. shop	D. slow
23. (sense)	A. senses	B. tense	C. spend	D. sense
24. (arrow)	A. allow	B. arrow	C. barrow	D. borrow
25. (hone)	A. hive	B. hone	C. honey	D. shone

Time elapsed: _____ minutes _____ seconds   Number correct: _____ out of 25

Name: _____ Date: _____ Period: _____

2   SOUNDING LIKE WHICH OTHER?

The English language contains some interesting letter combinations that make up various words. Try the *ough* combination in words such as *bough, dough, tough,* and *through,* and you will see the importance of recognizing words.

Recognizing words is an essential skill for you as a reader. This activity will test your word recognition abilities. In each blank, write the number of the word that rhymes with (sounds the most like) the first word in the row. Use a dictionary if necessary. If your answers are correct, the numbers in the blanks for each group will add up to 12. Enjoy!

Group One

A. _____ corps	(1) props	(2) drawer	(3) tarps
B. _____ plague	(1) plaque	(2) ague	(3) vague
C. _____ heard	(1) heart	(2) herd	(3) beard
D. _____ low	(1) brow	(2) tow	(3) cow
E. _____ ballet	(1) billet	(2) get	(3) okay

Total for Group One: _____

Group Two

A. _____ chalet	(1) wallet	(2) mallet	(3) bouquet
B. _____ tomb	(1) womb	(2) bomb	(3) comb
C. _____ very	(1) query	(2) berry	(3) cheery
D. _____ quay	(1) whey	(2) bay	(3) key
E. _____ though	(1) cough	(2) bough	(3) dough

Total for Group Two: _____

Group Three

A. _____ lover	(1) rover	(2) glover	(3) mover
B. _____ stranger	(1) anger	(2) manger	(3) clangor
C. _____ age	(1) foliage	(2) mirage	(3) gauge
D. _____ fury	(1) furry	(2) jury	(3) bury
E. _____ sieve	(1) weave	(2) grieve	(3) give

Total for Group Three: _____

3 WHAT A DIFFERENCE ONE LETTER MAKES!

Reading closely—in this activity, reading *very* closely—is important for many reasons, including logic and comprehension. Today, your eyes will have their work cut out for them, since there is one inappropriate word in each sentence that differs from the proper word by a single letter. Yet that one wrong letter changes the whole meaning of the sentence, sometimes in a humorous way. Read each sentence carefully, and then cross out the word that is off by one letter. Then, in the blank, write the word that belongs in the sentence, correctly spelled.

1. _____ The water lilies have grown beautifully in the pony.

2. _____ A hairy yeast chased the campers through the woods.

3. _____ These youngsters requested peanut butter and belly sandwiches.

4. _____ Very patiently, the magician pried to involve the children in his act.

5. _____ We are carefully looking for a winnow of opportunity to get the job done well.

6. _____ The carpenters installed the final window flame yesterday.

7. _____ To spice up the recipe even more, Mom will add more rhyme.

8. _____ Can you detect that willow of smoke coming from behind the counter over there?

9. _____ Three victims had been bitten by a poisonous wiper in the African jungle last year.

10. _____ Fourteen graduate school students attended the last night's seminal held in Fontell Hall.

3 WHAT A DIFFERENCE ONE LETTER MAKES! *(continued)*

11. _____ Our bus driver was inked by the selfish habits of the other drivers on the road.

12. _____ There was not a threat of evidence linking the suspect to the crime.

13. _____ My classmate's deport card indicated that she had shown significant improvement in two subjects.

14. _____ The commissioner called for wholesale chances in the way lawmakers oversee their daily operations.

15. _____ This cleanser will quickly rid your sink of dirt and crime.

16. _____ Some younger teens in your club are more outgoing than some of the otters in our club.

17. _____ Recent studies serve as evidence of a sport in the number of newly created jobs in our country.

18. _____ Could you please give me the gust of the short story that I did not find time to read last night?

19. _____ Do you remember the children's song titled "The Farmer in the Deli"?

20. _____ Our newspaper editor is pushing for a much-seeded change in the paper's format.

4   ONE LETTER DOES IT

Feeling hungry? Here is your chance to satisfy your taste buds (at least on paper). First, circle the word that is misspelled in each sentence. Then, in the blank for that sentence, write the letter that is missing from the misspelled word. If your answers are correct, when you read down the list of missing letters, you will have spelled out the names of three breakfast foods—and satisfied your taste buds!

1. _____ The dress was too lose on the lady.

2. _____ Those comittees will be meeting next Wednesday.

3. _____ Often audiences are turned off by such grusome scenes.

4. _____ Haloween is generally a fun day for most youngsters.

5. _____ Do not try to decive this very wise woman.

6. _____ I want to congraulate you on your extraordinary accomplishment.

7. _____ Could you imagine such bable coming out of his mouth?

8. _____ Ths is an unbreakable comb.

9. _____ How many of these myteries have you read?

10. _____ Will you write a reommendation for me?

11. _____ The humorous salesperson tried to sell us a vacum cleaner.

12. _____ Our attorney pointed out the town's neglgence in the accident.

13. _____ Seventh graders should be assigned at least four major wriing assignments a week.

14. _____ Would you please hand me some more wraping paper?

15. _____ Let us see if the community bazar is still open.

16. _____ Please listen to this morning's anouncements.

17. _____ As we all know, tonight is a very special ocasion.

18. _____ What an incredible and spectaculr feat!

19. _____ My extended family has always enjoyed picnicing.

20. _____ You are an essntial member of our team.

The three words you spelled out are _____, _____,

and _____.

5 LOOKING FOR POLES

Only one of the two words next to each number is spelled correctly. Circle the correctly spelled word, and write the word's one-letter answer code in the blank next to the number. Then copy your answer letters, in order, onto the line below item 25. If your answers are correct, you will see that they spell four words associated with poles.

1. _____ (n) library	(t) libary	
2. _____ (a) miniscule	(o) minuscule	
3. _____ (r) misspell	(k) mispell	
4. _____ (t) mitt	(e) mit	
5. _____ (i) monkies	(h) monkeys	
6. _____ (t) niece	(m) neice	
7. _____ (o) nickel	(a) nicule	
8. _____ (l) nineth	(t) ninth	
9. _____ (e) noticeable	(g) noticable	
10. _____ (m) occurred	(h) occured	
11. _____ (m) opportunity	(e) oppurtunity	
12. _____ (a) parallel	(l) paralell	
13. _____ (p) pasttime	(g) pastime	
14. _____ (r) peice	(n) piece	
15. _____ (s) potatoe	(e) potato	
16. _____ (s) recieve	(t) receive	
17. _____ (i) recommend	(l) reccommend	
18. _____ (c) rhythm	(m) rythm	
19. _____ (w) seperate	(f) separate	
20. _____ (i) seize	(c) sieze	
21. _____ (s) similar	(d) simillar	
22. _____ (h) speech	(f) speach	
23. _____ (b) tommorow	(i) tomorrow	
24. _____ (r) wierd	(n) weird	
25. _____ (n) writting	(g) writing	

The twenty-five letters are _____.

The words associated with poles are _____, _____,

_____, and _____.

6 SPELLING CAN BE MUCH FUN

You may not agree with the title of this activity, but if you do a perfect job on the activity, you will prove to yourself that spelling can be much fun. Circle the correctly spelled word in each row. Then write that word's one-letter answer code in the blank next to the number. Transfer the twenty letters to the line below item 20. If your answers are correct, you will see that spelling can be much fun!

1. _____ (s) address   (m) adress

2. _____ (a) acheive   (p) achieve

3. _____ (e) atheist   (o) athiest

4. _____ (r) autum   (l) autumn

5. _____ (t) beleive   (l) believe

6. _____ (s) cematary   (i) cemetery

7. _____ (n) committed   (e) commited

8. _____ (g) conceive   (t) concieve

9. _____ (o) definate   (c) definite

10. _____ (a) dispel   (u) dispell

11. _____ (n) embarrass   (v) embarass

12. _____ (c) extreemly   (b) extremely

13. _____ (t) Febuary   (e) February

14. _____ (o) fourty   (m) forty

15. _____ (u) friend   (i) freind

16. _____ (c) government   (a) govenment

17. _____ (h) grammar   (t) grammer

18. _____ (r) heigth   (f) height

19. _____ (u) independence   (w) independance

20. _____ (y) intresting   (n) interesting

The twenty letters are _____.

These letters spell out _____.

7   USAMNERBLC HET URNIENDELD WRDO

If this activity's title seems a bit odd, it will not after you have read the directions and completed these fifteen sentences. Each sentence contains one underlined scrambled word. If you can grasp the sense of the sentence, you should be able to unscramble the word. Write each of the unscrambled words between the parentheses. The first and last letters of each word are given to help you out. Gdoo lkuc!

1. The dolphins had <u>eenvr</u> (**n**_____**r**) been seen near this part of the island.

2. Five <u>uhlsbes</u> (**b**_____**s**) of corn had to be removed from the barn.

3. The train had been working its way through a major <u>swotnsmor</u> (**s**_____**m**).

4. Because of the <u>silamd</u> (**d**_____**l**) weather, we decided to move the party indoors.

5. Losing his temper, the outlaw pointed the <u>rvlreveo</u> (**r**_____**r**) at his enemy.

6. The <u>styur</u> (**r**_____**y**) machine could not be repaired.

7. After you <u>mcoelpte</u> (**c**_____**e**) the task, please bring the work up to my desk.

8. The boiling water <u>urldebm</u> (**r**_____**d**) and <u>ihseds</u> (**h**_____**d**).

9. She saw at a <u>gcenal</u> (**g**_____**e**) that her friend needed immediate help.

10. <u>hkniT</u> (**T**_____**k**) of an object in the room.

11. The soldier arrived in <u>aavdcne</u> (**a**_____**e**) of his comrades.

12. Crawling on all fours, the small children <u>esandek</u> (**s**_____**d**) around the large couch.

13. Her <u>galie</u> (**a**_____**e**) movements allowed her to dribble the ball with little trouble.

14. This was a <u>esnols</u> (**l**_____**n**) that Yvonne would not quickly forget.

15. Teddy stood <u>ilyd</u> (**i**_____**y**) by as his teammates ran through their drills.

Name: _____ Date: _____ Period: _____

8   MISSING LETTERS

Make sure your eyes are ready for this activity! Many, many letters have been left out of these sentences. Show your word-building skill by filling in the missing letters so that each sentence makes sense. Each line should be filled in with only one letter. When you are finished, share your answers with your classmates.

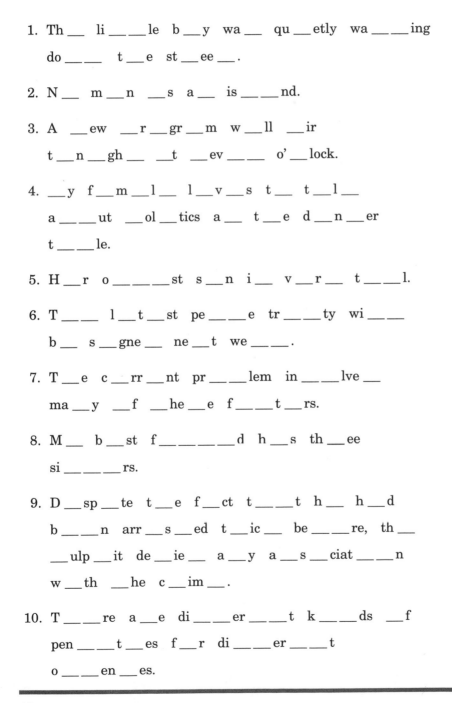

1. Th __ li __ __ le b __ y wa __ qu __ etly wa __ __ ing
   do __ __ t __ e st __ ee __ .

2. N __ m __ n __ s a __ is __ __ nd.

3. A __ew __r __gr __m w __ll __ir
   t __ n __ gh __ __ t __ ev __ __ __ o' __ lock.

4. __ y f __ m __ l __ l __ v __ s t __ t __ l __
   a __ __ ut __ ol __ tics a __ t __ e d __ n __ er
   t __ __ le.

5. H __ r o __ __ __ __ st s __ n i __ v __ r __ t __ __ l.

6. T __ __ __ l __ t __ st pe __ __ __ e tr __ __ ty wi __ __ __
   b __ s __ gne __ ne __ t we __ __ __ .

7. T __ e c __ rr __ nt pr __ __ __ lem in __ __ __ lve __
   ma __ y __ f __ he __ e f __ __ __ t __ rs.

8. M __ b __ st f __ __ __ __ __ __ d h __ s th __ ee
   si __ __ __ __ rs.

9. D __ sp __ te t __ e f __ ct t __ __ __ t h __ h __ d
   b __ __ __ n arr __ __ s __ ed t __ ic __ be __ __ re, th __
   __ ulp __ it de __ ie __ a __ y a __ s __ ciat __ __ __ n
   w __ th __ he c __ im __ __ .

10. T __ __ __ re a __ e di __ __ __ er __ __ __ t k __ __ ds __ f
    pen __ __ __ t __ es f __ r di __ __ __ er __ __ __ t
    o __ __ __ en __ es.

9 SWEET SIXTEEN WITH PLURALS

Of the choices presented below, only half give the correct plural form of the word. In each row, circle the correct plural, and then write the number next to it in the blank. If all your answers are correct, the numbers in each group will add up to sixteen—sweet sixteen!

Group One

A. _____   (3) x's   (4) xs'
B. _____   (4) monkies   (5) monkeys
C. _____   (2) brothers-in-law   (3) brother-in-laws
D. _____   (1) echoes   (2) echos
E. _____   (4) deers   (5) deer

     Total for Group One: _____

Group Two

F. _____   (3) crisises   (4) crises
G. _____   (2) woman   (3) women
H. _____   (3) roofs   (4) rooves
I. _____   (1) oxes   (2) oxen
J. _____   (3) gooses   (4) geese

     Total for Group Two: _____

Group Three

K. _____   (4) studios   (5) studioes
L. _____   (3) flys   (4) flies
M. _____   (1) tomatoes   (2) tomatos
N. _____   (2) soloes   (3) solos
O. _____   (3) mouthsful   (4) mouthfuls

     Total for Group Three: _____

Group Four

P. _____   (1) groupes   (2) groups
Q. _____   (3) facultys   (4) faculties
R. _____   (2) radioes   (3) radios
S. _____   (1) philosophys   (2) philosophies
T. _____   (4) babys   (5) babies

     Total for Group Four: _____

10 CONQUERING CLAUSES

Good reading requires joining ideas. Ideas are often brought together by the device called the clause. A *main* or *independent clause* has a subject and a verb and expresses a complete idea. A *subordinate* or *dependent clause* is not a complete thought and so cannot stand on its own. In the sentence "Because the turkey was so delicious, the diners asked for another serving," the main or independent clause is "the diners asked for another serving," and the subordinate or dependent clause is "Because the turkey was so delicious."

Match each of the twelve independent (main) clauses with its dependent (subordinate) clause. Write the letter associated with the dependent clause in the appropriate blank. Use each clause only once.

1. To get into the locked building, we needed to find the custodian _____.

2. _____, ask Mrs. Jenkins, our teacher, to assist you.

3. _____, the crowd erupted with loud applause.

4. _____, she developed lung cancer and died last June.

5. _____, Mr. Borritan spent two hours looking for it today.

6. Here is the flower arrangement _____.

7. _____, you need to send in your application this week.

8. _____, she becomes anxious and needs to take a deep breath.

9. We quickly perceived _____.

10. _____, the camper began to hear noises from the nearby woods.

11. _____, you will win $1 million a year for life.

12. The ticket _____ carried a fine of $100.

A. After Juanita scored the winning goal

B. Because he misplaced his wallet yesterday

C. As he crouched to fan the fire

D. If you need help with these math problems

E. If you would like to be a contestant on that television quiz show

F. Having smoked cigarettes for more than fifty years

G. that all the seats in the first ten rows were taken

H. that the traffic officer handed him

I. that we ordered over the phone last week

J. If you select the six correct numbers in the lottery

K. Whenever Monica sits for a math test

L. who had the keys

Name: _____ Date: _____ Period: _____

11 FINDING SUCCESS WITH ANALOGIES

Match the analogies from A to Y in Column A with their equivalent analogies numbered 1 through 25 in Column B. Write each letter in the appropriate space in the magic square. If your answers are correct, the rows, the columns, and the two diagonals will each add up to the same number. Five answers are provided to give you a head start. Find success now!

A =	B =	C = 18	D =	E =
F = 8	G =	H =	I =	J =
K =	L =	M =	N =	O = 14
P =	Q =	R =	S = 20	T =
U =	V = 10	W =	X =	Y =

Magic Number: _____

Column A

A. dirigible : air
B. quay : dock
C. margin : page
D. zoology : animals
E. pediatric : young
F. speedometer : speed
G. magician : wand
H. height : inches
I. human : arm
J. singular : plural
K. oil : lubricates
L. emerald : gem
M. harp : stringed
N. plumber : pipes
O. prefix : suffix
P. astronaut : space
Q. Sudan : Africa
R. patent : invention
S. tie : neck
T. glove : hand
U. baseball : inning
V. dune : beach
W. glacier : ice
X. immigrate : enter
Y. algebra : mathematics

Column B

1. glass : sand
2. explorer : land
3. electrician : wires
4. conductor : baton
5. geriatric : old
6. sock : foot
7. trumpet : brass
8. odometer : distance
9. botany : plants
10. sunscreen : face
11. submarine : water
12. emigrate : leave
13. Portugal : Europe
14. first : last
15. weight : pounds
16. doughnut : pastry
17. one : many
18. coast : land
19. hockey : period
20. belt : waist
21. octopus : tentacle
22. amendment : change
23. grammar : language
24. copyright : book
25. water : moisturizes

12   REASON IT OUT

Match the fifteen analogies in Column A with their logical partners in Column B. Write the two-letter answer code from Column B in the corresponding blank in Column A. Then copy those thirty consecutive letters onto the line below Column B. If your answers are correct, they will spell out an interesting sentence that deals with this activity's topic.

Column A

1. _____ bludgeon : weapon

2. _____ compact : car

3. _____ whole : hole

4. _____ shovel : dig

5. _____ college : higher

6. _____ general : army

7. _____ longitude : geography

8. _____ ball : sphere

9. _____ prologue : start

10. _____ *philo-* : love

11. _____ jeopardy : danger

12. _____ pediatric : young

13. _____ Italian : pizza

14. _____ catcher : baseball

15. _____ invention : patent

Column B

al. kitchenette : kitchen

an. basketball : game

ar. epilogue : end

ec. *soph-* : wisdom

en. Japanese : origami

gi. goalie : soccer

ha. harbor : safety

io. personification : English

ll. geriatric : old

ng. book : copyright

ns. pyramid : triangle

og. great : grate

st. admiral : navy

ue. elementary : lower

yq. crayon : color

The thirty letters spell out _____

_____.

13   PERFECTING PREFIXES (PART ONE)

Match the prefix from Column A with its definition in Column B. Write the corresponding number in the appropriate box. If your answers are correct, the rows, the columns, and the two diagonals will each add up to the same magic number. Enjoy!

A =	B =	C =	D =
E =	F =	G =	H =
I =	J =	K =	L =
M =	N =	O =	P =

Magic Number: _____

Column A

A. circum

B. bene

C. hemi, semi

D. hyper

E. dia

F. fore

G. ex

H. ambi

I. anti

J. dys

K. ante

L. ab

M. co (col, com, con, cor)

N. de

O. extra, extro

P. epi

Column B

1. beyond, outside

2. badly, ill

3. both, around

4. around

5. over, above

6. through, between

7. before

8. from, down

9. earlier

10. half

11. together, with

12. from, away

13. against

14. upon

15. well

16. out, former

14 PERFECTING PREFIXES (PART TWO)

All twenty-two answers in this crossword puzzle are prefixes. Write the answers in the appropriate spaces. The first letter of each answer has been provided for you.

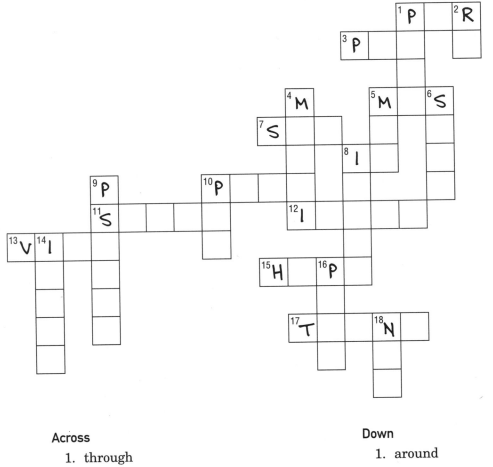

Across

1. through
3. before
5. incorrect
7. under
8. not
10. after
11. above
12. between
13. in place of
15. under
17. across

Down

1. around
2. again
4. many
5. bad
6. by oneself
8. into
9. false
10. forward
14. within
16. beside
18. new

Name: _____ Date: _____ Period: _____

15   NUMBER AND SIZE PREFIXES

Because mathematicians deal with numbers so often, they are quite familiar with number and size prefixes. Readers should also have a good knowledge of these prefixes to help them make sense of numerical concepts. For example, if a news article reported that a nation was celebrating its sesquicentennial, the reader would know that the country is 150 years old.

Match the prefixes from Column A with their definitions in Column B by writing the correct number in the square next to the prefix's letter. One has been done for you. If you have answered all the questions correctly, the rows, the columns, and the two diagonals will each add up to the same number. Start the countdown now!

A =	B = 13	C =	D =
E =	F =	G =	H =
I =	J =	K =	L =
M =	N =	O =	P =

Magic Number: _____

Column A

A. hept

B. sesqui

C. milli

D. cent

E. macro

F. tri

G. quadr

H. nano

I. micro

J. uni

K. penta

L. deca

M. oct

N. hex

O. bi

P. nov

Column B

1. one thousand

2. one

3. three

4. two

5. nine

6. large

7. small

8. one hundred

9. eight

10. one billion

11. ten

12. seven

13. one and a half

14. five

15. four

16. six

16 COUNTING WITH PREFIXES

Knowing number prefixes can help clarify specific details. In each of the following sentence pairs, the underlined word in the first sentence is formed with a number prefix. Complete the second sentence in the pair with the number indicated by that prefix. Use a dictionary if necessary.

1. Mr. Simmons was wearing a <u>monocle</u>. A monocle contains _____ glass lens.

2. Rafer Johnson was an Olympian <u>decathlon</u> champion. A decathlon consists of _____ athletic events.

3. My sister hit a <u>triple</u> in her softball game last night. That allowed her to run _____ bases.

4. The <u>octet</u> in this poem is very emotional. An octet contains _____ lines.

5. In 2076, the United States will celebrate its <u>tercentennial</u>. A tercentennial marks the passage of _____ hundred years.

6. The <u>Pentagon</u> houses many important military offices. The building has _____ sides.

7. Mrs. Robertson recently gave birth to <u>quadruplets</u>. The Robertsons have _____ new children.

8. This house has been standing for over a <u>century</u>. It has been here for more than _____ hundred years.

9. The rocket's interior took the form of a <u>hexagon</u>. A hexagon has _____ sides.

10. Poets often write verses in <u>tetrameter</u>. The lines contain _____ accented syllables.

11. Can you <u>bisect</u> this line for me? I'm asking you to divide it into _____ parts.

12. <u>September</u> was not originally the ninth month of the calendar year. It was the _____ month.

13. How many horns does a <u>unicorn</u> have? I count _____.

14. This <u>decade</u> just flew by! A decade has _____ years.

15. I have quite a few extra wheels for my <u>unicycle</u>. Yet I use only _____ at a time.

17 BY THE NUMBERS

An example for each of the roots in Column A is given to you in parentheses. That should help you match the roots in Column A with their definitions in Column B. Write each two-letter answer code in the blank next to the correct number. Then copy the thirty letters, in order, onto the line below the columns. If your answers are correct, they will spell out four words, each containing the name of a number. Underline the number portion of each of these words. You will have done this activity strictly by the numbers!

Column A	Column B	
1. _____ acer, acid, acri (acrid)	**at.**	bitter, sour, sharp
2. _____ ali, allo, alter (alias)	**es.**	star
3. _____ am, amor (amorous)	**et.**	self
4. _____ anim (unanimous)	**he.**	take
5. _____ anthrop (anthropology)	**ht.**	color
6. _____ arch (archenemy)	**ig.**	flesh
7. _____ aster, astr (asteroid)	**io.**	mind, will
8. _____ aud, aus (audible)	**me.**	short
9. _____ auto, aut (automatic)	**nl.**	man
10. _____ bibl (Bible)	**nt.**	love, liking
11. _____ bio (biography)	**om.**	hear, listen
12. _____ breve (abbreviate)	**on.**	chief, first, rule
13. _____ cap, cip, cept (capture)	**so.**	life
14. _____ carn (carnivore)	**te.**	other
15. _____ chrom (polychromatic)	**wo.**	book

The thirty letters are _____.

The four words are _____, _____, _____,

and _____. (Underline the names of numbers within these words.)

18   FLYING HIGH

It's time to go soaring! An example of each root in Column A is given to you in parentheses. Match the roots in Column A with their meaning in Column B by writing the corresponding two-letter answer code in the appropriately numbered blank. Then copy those thirty consecutive letters onto the line below the columns. If your answers are correct, they will spell out the names of six birds.

Column A	Column B
1. _____ cise (incision)	**ag.** people
2. _____ clemen (clemency)	**ar.** body
3. _____ cosm (cosmos)	**ee.** ten
4. _____ cord, cor, card (cordial)	**ha.** skin
5. _____ corp (corps)	**le.** tooth
6. _____ cresc (crescendo)	**nd.** run
7. _____ cred (credible)	**ot.** universe, world
8. _____ crit (critical)	**ov.** wheel, circular
9. _____ cur, curs (current)	**pa.** cut
10. _____ cycl, cyclo (bicycle)	**re.** truth
11. _____ deca (decade)	**ro.** rise, grow
12. _____ dem (democracy)	**rr.** merciful
13. _____ dent, dont (dentist)	**sp.** heart
14. _____ derm (dermatologist)	**wk.** say, speak
15. _____ dic, dict (diction)	**ww.** believe

The thirty letters are _____.

The six birds are the _____, the _____, the _____, the _____, the _____, and the _____.

19   LET'S PARTY

You're invited to a party! For each root in Column A, a word formed from that root is given. That should help you select the root's meaning from Column B. Write the two-letter answer code in the blank for each root. Then copy those answers, in order, onto the line below the columns. You will see that they spell out three party words! One answer has been done for you.

Column A

1. _de_ domin (dominate)

2. _____ dorm (dormitory)

3. _____ dox (orthodox)

4. _____ duc, duct (conduct)

5. _____ dynam (dynamic)

6. _____ equi (equidistant)

7. _____ fall, fals (fallacy)

8. _____ fid, fide, feder (fidelity)

9. _____ fin (finite)

10. _____ flex, flect (reflex)

11. _____ flu, fluc, fluv (influence)

12. _____ fort, forc (fortress)

13. _____ fract, frag (fraction)

14. _____ gastro (gastric)

15. _____ gen (genesis)

16. _____ grad, gress (upgrade)

Column B

at.   lead

ca.   end, ended, finished

cr.   opinion, praise

~~**de.**   master~~

de.   strong

en.   birth, race, produce

ep.   equal

in.   flowing

li.   faith, trust

mo.   sleep

nd.   stomach

ns.   bend

pe.   break

sr.   power

ts.   step

ub.   deceive

The answer letters are _____.

The three words associated with parties are _____, _____,

and _____.

Name: _____ Date: _____ Period: _____

20 ALL IN THE FAMILY

If you correctly match the roots in Column A with their meanings in Column B, your final answer will spell out the names of seven groups of creatures. Write the two-letter answer code in the appropriate space next to the number for each root, and then transfer the thirty letters, in order, to the line below the columns. Write the names of the seven groups at the bottom of the page. A word formed from the root is given in parentheses to help you along.

Column A

1. _____ graph, gram (telegram)
2. _____ greg (congregate)
3. _____ hema, hemo (hemoglobin)
4. _____ hetero (heterogeneous)
5. _____ homo (homo sapiens)
6. _____ hum, human (humus)
7. _____ hypn (hypnotize)
8. _____ hydr, hydro, hydra (hydrant)
9. _____ jud, judi, judic (judicial)
10. _____ juven (juvenile)
11. _____ levis (alleviate)
12. _____ liver, liber (liberate)
13. _____ loc, loco (location)
14. _____ log, logo, ology (logic)
15. _____ loqu, locut (elocution)

Column B

ac. earth, ground, man

ba. young

br. blood

ck. talk, speak

de. judge, lawyer

df. place

dp. same

he. write, written

kp. sleep

lo. word, study, speech

nd. light

oo. different

po. free

rd. herd, group, crowd

ri. water

The thirty letters are _____.

The groups are the _____, the _____, the _____, the _____, the _____, the _____, and the _____.

Building Words

21   PUNCTUATE IT

Match the roots in Column A with their definitions in Column B. Write the corresponding two-letter answer code in the blank next to each root. Then transfer your thirty letters to the line below the last question. If your answers are correct, they will spell out five "punctuate it" tools. A word formed from each root is given in parentheses as an example, and one answer has been provided to get you started. Good luck!

Column A

1. _____ luc, lum, lus, lun (luster)
2. _____ magn (magnify)
3. _____ mand (commandment)
4. _____ mania (maniac)
5. _____ mar, mari, mer (marine)
6. _____ matri, matro (matron)
7. _____ medi (medium)
8. *hh* mega (megalith)
9. _____ meter (centimeter)
10. _____ micro (microscope)
11. _____ mob, mot, mov (mobile)
12. _____ morph (morphology)
13. _____ mori, mort, mors (mortal)
14. _____ multi, multus (multiply)
15. _____ nasc, nat (innate)

Column B

ap.   command
as.   half, middle, between, halfway
co.   light
dd.   mother
em.   form
er.   madness
he.   small
~~**hh.**   great~~
ic.   death
io.   sea, pool
mm.   great
ns.   move
ol.   many, much
on.   be born, spring forth
yp.   measure

The thirty letters are _____.

The five "punctuate it" tools are the _____, the _____, the _____, the _____, and the _____.

22 AROUND THE WORLD

Feel like traveling today? Here's an easy way to go around the world. Match the roots in Column A with their meanings in Column B by writing the three-letter answer code in the blank next to the corresponding root in Column A. A word formed from each root is provided to help you along. Then transfer the forty-five letters, in order, onto the line below the columns. If your answers are correct, they will spell out five geographical names and their common association. You will truly have gone *around the world!*

Column A	Column B	
1. _____ neur (neurologist)	**áca.**	all
2. _____ nom (autonomy)	**aph.**	none
3. _____ nounce, nunci (announcer)	**cit.**	drive, urge
4. _____ nov (novel)	**del.**	straight, correct
5. _____ null (nullify)	**got.**	new
6. _____ omni (omnipotent)	**ibo.**	warn, declare
7. _____ ortho (orthodontist)	**ies.**	fear
8. _____ pac (pacifist)	**ila.**	all, every
9. _____ pan (panacea)	**lcu.**	father
10. _____ pater, patr (patriarch)	**nai.**	nerve
11. _____ path, pathy (sympathy)	**phi.**	peace
12. _____ ped, pod (pedal)	**rob.**	law, order
13. _____ pedo (pediatrician)	**saw.**	child
14. _____ pel, puls (compel)	**tta.**	feeling, suffering
15. _____ phobia (hydrophobia)	**war.**	foot

The forty-five letters are _____.

The five names are _____, _____, _____,

_____, and _____. All are _____.

23 ROLLIN' ON THE RIVER

It's time to hit the water! You'll find six ways to do so in this activity. Match each root in Column A with its definition in Column B. Write the two-letter answer code for the definition in the blank next to its root. A word formed from each root is given to help you along. Then copy the thirty letters, in order, onto the line beneath the columns. If your answers are correct, they will spell out the names of six things that are "rollin' on the river." Smooth sailing!

Column A	Column B
1. _____ phon (phonics)	**ac.** city
2. _____ photo (photosynthesis)	**ak.** follow
3. _____ plu, plur, plus (plural)	**ay.** feel
4. _____ polit (political)	**ca.** enough
5. _____ port (portable)	**di.** mind, soul
6. _____ prehend (comprehend)	**ek.** write
7. _____ proto (prototype)	**fe.** sound
8. _____ psych (psychology)	**ht.** carry
9. _____ reg, recti (regulate)	**hy.** break
10. _____ rupt (interrupt)	**ip.** first
11. _____ sat, satis (satisfy)	**ng.** straighten
12. _____ scope (periscope)	**no.** see, watch
13. _____ scrib, script (scribble)	**rr.** light
14. _____ sent, sens (sensitive)	**sh.** seize
15. _____ sequ, secu (sequential)	**yy.** more

The thirty letters are _____.

The six things that are "rollin' on the river" are a _____, a

_____, a _____ a _____, a

_____, and a _____.

24   TO AND FRO

Match each root in Column A with its definition in Column B by writing the appropriate two-letter answer code in the blank next to the root's number. A word formed from each root is given in parentheses. Then copy the thirty code letters, in order, onto the line below the columns. If all your answers are correct, they will spell out six words that contain either *to* or *fro*. Underline *to* or *fro* in each of them. One answer is already provided for you.

Column A

1. _____ simil, simul (similar)

2. _____ solv, solu (solve)

3. _____ soph (philosophy)

4. _____ spec, spect, spic (spectacles)

5. _____ spir (aspirate)

6. _____ string, strict (strictly)

7. _____ stru, struct (construct)

8. _²fr_ tact, tang (tactile)

9. _____ techni (technique)

10. _____ tele (telegraph)

11. _____ tempo (temporary)

12. _____ terra (terrain)

13. _____ therm (thermometer)

14. _____ tom (appendectomy)

15. _____ tox (toxic)

Column B

at.   like, resembling

ef.   wise

er.   build

¹fr.   heat

²fr.   touch

ic.   far

ll.   earth

mt.   breathe

ol.   skill, art

on.   loosen

os.   cut

ow.   draw, tight

ro.   look

to.   time

ty.   poison

The thirty letters are _____.

The six *to* and *fro* words are _____, _____,

_____, _____, _____, and

_____.

25   OUT IN THE WOODS

Here are fifteen roots that will help you to go, as the activity's title suggests, out in the woods. Match the roots in Column A with their definitions in Column B. A word formed from each root is presented in parentheses. Write the correct two-letter answer code in the blank next to the number, and then copy those thirty letters, in order, onto the line below the columns. If your answers are correct, they will spell out six types of things that you might find out in the woods.

Column A	Column B	
1. _____ tract (tractor)	**ak.**	turn
2. _____ trib (tribute)	**ar.**	conquer
3. _____ turb (turbine)	**bi.**	draw, pull
4. _____ ultima (ultimate)	**ca.**	call
5. _____ uni (unicycle)	**cy.**	one
6. _____ vac (vacate)	**es.**	come
7. _____ ven, vent (convene)	**he.**	disturb
8. _____ ver, veri (veritable)	**lm.**	last
9. _____ vert, vers (invert)	**mo.**	devour
10. _____ vest (vestment)	**pe.**	clothe, dress
11. _____ vict, vinc (victory)	**pr.**	empty
12. _____ viv, vita, vivi (vivacious)	**rc.**	pay, bestow
13. _____ voc (vocal)	**re.**	animal
14. _____ vor (voracious)	**so.**	true
15. _____ zo (zoo)	**sy.**	life

The thirty letters are _____.

The six types of things you might find out in the woods are _____,

_____, _____, _____, _____,

and _____.

26 RUNNING RAMPANT WITH ROOTS (PART ONE)

Match each root in Column A with **its** definition in Column B. Write the number for each answer after the corresponding letter in the magic square. Five answers are already provided. If your answers are correct, the rows, **the columns**, and the two diagonals will each add up to the same magic number. Run rampant and **have** some fun!

A = 6	B =	C =	D = 24	E =
F =	G = 25	H =	I =	J =
K =	L =	M =	N =	O = 21
P =	Q =	R = 22	S =	T =
U =	V =	W =	X =	Y =

Magic Number: _____

Column A	Column B
A. civ	1. year
B. cogn, gnosi	2. know
C. cosm	3. life
D. auto	4. flesh
E. ali, alter	5. bitter, sour, sharp
F. cide	6. citizen
G. arch	7. war
H. bibl	8. man
I. belli	9. time
J. bio	10. mind, will
K. cor, cord, card	11. love
L. anthrop	12. color
M. carn	13. universe, world
N. brev	14. kill
O. cise	15. short
P. acer, acid, acri	16. book
Q. am, amor	17. heart
R. clud, clus	18. hear, listen
S. aud, aus	19. sharp
T. chron	20. other
U. aster, astr	21. cut
V. acu	22. shut
W. anim	23. star
X. anni, annu	24. self
Y. chrom	25. chief, first, rule

Building Words

27   RUNNING RAMPANT WITH ROOTS (PART TWO)

Twenty-five roots are spelled backward, forward, diagonally, and vertically in this word-search puzzle. The clues listed below can help you find the words. The number next to the clue indicates how many letters are in the root. The letter next to the number indicates the root's first letter. Circle the hidden roots in the puzzle.

```
d d u c l c f q v h l c r e d f t k v r
r e i l q x i y c c j d b m e v t d z h
q d n i g b d k y g q j r k m q s r d x
r x u t k m k c h r d g r k j z z r v g
l q h r q n x b x a r q k p n s n v f g
e z w c l r k b z p k t c w k m f j p q
x y d h p y p b l h m p w z j p d q x y
f s n v l m b s r t v s r y n d v z x c
l y v f z t b l p n r y f r f z l r n t
g p n l s w q x b q d z q b z v n b p o
f k f m s q m t c p l d y z d t z g r h
r q d h j g f g l z d u e g o z g e v p
p x n g y r r l x r t r r r r a t v m m
g p e g h a t h e l l a f o m e h f i n
f o r t v s c m x d c u r h f r a c t
```

believe (4) c	equal (4) e	pleasing (4) g	tooth (4) d
bend (4) f	faith, trust (3) f	run (3) c	trick (4) f
blood (4) h	hard, lasting (4) d	say, speak (3) d	wheel, circular (4) c
break (5) f	heavy, weighty (4) g	skin (4) d	write, written (5) g
different (6) h	lead (3) d	sleep (4) d	
earth (3) g	marriage (3) g	step, go (4) g	
end (3) f	people (3) d	strong (4) f	

28 RUNNING RAMPANT WITH ROOTS (PART THREE)

Twenty-four roots are waiting for you to insert them into their proper places in this crossword puzzle. The first letter of each answer has been provided. Fill in the other letters as appropriate. Good luck!

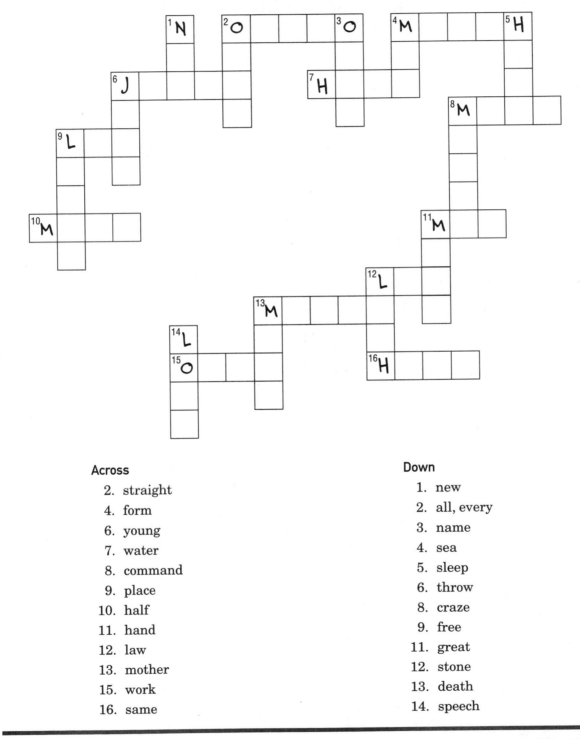

Across

2. straight
4. form
6. young
7. water
8. command
9. place
10. half
11. hand
12. law
13. mother
15. work
16. same

Down

1. new
2. all, every
3. name
4. sea
5. sleep
6. throw
8. craze
9. free
11. great
12. stone
13. death
14. speech

29 RUNNING RAMPANT WITH ROOTS (PART FOUR)

Match each root in Column A with its definition in Column B. Write your answers in the magic square. Three answers are already provided. If your answers are correct, the rows, the columns, and the two diagonals will each add up to the same magic number.

A =	B =	C = 17	D =	E =
F =	G =	H =	I =	J =
K =	L =	M =	N =	O =
P =	Q =	R =	S = 4	T =
U = 18	V =	W =	X =	Y =

Magic Number: _____

Column A

A. rupt (interrupt)
B. stru, struct (construct)
C. prim, prime, proto (primitive)
D. ped, pod (pedal)
E. port (transport)
F. vert, vers (convert)
G. plu, plur, plus (surplus)
H. scrib, script (scribble)
I. pend, pens (pendant)
J. phobia (hydrophobia)
K. scope (periscope)
L. pan (pandemonium)
M. voc (vocal)
N. satis (satisfy)
O. simil, simul (similar)
P. pater, part (paternal)
Q. tele (telegraph)
R. psych (psychology)
S. phon (phonics)
T. vac (vacate)
U. poli (metropolis)
V. spec, spect (spectator)
W. pel, puls (compel)
X. phil (philosophy)
Y. path, pathy (sympathy)

Column B

1. write
2. break
3. look
4. sound
5. like
6. far
7. enough
8. carry
9. urge, drive
10. turn
11. love
12. fear
13. call
14. father
15. build
16. empty
17. first
18. city
19. all
20. hang, weight
21. see
22. more
23. foot
24. feeling
25. mind

30 SETTLING IN WITH SUFFIXES (PART ONE)

Match each suffix in Column A with its definition in Column B. Write your answers in the magic square. Three answers are provided for you. If your answers are correct, the rows, the columns, and the two diagonals will each add up to the same magic number.

A =	B =	C =	D =
E =	F = 10	G =	H =
I = 11	J =	K =	L =
M =	N =	O =	P = 7

Magic Number: _____

Column A	Column B
A. cian (physician)	1. cause
B. ee (interviewee)	2. quality, realm, office
C. cide (suicide)	3. receiver of the action
D. esque (grotesque)	4. action, process, state
E. able, ible (renewable)	5. relating to
F. ence, ency (resilience)	6. kill
G. ar, er, or, are, art (author)	7. native of, relating to
H. ate (insinuate)	8. able
I. et, ette, illo (kitchenette)	9. female
J. al (familial)	10. action, state, quality
K. ance, ancy (maintenance)	11. small
L. cule, ling (minuscule)	12. like, in the style of
M. dom (kingdom)	13. skilled pratitioner
N. en (leaden)	14. very small
O. ess (princess)	15. doer, one who, thing that
P. an, ian (American)	16. made of, make

31   SETTLING IN WITH SUFFIXES (PART TWO)

Match each suffix in Column A with its definition in Column B. Write your answers in the magic square. Three answers have already been provided. If your answers are correct, the rows, the columns, and the two diagonals will each add up to the same magic number.

A = 2	B =	C =	D =
E =	F =	G =	H = 1
I =	J =	K = 9	L =
M =	N =	O =	P =

Magic Number: _____

Column A

A. ward (backward)

B. ize (materialize)

C. ite (Israelite)

D. ness (coldness)

E. ion, sion, tion (tension)

F. ly (fully)

G. less (faultless)

H. ish (foolish)

I. ology (biology)

J. ic (caustic)

K. tude (fortitude)

L. ile (juvenile)

M. ive (constructive)

N. ism (Judaism)

O. ous (generous)

P. ist (guitarist)

Column B

1. resembling, like

2. in the direction of

3. make, act on

4. without

5. of that nature, like

6. full of, having

7. one who, that which

8. study, science

9. state, condition

10. doctrine, belief

11. causing, making

12. relating to, suited for, capable of

13. action, result

14. state, condition

15. resident, dweller

16. in the manner of

32 PUTTING WORDS TOGETHER

Here's your chance to show how well you can put words together. The first part of a word is in Column B, and its second part is in Column C. Match the two parts, and complete the word in Column B. Then write in Column A the letter code for the part inserted from Column C. If your answers are correct, your consecutive answers in Column A will spell out a six-letter word, a five-letter word, a four-letter word, a three-letter word, and a two-letter word. Write those words on the lines at the bottom of the page. The first answer is provided as an example.

Column A	Column B	Column C
1. _f_	co_ordinate_	**u.** age
2. ___	di_____	**n.** al
3. ___	dis_____	**y.** ary
4. ___	en_____	**w.** commend
5. ___	extreme_____	**a.** convenient
6. ___	for_____	**h.** courage
7. ___	heal_____	**g.** ease
8. ___	host_____	**d.** form
9. ___	in_____	**o.** gress
10. ___	maxi_____	**t.** ly
11. ___	mean_____	**m.** ment
12. ___	move_____	**r.** meter
13. ___	no_____	**c.** mum
14. ___	norm_____	~~**f.** ordinate~~
15. ___	per_____	**b.** pass
16. ___	peri_____	**q.** thy
17. ___	pro_____	**i.** vision
18. ___	re_____	**s.** ward
19. ___	under_____	**e.** where
20. ___	vision_____	**k.** while

The six-letter word is _____.

The five-letter word is _____.

The four-letter word is _____.

The three-letter word is _____.

The two-letter word is _____.

Building Words

Section Two

MAKING SENSE WITH WORDS

The seventeen activities in Section Two familiarize students with more words, expressions, and idioms to help them improve their reading comprehension and appreciation. Idioms and other expressions are featured in the first four activities, 33 through 36. Students will concentrate on word connotations and denotations in Activities 38 and 39. Your students will find word origins of interest in Activities 41 and 42 and word and idea interpretations in Activity 43. Three activities (37, 44, and 45) focus on vocabulary. Three others (46, 48, and 49) clarify words that are often confused. Students will also enjoy constructing words in Activity 40 and working with adages in Activity 47.

Like Section One, this section makes use of magic squares, crossword puzzles, matching columns, and other interesting formats to pique students' interest. Self-check answers are provided here as well.

33 IDIOMATICALLY SPEAKING (PART ONE)

Idioms are those cute and curious untranslatable expressions that often have meanings unrelated to the words they contain. Idioms are more common in speech than in writing. Nevertheless, knowledge of their meanings is essential if readers are to grasp the intended sense of the reading passage. So let's review our idioms.

Match the idioms in Column A with their meanings in Column B by writing the correct number in the appropriate box in the magic square. If your answers are correct, the rows, the columns, and the two diagonals will each add up to the same magic number. So let's make no bones about it and cut to the chase. (Three answers are provided to get this show on the road.)

A = 12	B =	C =	D =
E =	F =	G =	H = 10
I =	J =	K =	L =
M =	N =	O = 4	P =

Magic Number: _____

Column A	Column B
A. a fly on the wall	1. I refuse
B. hocus pocus	2. pulled muscle
C. no dice	3. get to the main point
D. shake a leg	4. exact duplicate
E. wash one's hands of it	5. dying in great numbers
F. cut to the chase	6. reject present or future responsibility
G. green room	7. speak openly about it
H. go out on a limb	8. hurry up
I. make no bones about it	9. unemployed and collecting compensation
J. charley horse	10. take a risk
K. tie the knot	11. rich and well fed
L. living high on the hog	12. an unseen observer
M. on the dole	13. magic; trickery
N. put a sock in it	14. marry
O. dead ringer	15. backstage relaxation area
P. dropping like flies	16. stop talking

Name: _____ Date: _____ Period: _____

34 IDIOMATICALLY SPEAKING (PART TWO)

It is time to show that for you, mastering idioms is a piece of cake. Your future success will be in the bag, and you will not be running around like a chicken with its head cut off!

Match the idioms from Column A with their definitions in Column B by writing the definition number in the appropriately lettered box. Three answers are provided to give you a leg up. If your answers are correct, the rows, the columns, and the two diagonals will each add up to the same magic number. If not, keep your chin up, go the extra mile, and keep your fingers crossed!

A =	B =	C =	D = 10
E = 4	F =	G =	H =
I =	J =	K =	L =
M =	N =	O = 9	P =

Magic Number: _____

Column A

A. gilding the lily

B. top-notch

C. read the handwriting on the wall

D. hit the hay

E. in the bag

F. field day

G. over the top

H. like a chicken with its head cut off

I. keep your chin up

J. pipe down

K. Murphy's law

L. cup of joe

M. go the extra mile

N. escape by the skin of your teeth

O. raising Cain

P. Elvis has left the building.

Column B

1. exaggerating

2. avoid a risk at the last possible moment

3. be quiet

4. secured

5. excessive

6. coffee

7. "The show is over."

8. realize that bad things are going to happen

9. cause trouble

10. go to bed

11. confused; frenzied

12. "If anything can go wrong, it will."

13. remain cheerful in a difficult situation

14. a special or enjoyable time

15. excellent

16. do more than is required

35   A FEATHER IN YOUR CAP

You will earn a feather in your cap when you successfully complete this crossword puzzle featuring common expressions. Write your answers in the appropriate spaces. The first letter of each answer is provided. So get real, be quick on the draw, and raise the roof with this puzzle!

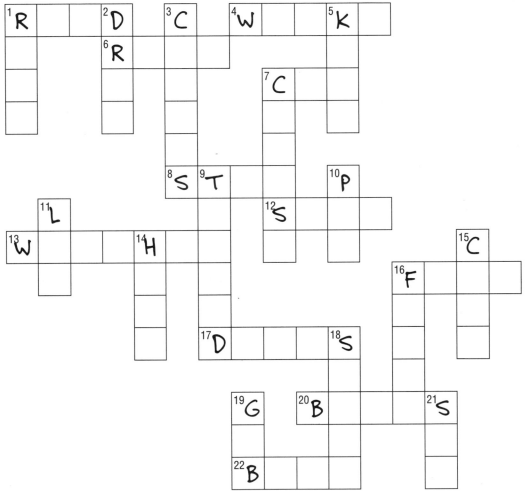

Making Sense with Words

35   A FEATHER IN YOUR CAP *(continued)*

Across

1. begin a trip; leave: hit the _____

4. a short nap: forty _____

6. have a good time; party: raise the _____

7. reveal a secret: let the _____ out of the bag

8. aim high: hitch your wagon to a _____

12. fail or succeed on one's own: sink or _____

13. sick or ill: under the _____

16. in a reversed situation: the shoe is on the other _____

17. sad: down in the _____

20. worthless; silly: for the _____

22. employ an illegal maneuver or unfair tactics: hit below the _____

Down

1. face the facts: get _____

2. sharp-minded: quick on the _____

3. let people know what you are really like: show your true _____

5. go away; stop pestering me: go fly a _____

7. typical; usual: par for the _____

9. be in a dangerous position: hang by a _____

10. admit guilt: eat humble _____

11. an advantage: a _____ up

14. the very last minute: the eleventh _____

15. the opposite point of view: the other side of the _____

16. deceitful: two-_____

18. suffer a great loss of money or resources: lose your _____

19. the ability to talk easily and interestingly: the gift of _____

21. unrealistic hopes: pie in the _____

36 EXPRESSING YOURSELF

You will frequently encounter idiomatic expressions in your reading. It is good to know the meaning of these expressions. This activity will test your knowledge of some common expressions. Match each expression from Column A with its meaning in Column B. Write the corresponding two-letter answer code in the blank next to the number. When you are done, copy the answer codes onto the line below the columns. If your answers are correct, they will spell out two more idiomatic expressions.

Column A

1. _____ bend over backward
2. _____ cakewalk
3. _____ cold feet
4. _____ dodge the issue
5. _____ done to a T
6. _____ egg on your face
7. _____ feeling blue
8. _____ foot the bill
9. _____ in the nick of time
10. _____ one brick shy of a load
11. _____ pulling your leg
12. _____ rolling in dough
13. _____ take the plunge
14. _____ turn over a new leaf
15. _____ winging it

Column B

ab. avoid the facts

ce. very easy job

em. embarrassment

eo. get married; enter a new situation

in. apprehension or doubt

lu. perfectly made

nb. pay for something

ne. start anew (usually in a positive way)

om. wealthy

on. do all that one can

oo. being sad

rs. joking

te. dumb

up. acting without practice or experience

ut. just before the deadline

The thirty letters are _____.

The two expressions are _____

and _____.

37   ACCORDING TO FORBES

Match each of the fifteen words in Column A with its opposite found in Column B. Write the two-letter answer code in the blank next to the number in Column A. One answer has already been provided. When you are done, copy the answer codes, in order, onto the line below the columns. If your answers are correct, they will spell out a quote by the magazine publisher Malcolm Forbes.

Column A		Column B	
1. _____ frigid		**as.**	puny
2. _____ excitement		[1]**ea.** ~~blurry~~	
3. _____ gigantic		[2]**ea.**	attach
4. _____ brilliant		**et.**	smile
5. _____ grimace		**he.**	humorous
6. _____ serious		**hi.**	conceal
7. _____ polished		**ma.**	dull
8. _____ rigid		**me.**	boredom
9. [1]_ea_ clear		**nm.**	relaxed
10. _____ ordinary		**re.**	charity
11. _____ greed		**rt.**	few
12. _____ present		**sh.**	unfair
13. _____ equitable		**su.**	bizarre
14. _____ disconnect		**to.**	torrid
15. _____ numerous		**ur.**	unintelligent

The thirty letters are _____.

The quote from Malcolm Forbes is _____

_____.

38 POSITIVELY—OR NEGATIVELY—SPEAKING

Twenty adjectives are listed below. Ten of them have positive associations or connotations, and ten of them have negative associations or connotations. For each adjective, circle the letter associated with the positive or negative association. If your answers are correct, the positives will spell a positive ten-letter adjective, and the negatives will spell a negative ten-letter adjective. Write those two adjectives on the lines indicated. Use the dictionary if necessary.

Adjective	Positive	Negative
1. charitable	(d)	(e)
2. malnourished	(c)	(d)
3. overwrought	(h)	(i)
4. prudent	(e)	(f)
5. selfish	(z)	(a)
6. mature	(t)	(u)
7. spectacular	(e)	(f)
8. officious	(a)	(b)
9. grisly	(n)	(o)
10. guileless	(r)	(s)
11. angry	(k)	(l)
12. overbearing	(h)	(i)
13. loving	(m)	(n)
14. sunny	(i)	(j)
15. inclement	(b)	(c)
16. furtive	(z)	(a)
17. mild	(n)	(o)
18. hardworking	(e)	(f)
19. arrogant	(k)	(l)
20. peaceful	(d)	(e)

The answer letters for the positive adjectives spell _____.

The answer letters for the negative adjectives spell _____.

Name: _____ Date: _____ Period: _____

39 FOR THE BIRDS

Readers expect that an author will use the most appropriate word to describe a person, an action, a place, or an idea. For example, although the words *guffaw* and *chuckle* both describe a type of laugh, *guffaw* would be the more appropriate word to describe a loud laugh, and *chuckle* would describe a softer laugh.

     Circle the more appropriate word for each numbered item. Then write the letter code for that answer in the blank. When you are done, copy the twenty answer codes, in order, onto the line beneath item 20. If your answers are correct, they will spell out the names of five birds. Thus you will have done this activity *for the birds*.

1. _____ a quick look: **(l)** glance **(m)** examination
2. _____ the more formal word for giving something to another person: **(a)** present **(b)** hand off
3. _____ beat or pound continually: **(q)** meddle **(r)** batter
4. _____ move in a sneaky way: **(j)** mince **(k)** slink
5. _____ excited: **(v)** content **(w)** gleeful
6. _____ extended in time: **(r)** prolonged **(s)** brief
7. _____ a brief encounter: **(e)** skirmish **(f)** ordeal
8. _____ easily frightened or jumpy: **(m)** complacent **(n)** skittish
9. _____ hard work: **(g)** snap **(h)** labor
10. _____ crowded together: **(a)** dense **(b)** spacious
11. _____ a handle or a grouchy person: **(v)** lever **(w)** crank
12. _____ kind and merciful toward others: **(j)** human **(k)** humane
13. _____ on time or suggest something to someone: **(d)** prompt **(e)** punctual
14. _____ total destruction or devastation: **(o)** havoc **(p)** fraternity
15. _____ an unsupported claim: **(v)** pretense **(w)** intense
16. _____ a person who is regularly seen at a location: **(e)** fixture **(f)** robot
17. _____ gather people for an army: **(f)** fluster **(g)** muster
18. _____ great evil: **(g)** peculiarity **(u)** enormity
19. _____ suppress or silence: **(l)** squelch **(m)** gratify
20. _____ sell by going from place to place: **(k)** pedal **(l)** peddle

The twenty letters are _____.

The names of the five birds are _____, _____, _____, _____, and _____.

Copyright © 2005 by John Wiley & Sons, Inc.

40   CONSTRUCTING FIFTEEN WORDS

The blueprint is quite simple. You will construct fifteen words by taking the first part in the numbered list and combining it with a second part from the word bank. Each first part is used only once. The same holds true for the second part. Write the appropriate word bank portion in each blank. Now start constructing words!

back	inate	nourished	soever
dreaming	lessness	placement	sole
fortunately	mental	sanity	theless
grace	national	ship	

1. dis _____

2. un _____

3. never _____

4. funda _____

5. inter _____

6. in _____

7. re _____

8. mal _____

9. day _____

10. care _____

11. con _____

12. dom _____

13. champion _____

14. what _____

15. quarter _____

Name: _____ Date: _____ Period: _____

41 WHERE WORDS COME FROM

Here's your chance to show your knowledge of where words come from. Match the word in Column A with its origin in Column B. Write your answers in the magic square. Three answers have been provided for you. If your answers are correct, the columns, the rows, and the two diagonals will each add up to the same magic number.

A =	B =	C =	D =
E =	F = 9	G =	H =
I = 13	J =	K =	L =
M =	N =	O =	P = 14

Magic Number: _____

Column A

A. humongous

B. Ivy League

C. scuba

D. hick

E. fender

F. debonair

G. Motown

H. malaria

I. dollar

J. funny bone

K. infantry

L. goatee

M. Jerusalem artichoke

N. howdy

O. ZIP Code

P. lunatic

Column B

1. an acronym for the U.S. Postal Service's Zoning Improvement Plan

2. its medical name sounds like a word meaning "funny"

3. bad air

4. a combination of *huge* and *monstrous*

5. an old rural nickname for Richard

6. short for *defender*

7. the youngest foot soldiers in the army

8. "How do you do?"

9. French for "of good breeding"

10. an acronym for *self-contained underwater breathing apparatus*

11. Italian *girasole,* meaning "sunflower"

12. the hairs on a billy goat's chin

13. *Taler,* "of the valley," referring to the place where certain coins were first used

14. the belief that the moon influences people's moods

15. the vines covering old university buildings

16. Detroit, known as the Motor City

42   AMERICANISMS

All of the following words have been added to the English language by Americans since the 1550s. Knowing them can help your reading comprehension. Underline the correct answer; then write the corresponding letter in the blank. If your answers are correct, they will spell out a fifteen-letter word that was introduced into the English language in 1896.

1. _____ What color describes sensational journalism?
   (t) blue (u) yellow (v) red

2. _____ What word meaning "a person who takes an independent stand (as in politics) and refuses to conform to that of a party or group" was named after a Texas cattleman in 1867?
   (n) maverick (m) protester (o) radical

3. _____ This word, coined in 1748, was a trading term used between the Indians and the European settlers.
   (c) dollar (d) buck (e) greenback

4. _____ These types of laws enforcing a strict morality and godly behavior entered the English language in the last twenty years of the eighteenth century.
   (e) blue laws (f) black codes (g) white laws

5. _____ Which expression means "follow an incorrect assumption"?
   (q) whistle in the dark (r) bark up the wrong tree (s) bob for apples

6. _____ This word, originally meaning a coffee shop, was introduced into English in 1853.
   (n) infirmary (o) gymnasium (p) cafeteria

7. _____ This toy was named after a U.S. president who spared a cub in 1906.
   (q) yo-yo (r) teddy bear (s) Lego blocks

8. _____ This term, meaning "sudden withdrawal," refers to giving up a substance, such as narcotics or alcohol, to which one was addicted.
   (j) saying good-bye (k) peace pipe (i) cold turkey

42   AMERICANISMS *(continued)*

9. _____ This political term, coined during the 1964 presidential race between Lyndon Johnson and Barry Goldwater, refers to voters who are sitting on the political fence waiting to be persuaded by one of the political parties' candidates.

   (**v**) swing voter (**w**) hack (**x**) party animal

10. _____ This pejorative term for someone who vegetates in front of the television and eats junk food became popular in 1976.

    (**g**) boob tube (**h**) Slinky (**i**) couch potato

11. _____ What hairstyle was named after Civil War General Ambrose Burnside in 1887?

    (**j**) crew cut (**k**) Afro (**l**) sideburns

12. _____ In IQ, a concept dating from 1916, what do the letters stand for?

    (**e**) intelligence quotient (**f**) intelligently qualified (**g**) infinitely qualified

13. _____ Which term meaning the main theme or the final result became popular in the early 1970s?

    (**f**) Watergate (**g**) bottom line (**h**) Murphy's law

14. _____ Which of the following is the nickname of the state of Indiana?

    (**c**) Bluegrass State (**d**) Wolverine State (**e**) Hoosier State

15. _____ In 1856, this word described people who took the law into their own hands and enforced it as they chose, answering to no higher authority. Today the word means "one who belongs to a group outside of legal authority to keep order and punish crime because the usual law enforcement agencies do not exist or are alleged to be inefficient."

    (**c**) sheriff (**d**) vigilante (**e**) posse

The word introduced into the English language in 1896 is

_____ .

43   MULTIPLE MEANINGS

When words have more than one meaning, good readers determine which meaning is appropriate from the word's context within its sentence. Each of the answers in this activity is a word with multiple meanings. Write the word in the blanks next to the word's definitions, one letter in each blank. The first and last letters of each answer are provided.

1. **i** ____ ____ **n:** press clothes; a mineral; a device with a handle and a flat, smooth undersurface

2. **p** ____ ____ ____ ____ ____ **m:** execute; carry out; meet the requirements

3. **c** ____ ____ ____ ____ ____ **l:** most important; principal; chief; wealth used to produce more wealth

4. **i** ____ ____ ____ **x:** an alphabetical list of names; a finger; a number used to measure changes in prices, wages, and unemployment; a sign; a representation

5. **p** ____ ____ ____ ____ ____ **t:** a proposal; a specific task or undertaking; a complex of inexpensive houses or apartments; jut out

6. **b** ____ ____ **y:** the physical substance of a human being, animal, or plant; a group of people or things functioning as a unit; a mass of matter

7. **r** ____ ____ ____ ____ ____ **e:** get or obtain; undergo or suffer; greet guests or visitors

8. **b** ____ ____ ____ ____ **m:** the lowest point; the part of a ship's hull that is normally below water; the lower unit of a two-piece garment; the bed or ground beneath a body of water

9. **r** ____ ____ **e:** a flower; a pinkish or purplish red; past tense of *rise*

10. **c** ____ ____ **l:** wind or twist into ringlets; raise the corner of the upper lip; a little coil of hair

11. **p** ____ ____ ____ **f:** a test or trial; conclusive evidence; a trial print of a negative

12. **d** ____ ____ ____ ____ **t:** a condensed but comprehensive account; a book of summaries; break down food in the stomach and intestines

44 THE HIDDEN TITLE

Underline the word that means the same as the first word in each numbered row. Write the synonym's one-letter answer code in the blank. Then copy the fifteen answer letters onto the line below item 15. If your answers are correct, they will spell out the name of a play by Lorraine Hansberry that was originally a line from a poem by Langston Hughes.

1. _____ akin: **(a)** showing similar features or qualities **(b)** stuttering **(c)** coordinated

2. _____ peruse: **(p)** flexible **(q)** indicated by nodding the head **(r)** read attentively

3. _____ ennui: **(z)** pleasure **(a)** boredom **(b)** probability

4. _____ plethora: **(g)** excessive pride **(h)** light **(i)** abundance

5. _____ mundane: **(s)** ordinary; everyday **(t)** very special; extraordinary **(u)** frequent; often

6. _____ cumbersome: **(h)** crazed **(i)** hard to manage; unwieldy **(j)** productive

7. _____ arbiter: **(m)** contestant **(n)** judge; mediator **(o)** diligent worker

8. _____ meander: **(i)** follow a winding path **(j)** recall vividly **(k)** spend freely

9. _____ qualm: **(l)** stillness **(m)** freedom **(n)** misgiving or pang of conscience

10. _____ formidable: **(t)** capable of inspiring fear or respect **(u)** capable of failure
      (v) capable of finding work

11. _____ visage: **(g)** nose **(h)** face **(i)** mouth

12. _____ macabre: **(e)** horrifying **(f)** pleasant **(g)** loud

13. _____ bestow: **(s)** give **(t)** remain **(u)** suspect

14. _____ disparity: **(t)** wellness **(u)** inequality **(v)** illness

15. _____ malinger: **(n)** exaggerate one's incapacity or illness **(o)** avoid bad weather
      (p) get into trouble

The letters are _____.

The name of the play is _____.

45   MATCHING THE WORDS

Here is a little vocabulary activity that will help you increase your word recognition. Match the words from Column A with their definitions in Column B by writing the corresponding number next to the appropriate letter in the magic square. Three answers are already provided. If your answers are correct, the rows, the columns, and the two diagonals will each add up to the same magic number.

A = 4	B =	C =	D =
E =	F =	G = 2	H =
I =	J =	K =	L = 3
M =	N =	O =	P =

Magic Number: _____

Column A

A. etiquette

B. yield

C. fatal

D. nomadic

E. rigorous

F. segregate

G. lofty

H. taboo

I. fitful

J. complex

K. upgrade

L. unrivaled

M. adversity

N. weird

O. debt

P. techniques

Column B

1. odd; strange

2. high

3. without competition

4. proper behavior

5. improve; advance to a higher level

6. give in

7. problems

8. prohibited; not allowed

9. stringent; tough

10. methods

11. deadly

12. involved; complicated

13. wandering

14. irregular; intermittent

15. separate

16. repayment obligation

46 MUSIC TO YOUR EARS

Let us not be confused with these words that sound and in some cases look very much alike. Instead, let's have this activity make music to your ears by selecting the correct word in each pair of words. Write the two-letter answer code in the blank next to the item number. Then copy the answer codes, in order, onto the line below item 15. If your answers are correct, they will spell out five things that can bring music to your ears.

1. _____ Which is a food found in the sea? **(ob)** mussel **(tr)** muscle

2. _____ What does old garbage do? **(um)** wreak **(oe)** reek

3. _____ What is the opposite of left? **(cl)** right **(de)** rite

4. _____ What do kings do? **(ar)** reign **(br)** rein

5. _____ What is a word for a person's midsection? **(ed)** waste **(in)** waist

6. _____ What is a word for long ago? **(et)** yore **(is)** your

7. _____ To obtain a sum, what must you do? **(or)** add **(wo)** ad

8. _____ What does your ear do? **(th)** here **(ga)** hear

9. _____ What is the name for the inside of an apple? **(ng)** core **(as)** corps

10. _____ What was the beautician doing to her client's hair? **(ui)** dyeing **(th)** dying

11. _____ What is the opposite of war? **(ta)** peace **(th)** piece

12. _____ How do you get water into a glass? **(se)** pore **(rt)** pour

13. _____ Where might you go on the World Wide Web? **(ru)** site **(wn)** sight

14. _____ What did the winner of the race receive? **(mp)** medal **(me)** meddle

15. _____ What do you do when you look at something when you probably shouldn't? **(et)** peek **(rs)** peak

The thirty letters are _____.

The five things that can bring music to your ears are the _____,
the _____, the _____, the _____,
and the _____.

47 WISE WORDS IN OTHER WORDS

Adages are wise sayings or "words of wisdom." Each of the fifteen adages in Group One is para-phrased in Group Two. Match each of them by writing the corresponding three-letter answer code from Group Two in the appropriate blank in Group One. One answer is provided already. If your answers are correct, the consecutive three-letter answer codes will spell out three more adages. Write the forty-five letters, in order, on the line below Group Two. Then write out the three adages. Your actions will speak louder than words!

Group One

1. _____ Actions speak louder than words.

2. _____ To err is human.

3. _____ The truth will set you free.

4. _____ Two heads are better than one.

5. _____ A house divided against itself cannot stand.

6. _____ You can lead a horse to water, but you can't make it drink.

7. _____ There was never a good war or a bad peace.

8. _____ Waste not, want not.

9. _____ Early to bed and early to rise makes a man healthy, wealthy, and wise.

10. [1]ndt An ounce of prevention is worth a pound of cure.

11. _____ Vision is the art of seeing things that are invisible.

12. _____ Knowledge is power.

13. _____ Fools rush in where angels fear to tread.

14. _____ God gives every bird food, but he does not throw it into the nest.

15. _____ The worst man is least troubled by his conscience.

Making Sense with Words

47   WISE WORDS IN OTHER WORDS *(continued)*

Group Two

bli.   Honesty brings freedom.

eis.   We all make mistakes.

ide.   Foresight is seeing what no one else can see.

ime.   Unity brings solidarity.

ism.   You can show a man the right way to do something, but he must want to do it himself.

lov.   Don't just say it—do it!

man.   A villain is not bothered by guilt.

mea.   Going to sleep early and waking up early will improve your quality of life.

¹**ndt.**   Sometimes it takes very little to prevent what it would take a great deal to fix.

²**ndt.**   The more people you have thinking about a solution, the more ideas the group will provide.

one.   War is bad; peace is good.

rno.   The Lord may provide us with things, but we must learn to provide for ourselves as well.

tfo.   The wise are cautious.

wai.   Learning gives people influence and strength.

yti.   Be thrifty, and you will never go without the things you need.

The forty-five letters are _____.

The three adages are _____,

_____, and

_____.

48   CEASE TO ERR

Match the word from Column A with its meaning in Column B. Write the correct number in the appropriate square. Four answers are provided. If your answers are correct, the rows, the columns, and the two diagonals will each add up to the same magic number.

A = 2	B =	C =	D =	E =
F =	G =	H =	I =	J = 12
K =	L = 19	M =	N =	O =
P =	Q =	R =	S = 4	T =
U =	V =	W =	X =	Y =

Magic Number: _____

Column A

A. for
B. seize
C. knew
D. chute
E. new
F. four
G. heir
H. sent
I. no
J. fore
K. alter
L. aisle
M. cereal
N. serial
O. scent
P. air
Q. altar
R. eight
S. ate
T. cent
U. cease
V. err
W. shoot
X. isle
Y. know

Column B

1. past tense of *send*
2. preposition indicating purpose
3. to make a mistake
4. past tense of *eat*
5. aroma
6. raised platform in a church
7. arranged in a sequence
8. opposite of *old*
9. launch a basketball; fire a weapon
10. two plus two
11. small island
12. toward the ship's bow
13. grain used for food
14. atmosphere
15. grasp or grab; confiscate
16. penny
17. past tense of *know*
18. stop
19. walkway between seats
20. opposite of *yes*
21. change
22. person who inherits
23. waterfall; river rapids
24. have knowledge of
25. seven plus one

Making Sense with Words

49 MEET AT THE RIGHT PAIR

Match the word in Column A with its definition in Column B. Write the correct number in the appropriate square. Five answers are provided. If your answers are correct, the rows, the columns, and the two diagonals will each add up to the same magic number.

A = 11	B =	C =	D =	E =
F =	G =	H =	I = 21	J =
K =	L –	M –	N =	O – 14
P =	Q =	R = 24	S =	T =
U =	V = 10	W =	X =	Y =

Magic Number: _____

Column A

A. pare
B. flue
C. vein
D. pair
E. to
F. vane
G. bored
H. mete
I. flu
J. rite
K. pear
L. too
M. rote
N. holey
O. holy
P. right
Q. vain
R. write
S. wholly
T. meat
U. flew
V. two
W. meet
X. board
Y. wrote

Column B

1. join; come face to face with
2. opposite of *left*
3. perforated
4. finding nothing of interest
5. in the direction of
6. animal flesh used as food
7. in an unthinking or mechanical manner
8. wind direction indicator
9. two of a kind
10. five minus three
11. cut or trim away
12. piece of wood
13. worthless; empty; insignificant
14. sacred
15. boundary
16. also
17. ceremony
18. blood vessel
19. past tense of *fly*
20. totally
21. short for *influenza*
22. chimney passageway
23. past tense of *write*
24. inscribe
25. a fruit

Section Three

BECOMING A BETTER READER

The twenty-three activities in this section help students see the bigger picture in reading as they move away from words into ideas and purposes. Students will study how writers begin their pieces (Activity 50), what clue words are essential to understanding an idea (Activity 51), and how important tone is to reading comprehension (Activities 52, 55, and 56). Students will distinguish between facts and opinions in Activity 53. Context clues are featured in Activity 54 and then again in Activities 57 through 63. Cause-and-effect strategies are reviewed in Activities 64 through 66. Anticipating what comes next is exemplified in Activities 64 through 66. Everyday activities such as reading travel directions and following directions make up the section's final activities.

50   INTERESTING A READER FROM THE START

Strong writers get each piece of writing off to an effective start. They know how important it is to capture the reader's interest and attention from the very beginning.

Seven techniques for doing just that are listed below. Each numbered item is the opening from a piece of writing. In the blank, write the letter corresponding to the technique the writer is using. Each technique is used twice. Discuss your answers with your classmates.

> A. Cite a statistic.
>
> B. Use a quotation.
>
> C. Pose a rhetorical question.
>
> D. Relate an incident.
>
> E. State a thesis.
>
> F. Show the opposite condition.
>
> G. Give supporting evidence of your position.

1. _____ How often can a team sign a player of her ability—one who has won as many championships, has led the league in scoring five times, and has won the hearts of as many sports fans?

2. _____ "I always wanted to be a Laker. It's in my heart. This is what I want to do. This is the team I want to play for and have a chance to finish out my career here," the former free agent announced to an appreciative audience of hometown fans.

3. _____ Elected to the Hall of Fame three years ago, home run leader six times in his twenty-year career, named best fielding centerfielder of all time, chosen as the finest left-handed hitter of the past fifty years—these are just a few of the many outstanding feats of tonight's award recipient.

4. _____ Mike O'Brien, basketball analyst for this network, believes that no one could ever match Michael Jordan as a player, teammate, or representative of the NBA.

5. _____ Do you really believe that students will camp outside the stadium for several days just to be able to sit in the top row at the college basketball game? If you're talking about students at Duke University, you had better believe it!

6. _____ According to a recent poll, although nearly three million people reside in the city today, only five hundred are in favor of the proposed sports stadium to be built on the banks of the river.

50   INTERESTING A READER FROM THE START (continued)

7. _____ The count was three balls and two strikes. The league's best softball pitcher was up against the league's most talented and productive hitter. Finch had been there many times before, often cutting down the opponent's hitters with poise and confidence. After getting the catcher's signal, the tall blonde reared back and unleashed a curve ball that once again fooled the batter. Strike three, three outs, no runs, no runners left on base. This was just another day on the mound for superstar Jennie Finch.

8. _____ It seems that more than $136 million over seven years was enough to keep this three-time NBA champion in his current uniform.

9. _____ Indisputably, the greatest shortstop to play the game in the past fifty years wears the number 21 for the Cardinals.

10. _____ The Miami Heat will be a much improved team now that Shaq will wear 32 and play center.

11. _____ "Why would anyone ever want to work for that guy?" the recently traded player said of his former boss at this morning's news conference announcing his trade to the division's last-place team.

12. _____ Do you want empty seats in your arena each night? Do you want your fans to think you have lost your minds? Do you need sportswriters and sportscasters to challenge your football knowledge and player selection abilities? If you do, then do not pick Bobby Runyon in tomorrow night's draft.

13. _____ A quick note to you baseball players:

Go on strike, and your fans will love you.
Go on strike, and they will send you flowers.
Go on strike, and they will feel sorry for you millionaires.
Go on strike, and they will side 100 percent with your decision.
Go on strike, and they will always believe that you are selfless people who think of the fans' best interests over your own.

14. _____ With a quick spin dribble, he moved past his defender, switched the ball from his right hand to his left, jumped nearly three feet, and deftly laid the ball over the front of the rim. Though many appreciative fans cheered, few were surprised by this skillful maneuver. Such feats have become routine for this gifted player.

51   UNLOCKING THE IMPORTANT WORDS

The key to understanding the purpose of a sentence is to recognize or unlock the important words in it. Who did what? What did that person do? Where did it happen? Does the sentence include descriptive words? Underline the words that you think are important in each sentence below, and be ready to explain why you think they are important. A sentence can have any number of important words. Discuss your ideas with your classmates.

1. Last night, my older sister lost her purse at the movie theater.

2. The misbehaving children were not allowed to watch television because they were rude to the baby-sitter.

3. The delicatessen owner won the state lottery last weekend.

4. My father's tool box has all the tools that we need to make the bench.

5. Just do it and do not complain about it.

6. An angry motorist did not want to forgive the driver who cut him off on the crowded highway.

7. Holding on to anger can weaken the body's immune system.

8. To avoid injury and boredom, try different types of cardiovascular exercises.

9. The model's clothes were colorful and attractive.

10. Take all of your books and belongings with you after you complete the exam.

11. Interrogators questioned those who had been at the accident scene.

12. The filly extended her streak of victories to seven, outrunning her closest competitor down the stretch.

13. The legislators debated the various problems concerning the town's natural resources.

14. Two celebrities were honored by the Red Cross for their work in recruiting volunteers to work overseas.

15. Reports from the commission investigating the robberies fault the alarm systems, which were deemed inadequate.

52   CREATING THE MOOD

Readers must tune in to the words and phrases that create a mood in the text they are reading. Is the intended mood one of happiness? Horror? Surprise? Something else? The carefully selected words and phrases create the mood.

Fill in a word or a phrase in each blank to create a specific mood for each sentence. On the line following the sentence, write a word or two to describe the mood you intended to create with the words and phrases that you inserted. The first item is done for you. Discuss your sentences with your classmates.

1. The _____arguments_____ created such a _____bad_____ feeling that _several members stormed out the meeting_. _____anger_____

2. Two _____ _____ along the _____ _____ at midnight. _____

3. Under the _____ eyes of their watchful coach, the _____ players learned how to play _____, _____ football. _____

4. _____, several _____ _____ the dog so that _____. _____

5. _____ graduates _____ by _____ in the _____ near the campus. _____

6. Waves _____ _____ the _____ as the three women _____. _____

7. Only _____ will _____ buy a _____. _____

8. Her offer to help us _____. _____

9. Miguel _____ said that the other runners had _____ him during the _____. _____

10. The _____ game show host _____ the contestant for _____. _____

53   JUST THE FACTS, PLEASE!

Distinguishing between fact and opinion is important to every reader. Below are fifteen sentences. Seven of them state facts; the other eight express opinions. In the blank next to each number, write the letter O for sentences that are opinions and the letter F for sentences that are facts. Then on the line below sentence 15, write the four letters that follow each of the eight opinion sentences. Then on the line below that one, do the same with the letters that follow the factual sentences. The two sets of letters will spell out a humorous comment about facts by a famous American author whose initials follow the quotation.

1. _____ Mathematics is the most difficult subject to learn. **(gety)**

2. _____ Some of today's television shows are a bad influence on young children. **(ourf)**

3. _____ California is more populated than Connecticut. **(stor)**

4. _____ Officials acknowledged that they had used flawed methods to build their list of candidates. **(tthe)**

5. _____ The critics said that he had ignored some aspects of the movie. **(masm)**

6. _____ Abraham Lincoln was America's best president ever. **(acts)**

7. _____ This law should be repealed. **(firs)**

8. _____ The company's vice president is to blame for all this trouble. **(tand)**

9. _____ Two hundred workers lost their jobs after the stock market plummeted. **(ucha)**

10. _____ The report stated several reasons for the company's later successes. **(syou)**

11. _____ She is friendly with that family only because they have lots of money. **(then)**

12. _____ Friday is the best day of the week. **(youc)**

13. _____ The Vikings have the best record in our town's football league. **(plea)**

14. _____ The panel's recommendations were discussed on yesterday's radio broadcast. **(semt)**

15. _____ Saint Croix is the best vacation spot in this hemisphere. **(andi)**

The letters following the opinion sentences are _____.

The letters following the factual sentences are _____.

The two sets of letters combine to spell out this quotation and its author's initials:

_____

_____

_____

54   LOOKING FOR CLUES

Even though many of the words in this paragraph are not really words, you will be able to figure out which part of speech they are from the words around them. Using the legitimate English words as clues to the other "words," answer the fifteen questions. Underline the correct answer, and write the corresponding letter in the blank for that question. If your answers are correct, you will have five of each response (*a*, *b*, and *c*).

Mytei was khkjuing and iwejsaaing next to the ljlj tree. Tnffely, she joiasd a nppjswd without emcps. A few ijys in the olasscw remembered to wjwlrg an pwdnko oojhdw. Often the oqwecas lifted some prtgnhs lhjd carefully. Rarely did Tkkjhde hide these popqwqws. Today qweqw and iwlfie will outsghq some ertoys. This is the kgwq of our ohoeld.

1. _____ *Khkjuing* and *iwejsaaing* are probably **(a)** verbs **(b)** nouns **(c)** adjectives.

2. _____ *Ljlj* is probably **(a)** an adjective **(b)** a verb **(c)** both *a* and *b*.

3. _____ *Tnffely* is probably **(a)** an adjective **(b)** an adverb **(c)** a verb.

4. _____ *Joiasd* is probably **(a)** an adjective **(b)** a noun **(c)** a verb.

5. _____ *Emcps* is probably either a noun or **(a)** a verb **(b)** a conjunction **(c)** a pronoun.

6. _____ *Ijys* is probably **(a)** a noun **(b)** an adjective **(c)** a verb.

7. _____ *Wjwlrg* is probably **(a)** a noun **(b)** an adjective **(c)** a verb.

8. _____ *Oojhdw* can be either a noun or **(a)** an adverb **(b)** an adjective **(c)** an adverb.

9. _____ *Prtgnhs* can be either a noun or **(a)** a verb **(b)** an adjective **(c)** a conjunction.

10. _____ *Tkkjhde* is probably **(a)** a conjunction **(b)** an adjective **(c)** a noun.

11. _____ *Popqwqws* is either a noun or **(a)** a verb **(b)** an adverb **(c)** an adjective.

12. _____ *Qweqw* and *iwlfie* are **(a)** verbs **(b)** nouns **(c)** adjectives.

13. _____ *Outsghq* is probably **(a)** a verb **(b)** an adjective **(c)** a noun.

14. _____ *Kgwq* is **(a)** a noun **(b)** a verb **(c)** an adjective.

15. _____ *Ohoeld* is **(a)** an adverb **(b)** a noun **(c)** an adjective.

55   TONING UP THE TONE

Tone helps readers make sense of sentences. Tone can create such moods as happiness, sadness, anger, frustration, confusion, and beauty. Words set the tone for each of the eight sentences below. On the short line after the sentence, identify the sentence's tone. On the long line, explain (using specifics) what brought you to that conclusion. Discuss your answers with your classmates.

1. Unfortunately, both men agreed to the plan, and eventually both paid the price for their choice. _____

    _____

2. She moved quickly past the dark and vacant street corner, hoping that she would not be noticed. _____

    _____

3. Unsure of his next move, the champion chess player hesitated several times before finally moving his rook. _____

    _____

4. Removing herself from the chaotic scene, the mayor sought shelter away from the crowd. _____

    _____

5. Wringing her hands, our neighbor pleaded with the policewoman. _____

    _____

6. Several of the runners in the lead pack jostled for position as they neared the halfway mark of the race. _____

    _____

7. The youngster immediately sank into her mother's arms and sighed deeply. _____

    _____

8. Laughing uncontrollably, the children were enjoying the clown's performance. _____

    _____

56   THE LONG DAY

The writer who wrote the following brief essay has developed a tone (or several tones) in this writing. *Disbelief, amazement, loss, affection,* and *contentment* are examples of tone words. Read the essay several times, underlining what you consider to be important ideas. Then in the space at the bottom of the page, discuss the ways in which the writer develops the tone or tones. Discuss your answers with your classmates. The sentences have been numbered for easy reference.

(1) The day never seems long enough. (2) There are just so many great things to do that I often cannot do all of the things that I want to do. (3) For instance, take school. (4) From 8:00 until 3:00 each weekday, I go to school. (5) Then for the next two hours or so, I am on one sports team or another. (6) By the time I eat supper, practice my drums, and finish my homework, I am too exhausted to do much else.

(7) When will I get the time to do some of the things that I really want to do? (8) I realize that school is important and all, but why do I have to go for six straight hours? (9) Sports are a good release after my day in school. (10) Playing the drums also helps. (11) But there are so many other things that I would like to do, and there is no time to do them. (12) Television watching is out, and so is having a part-time job.

(13) I hope that summer vacation comes quickly. (14) Then, at least and at last, I will have the time to do some of the things that I would really like to do.

_____

_____

_____

_____

_____

_____

57   TWO BY TWO

Each of these fifteen sentences has two words missing. From the word bank, select the pair of words that makes the most sense in each sentence, in the order in which they appear, and write the words in the appropriate blanks. Each pair of words will be used only once.

caterpillar, crawled	paunchy, memorable
considered, amnesty	police, mourners
deposits, geologists	protesters, convince
failed, haunt	rates, bills
flight, discontinued	reaction, enthusiastic
freely, water	sound, newcomer
grasp, nervously	tribute, fallen
old, renovation	

1. The _____ barn needed a major _____.

2. The crowd's _____ to the news was nothing short of

    _____.

3. A _____ character actor, Fred Hickens had some

    _____ roles in several sitcoms.

4. Many of the senators _____ passing a bill to grant

    _____ to the rebels.

5. The _____ policies of the past school administration may come back to

    _____ the community for some time.

6. Mineral _____ were spotted by the _____.

57 TWO BY TWO (continued)

7. Fully able to _____ the importance of the moment, the candidate _____ approached the podium to deliver the most important speech of his political career.

8. Antiwar _____ attempted to _____ others to join them at the rally this weekend.

9. Dozens of _____ vehicles and cars of _____ crowded the narrow streets around the funeral parlor.

10. The poem is a _____ to the _____ hero who saved many lives before losing his own.

11. A _____ _____ along the driveway leading to David's house.

12. Reeling from his _____ defeat at the hands of the _____, the champion considered retirement.

13. Nearly two thousand _____ attendants voted to walk off the job if negotiation talks were _____.

14. Higher interest _____ and larger tax _____ are hurting the family's ability to save.

15. All the flags waved _____ in the breeze coming off the _____.

58   WHAT WORDS ARE MISSING?

The sentences presented below have many blanks waiting to be filled. Fill them with words that you think make sense within the context of the sentence. Discuss your answers with your classmates. Have _____!

1. Unaware of the _____, the fisherman seemed to _____ the _____ during the early morning hours.

2. _____ and _____, the third-grade students hurried out of their classroom to enjoy _____.

3. A bit _____ awaiting the doctor's arrival, the patient _____ about the possible _____ of his blood tests.

4. As we _____ here looking out at the sea, we _____ that we are very _____.

5. _____ the children to _____ themselves during the _____ later this evening.

6. _____ sipped the _____ that his wife had _____ for _____ earlier that _____.

7. _____ host comes into the main _____ ready to _____ the visitors.

8. Smith is a _____ who got _____ by _____ many of his clients.

9. Criticized as _____ and _____, the candidate is certainly not as _____ as many people would think.

10. _____, who will attend the _____, is _____ the _____.

11. _____ of the _____ spoke before the _____ at last _____ meeting.

12. Judging from your _____, I would _____ that you _____ a good _____.

Copyright © 2005 by John Wiley & Sons, Inc.

59 MONEY, MONEY, MONEY

Two words have been left out of each sentence below. From the word bank, select the pair of words that make the most sense in each sentence. Circle the first letter of the first word you filled in. If your answers are correct, the circled letters, in order, will spell out three words that are related to money. Write them in the blanks at the end of this activity.

avidly, favorite	often, scary
burrowed, dirt	opinionated, view
cheetahs, elephants	sailors, deck
colors, resin	scholarship, job
dutifully, camp	strong, granite
harried, motorist	systematically, components
kangaroo, baby	necessarily, only
teacher, specific	

1. Two of the _____ cleaned the _____ last night.

2. Joanna's _____ told her to include additional _____ examples in her story.

3. A person who is _____ seldom wants to listen to another person's point of _____.

4. My younger sister enjoys watching the _____ and the _____ at the zoo.

5. Each _____ carried her _____ in her pouch.

6. It takes _____ laborers to drill _____ from the

mountain.

59 MONEY, MONEY, MONEY (continued)

7. Tiny insects _____ their way into the _____ underneath our porch.

8. Young children are _____ afraid of _____ creatures in movies.

9. Your response was not _____ the _____ correct answer.

10. The soldiers _____ stood watch over the military

    _____.

11. The repairman _____ arranged the _____ of the watch in place.

12. The paint _____ were mixed with wax and _____.

13. Baseball fanatics _____ follow their _____ players and teams.

14. Having earned a _____, the student was able to give up his weekend

    _____.

15. Feeling _____ by the number of cars on the road, the

    _____ tried to calm himself down.

The three words related to money are _____, _____, and _____.

60 SENTENCE CLUES

Readers use clues to make sense of sentences and paragraphs. In the sentence "The _____ track runner set a world record in the mile run," a logical word that could fill in the blank is *fast* or *speedy.* Use the word bank to fill in the fifteen words that have been omitted from these sentences. Each word is used only once.

abandoned	gourmet	or
anxiety	gruesome	robust
chestnut	imply	smuggle
commissioned	microwave	stretcher
eventually	nostalgia	wrest

1. She intended to _____ a slice of last night's pizza.

2. Stuart _____ the puzzle and went to answer the phone.

3. The sight of their child on the _____ caused the parents' eyes to fill with tears.

4. Yesterday, they ran into each other while shopping at the local _____ grocery store.

5. She couldn't shake the _____ that gripped her every time she had to speak in public.

6. The actor hoped to _____ at least a shred of dignity from the humiliating audition.

7. The couple _____ a mural depicting their entire family.

8. That shade of _____ brown is very flattering on you.

9. We waited quite a long time, but the fish _____ began to bite.

10. It took several _____ men to push the stalled car away from the traffic.

11. The Black Death that devastated London in the Middle Ages was particularly _____.

12. "This is not the time for fooling _____ laughing," said the teacher.

13. "What are you trying to _____ about the officer's integrity?" the lawyer asked the witness.

14. Those criminals tried to _____ the drugs into the country.

15. Walking through my childhood neighborhood, I was overwhelmed by a wave of _____.

61   FILLING THEM IN

Effective readers know how to anticipate the words that are coming and then to fit them into the context of the sentence. Here are fifteen sentences that will test your ability to put words in their proper place. Three words have been left out of each sentence. Select the most suitable three-word set from the word bank, and write those words in the blanks in the appropriate sentence. Each set of words is used only once.

anxiety, assure, sedated	hair, shrimp, affair
astute, solved, minutes	hours, explosion, extinguish
botanist, acknowledged, existence	missing, intended, ricocheted
carefully, sliver, knee	problems, mentor, crucial
character, novel, heroine	ramifications, actions, heed
colorful, roadway, trotted	shouldered, burden, crisis
engaged, delicate, wits	understand, concepts, theory
established, based, year	

1. Several _____ after the _____, the firefighters were still trying to _____ the flames.

2. Completely _____ the _____ target, the bullet _____ off the wall.

3. Many _____ umbrellas lined the _____ as the joggers _____ by.

4. You will _____ these _____ better once the _____ have been explained in greater detail.

5. The _____ _____ the _____ of an infection among the maple trees.

61   FILLING THEM IN *(continued)*

6. Mitch _____ much of the _____ during the

   _____.

7. The _____ mathematician _____ the challenging

   problem in just a few _____.

8. Angel _____ pasta with _____ was the featured

   dish at the catered _____.

9. I reviewed the _____ with my _____ before the

   _____ exam.

10. The doctor _____ removed the _____ of wood from

    the patient's _____.

11. Though she understood his _____ about the surgery, she wanted to

    _____ him that he would be fully _____.

12. The couple had been _____ in a _____ battle of

    _____.

13. Even though you might not understand the _____ of your

    _____, I suggest that you _____ my advice.

14. Hester Prynne, a _____ in Nathaniel Hawthorne's

    _____ *The Scarlet Letter,* is regarded as a _____.

15. The Julian calendar, _____ by Julius Caesar more than two thousand

    years ago, was _____ on a _____ of 365¼ days.

62 FILLING IN THE BLANKS

Often readers anticipate the words a writer will use in a story. Here is your chance to anticipate and then fill in the most appropriate words. Each group of five sentences is preceded by five words that can fill in the blanks. Use each word only once.

builders	he	into	reverberating	satisfied

1. Many of the wedding guests walked slowly _____ the reception hall.

2. Echoes were _____ throughout the cave.

3. Skillful _____ constructed the forty-story hotel.

4. Are you _____ with the teacher's explanation of this solution?

5. Do you think that _____ would like to visit the Bahamas with us?

after	befuddled	despite	neither	placid

6. We moved along the trail _____ the oppressive heat.

7. Do you think that we can see the movie _____ we finish our chores?

8. I believe that _____ of the paintings was done by Matisse.

9. Canoeists love both rough and _____ waters.

10. Most of the college math students were _____ by the problem.

62   FILLING IN THE BLANKS *(continued)*

commander	gratified	resounding	themselves	wonderment

11. All of us looked at the huge mountain in _____.

12. My sister was _____ by the gifts she received after her operation.

13. The navy _____ gave the sailors specific instructions.

14. All of the kindergarten students drew pictures of _____.

15. The convention participants gave the candidate a _____ round of applause.

breathtaking	expertly	magician	numb	persuasive

16. The video featured _____ views of New York City.

17. The dentist had to _____ my gums before she started drilling.

18. She _____ demonstrated how to sew the hem.

19. The youngsters were amazed by the skills and tricks of the _____.

20. Several _____ police officers addressed the audience.

63   IMPROVING SENTENCES

Readers need sentences that include just enough detail to allow them to picture the scene in their mind. Too much detail can be boring, but too little detail can keep the reader in the dark.

Group One contains fifteen sentences. Although these sentences make sense as they are, they can be improved with more detail, by inserting a word, a phrase, or a clause in the blank. That is where Group Two comes in handy. Each of the selections in Group Two can be added to improve one of the sentences in Group One.

Figure out which selection from Group Two will complete each sentence in Group One, and then write the Group Two letter code in the blank next to its match in Group One. If your answers are correct, the letters will consecutively spell out three five-letter words. Good luck!

Group One

1. _____ He had to get to the store _____.

2. _____ The criminal had hidden the _____ merchandise.

3. _____ When the early morning came, the owner went into town _____.

4. _____ _____ these roads are now major highways.

5. _____ The winds _____ were quite ferocious.

6. _____ The nurse slapped the man's cheek _____.

7. _____ Her Majesty's jaw dropped _____.

8. _____ The disease _____ broke out in 1592.

9. _____ Good writers know what to include in stories _____.

10. _____ _____ you can fit two basketballs within the rim at the same time.

11. _____ _____ for a short time, the mountain climbers would be safe.

12. _____ Instantaneously _____ the police officer lunged for the falling child.

13. _____ _____ a total cholesterol reading of 200 was considered safe.

14. _____ _____ the contestants took their turn at completing the intricate puzzle.

15. _____ Read this passage at least twice _____.

63   IMPROVING SENTENCES (continued)

Group Two

A. to search for her lost dog

E. stolen

F. in a hurry

G. As amazing as it may seem,

J. At least

M. Until recently,

N. to capture a reader's interest

O. that took the lives of so many Londoners

P. One by one,

R. at the sight of the citizens rioting in the streets

S. Crooked little paths just a few years ago,

T. that beat against the beach cottages

U. and without the slightest hesitation,

W. to see if he was still unconscious

Y. or until you think you understand it

The three five-letter words are _____, _____, and _____.

64 COMPLETING THE THOUGHTS

Often writers write sentences that express more than a single thought. Good readers anticipate how a sentence might end. What is the effect of a person's actions? Why does a person do what he or she does? These are some questions that readers ask themselves and that you will be asked to think about as you complete these fifteen sentences. On the lines provided, write the part of the sentence that has been left out. There are many possible answers. Share your responses with your classmates.

1. Because he could not see well under water, _____

   _____

   _____.

2. After receiving more than enough votes to win the election, _____

   _____

   _____.

3. Hurt on the straightaway, _____

   _____

   _____.

4. Having stayed out in the sun for too long, _____

   _____

   _____.

5. Due to inclement weather, _____

   _____

   _____.

6. Since there was hardly any time left to finish the project, _____

   _____

   _____.

7. Impressing the interview committee, _____

   _____

   _____.

8. Thirsty from the long hike, _____

   _____

   _____.

64   COMPLETING THE THOUGHTS *(continued)*

9. Given another opportunity to make the cheerleading team, _____

_____

_____.

10. Locating the submarine, _____

_____

_____.

11. Since the ship had been battered by the rough waves, _____

_____

_____.

12. Because there were so many contestants, _____

_____

_____.

13. _____

_____

_____ because he had lost his wallet.

14. _____

_____

_____ so that others could help in the house's
construction.

15. _____

_____

_____ after Melanie had written a letter to the
editor of her local paper.

65   CAUSE AND EFFECT

A *cause* is why an *effect* happens. In the sentence "Our flight was delayed due to the hurricane," the hurricane is the *cause* and the flight's being delayed is the *effect*. In the sentence "Because she scored so well on the state exam, Kendra was given a special award," the *cause* is "Because she scored so well on the state exam," and the *effect* is "Kendra was given a special award."

Some of the following sentences simply state facts, and others make cause-and-effect statements. In the cause-and-effect sentences, underline the cause and put brackets around the effect. Discuss your answers with your classmates.

1. Theodore bought a new car after his old one was totaled in an accident.

2. Luis brushed his hair each morning before school.

3. After the children left the zoo, they boarded the bus to go home.

4. Because there were only five tickets to the opera, you and I will be forced to stay home.

5. Due to inclement weather, our trip to the park will be postponed until tomorrow.

6. Having fallen victim to a disease, this apple tree will have to be cut down and destroyed.

7. Yesterday's concert ended later than the one the night before.

8. The laboratory workers took four breaks today and five breaks yesterday.

9. Vivian had no time to go back to the cafeteria, for her next class was starting in less than a minute.

10. My sister is always happy whenever Mom is cooking a steak dinner.

11. There is no opportunity like this one to make you a rich person.

12. The machine's incessant noise forced us to keep our windows closed.

13. The wind was blowing so furiously that the sunbathers were unable to open their umbrellas.

14. Miriam sang at last year's school musical celebration.

15. Hordes of summer travelers will soon be making their way through these two bus terminals.

66 CAUSE AND EFFECT, HISTORICALLY SPEAKING

The beginnings of ten sentences are given in Column A. Match each with its logical completion in Column B. Write the one-letter answer code from Column B in the blank in Column A. Then copy the ten answer letters, in order, onto the line below Column B. If your answers are correct, they will spell out two names that are famous in U.S. history.

Column A

1. _____ When the rain started to fall heavily,

2. _____ After the test was completed,

3. _____ My brother missed the concert

4. _____ As long as he is healthy,

5. _____ Even though the streets were very crowded,

6. _____ Because the subway car was very stuffy,

7. _____ Whenever my sister sees her friends,

8. _____ As soon as the movie began,

9. _____ While the scientist recorded the experiment's data,

10. _____ Before you enter the house,

Column B

A. the taxi driver was able to get us to school on time.

K. please wipe your muddy shoes on the mat.

L. her three assistants cleaned the lab.

M. my grandfather will not retire from his job.

N. several passengers became ill.

O. the people behind me started to talk.

P. they always have a great time together.

R. the proctors collected the papers.

T. the umpire called the game.

U. because he misplaced his tickets.

The ten letters are _____.

The famous names in U.S. history are _____ and _____.

67   WHAT IS THE NEXT LINE?

Anticipating the next line when reading is often crucial. Here is your chance to develop a sense of what is ahead of you in the text. Match each sentence in Group One with the sentence that logically follows it in Group Two. Write the Group Two three-letter answer code in the blank next to the appropriate number in Group One. Then copy those letters, in order, onto the line below Group Two. If your answers are correct, they will spell out the names of four items typically found on an office desk.

Group One

1. _____ Early this morning, the sheriff knocked on my front door.

2. _____ Building the mansion was hard work.

3. _____ Surfers often wait a long time for the perfect wave to carry them in near the shore.

4. _____ The houselights dimmed, the audience hushed, and the musicians readied themselves.

5. _____ After putting my three-year-old son to sleep last night, I paused for a second and began to reminisce.

6. _____ The morning after Sam married his longtime girlfriend, Louise, the two happily left for France on their honeymoon.

7. _____ Neither had been back to Chile in years.

Group Two

bin. Their happiness would be short-lived.

der. What both remembered most was strolling along the streets of Santiago, just looking at the sights and people around them.

npa. The opera was about to begin.

per. Was it not just yesterday that he came into our lives?

ple. Several crews worked long hours simply laying its foundation.

rpe. At times they may lose patience—or even hope—out there on the water.

sta. He said that he wanted to ask me a few questions.

The twenty-one letters are _____.

The four items found on a desk are a _____, a _____,

_____, and a _____.

68 ANTICIPATING WHAT HAPPENS NEXT

How often have you wondered what will happen next in a story that you are reading? You, like many other readers, have probably done this quite frequently. In the reading process, even though your eyes and mind are working to understand the written words on the page, your mind is doing double duty since it is also thinking ahead a bit, trying to anticipate what will happen next in this story.

This process is part of the fun of reading stories, for your curiosity comes alive and makes the reading experience enjoyable and creative at the same time.

Below are the beginnings of two different stories. As you read each of them, your mind will be actively thinking about the scene, the characters, the action, and other details. You will also be anticipating what will happen next in each story. On the back of this page or a separate piece of paper, continue the story, and if your teacher asks you to, conclude it. Be aware of how you, as the story's new author, create anticipation for your readers. When you have finished your writing, share your story with your classmates.

Story A

Bob and Alberto, both fifteen, had had a great time at the crowded movies that late October night. Along with the hundreds of others in the movie house, they had really been scared by the horrifying characters and the gruesome scenes featured in the sci-fi thriller. Several times during the movie, both boys had been truly frightened. Now they were starting the walk to their suburban homes about a mile away. Ten minutes into their walk down the dark street, they noticed that there were no other people near them. No cars had gone by them for at least five minutes. Few houses on the street were lit, for most people had gone to bed for the night. Suddenly, a car slowly approached the two boys from behind. . . .

Story B

The sun had been up for only an hour when the three lifeguards appeared on the empty beach. Twenty-year-old Juan, the most experienced of the three, helped Richie and Duayne, both seventeen, the newest guards on the beach this summer, with the chores of setting up for the day. The young men set up the lifeguards' stand, took the life preservers out of the wooden box behind the stand, and attached tow lines to the lifeboat and stashed the oars inside it. Looking out at the surf, Juan realized that he had seldom seen the waves so rough. They came in with such force that he doubted that many people would take the chance of going in the water today. These riptides had taken the confidence out of many bathers over the years. Today would be a test for the lifeguards, old and new.

Just after the three had settled in on the stand, they saw a man in the distance running toward them shouting something that they could not understand. As the man neared the guards, they saw that he had a terrified look on his face. . . .

69   SORTING THINGS OUT

The phrases in Group Two have been excerpted from five articles on different topics. Sort them under the proper topic heading in Group One by writing the two-letter answer code in the correct blank in Group One. The number in parentheses after each phrase indicates its order in the article. The answer codes for each article spell out an eight-letter word that was found in the same article. Each phrase in Group Two is used only once.

Group One

Article 1: "Whales and Dolphins"

(1) _____ (2) _____ (3) _____ (4) _____: _____

Article 2: "Languages"

(1) _____ (2) _____ (3) _____ (4) _____: _____

Article 3: "Firefighting"

(1) _____ (2) _____ (3) _____ (4) _____: _____

Article 4: "Circuses and Carnivals"

(1) _____ (2) _____ (3) _____ (4) _____: _____

Article 5: "The U.S. Supreme Court"

(1) _____ (2) _____ (3) _____ (4) _____: _____

69   SORTING THINGS OUT *(continued)*

Group Two

al.   words change their meaning for many reasons (2)

an.   may freeze and cause slippery conditions (3)

at.   return to the surface to breathe (3)

aw.   hunts seals and penguins (2)

co.   Chief Justice John Marshall (1)

di.   they became bilingual (1)

dr.   unable to control the sparks (2)

ec.   a fixed number of letters and symbols (3)

er.   most important sense is hearing (4)

gg.   P. T. Barnum's "Greatest Show on Earth" featured animals as well (2)

hy.   carry heavy hoses up many stairs (1)

ju.   trained bears and clowns (1)

le.   parades of colorful floats and talented performers (3)

ng.   hands down many important judicial decisions (2)

re.   interprets the Constitution (3)

rs.   deeds of skill and daring on the trapeze (4)

se.   flat forelimbs to help steer (1)

ss.   examines and presents its findings (4)

[1]**ts.**   a type of writing called cuneiform (4)

[2]**ts.**   the danger of blazing buildings (4)

70 GIVING DIRECTIONS

It's time to travel! Carefully read the directions that Yvonne gave to Tomas, who has to drive from New York City to Robert Moses Beach on Long Island. Then answer the ten questions that follow Yvonne's directions.

The easiest way to get to Robert Moses State Parkway from New York City is to take the Midtown Tunnel out of Manhattan into the borough of Queens. As soon as you come out of the tunnel, you will be on the Long Island Expressway, otherwise known as Route 495. Continue along Route 495 heading east, passing through Nassau County and then entering Suffolk County. Look for the Long Island Expressway's exit 53, Sagtikos Parkway South. Take this exit and head south. After approximately 3 miles, the parkway splits. Take the right fork, which is labeled Southern State Parkway, heading west. Stay on that road for less than a mile, and look for the sign that says "Ocean Beaches/Robert Moses Causeway." Turn at that sign and follow that road for approximately 4 miles. You will be heading south again and cross over Sunrise Highway (Route 27), Montauk Highway (Route 27A), a long bridge, and then two shorter bridges. Once you have crossed over the third bridge, you will see a tall water tower. You are now at Robert Moses State Park. Fields 2 and 3 are to your right, and Fields 4 and 5 will be on your left. Be aware of all the signs, and I'm sure you'll do just fine, Tomas!

1. In which two directions will Tomas mainly be driving?
_____ and _____

2. What borough is to the east of Manhattan? _____

3. What two counties will Tomas drive through once he leaves Queens?
_____ and _____

4. Which parkway will split? _____

5. Which fork in the parkway should Tomas take? _____

6. Which road will Tomas be on for the shortest time and distance?
_____

7. On how many different roads will Tomas be heading south?
_____

8. How many bridges will Tomas cross over once he has crossed over Montauk Highway?
_____

9. What landmark should Tomas look for as he is crossing over the last bridge before the beach? _____

10. Is Field 5 to Tomas's right or left as he crosses the last bridge?
_____

71   FIXING A FLAT

How would you like to save time and money the next time you have to fix a bicycle tire flat? Below are fourteen steps to help you successfully complete the job.

Read the steps at least twice. Then on the next page, place the steps in order by writing the numbers 1–14 next to the appropriate steps. If your answers are in the correct order, you'll be on your way! Happy biking!

1. Place the bicycle in a position that makes it easy to work on—either right side up or upside down.

2. Detach the chain from the wheel that you will be working on.

3. Remove the wheel from the bike by loosening the nuts on both sides.

4. Remove the tire from the rim.

5. Remove the inner tube from either the rim or the tire, wherever it may be.

6. Clean the surface around the hole in the tire, and apply adhesive to the area around it.

7. Place a patch over the hole in the tire.

8. Fill the inner tube with enough air to make sure that the tube is no longer leaking.

9. Place the inner tube on the rim.

10. Place the tire with the inner tube on it back onto the rim.

11. Fill the inner tube completely with air.

12. Reattach the chain to the axle, making sure the chain is on tightly.

13. Reattach both nuts onto both bolts and tighten the nuts.

14. Stand the bicycle back up on its two tires.

71 FIXING A FLAT *(continued)*

_____ Place the tire with the inner tube on it back onto the rim.

_____ Remove the wheel from the bike by loosening the nuts on both sides.

_____ Fill the inner tube with enough air to make sure that the tube is no longer leaking.

_____ Stand the bicycle back up on its two tires.

_____ Place the bicycle in a position that makes it easy to work on—either right side up or upside down.

_____ Fill the inner tube completely with air.

_____ Detach the chain from the wheel that you will be working on.

_____ Place a patch over the hole in the tire.

_____ Reattach the chain to the axle, making sure the chain is on tightly.

_____ Place the inner tube on the rim.

_____ Remove the tire from the rim.

_____ Remove the inner tube from either the rim or the tire, wherever it may be.

_____ Clean the surface around the hole in the tire, and apply adhesive to the area around it.

_____ Reattach both nuts onto both bolts and tighten the nuts.

72   CELLULAR PROBLEMS

Michelle Perkins has experienced problems with her new cell phone. She has written to the manufacturer in hopes of resolving this situation. Read her letter; then answer the questions that follow it.

439 Smith Street
Anytown, US 00000
September 28, 2005

World's Finest Cell Phones
3009 Manufacturer's Way
Industryville, US 00000

Dear World's Finest:

When I spoke to the salesperson who sold me my cell phone, he said that I would have to deal directly with you, the manufacturer. Therefore, I will explain the problems I am having.

Two weeks ago, I purchased one of your cell phones, and it has not worked properly since that very day. First, there is constant static whenever I make or receive a call. This annoying noise prevents me from hearing the other party clearly. And my voice is almost inaudible to the people I call.

Another problem involves my message function. When callers leave me messages, I can hear only some of their words. Sometimes the message just cuts off; at other times, the words are garbled. Unfortunately, I have missed several important messages because of this problem.

A third problem with my cell phone involves the ringer and the vibrator. The phone does not ring and does not vibrate! I have frequently checked my phone messages only to find that several people have called without my being aware of it. I have changed the batteries several times, so I know that this is not the reason for the problem.

I trust that you will be able to solve my cell phone problems by either replacing this phone with a new one or by refunding the money I paid for it. Please respond via regular mail to the above address or call my home phone at (555) 555-1111. Hoping that you fully appreciate my situation, I thank you in advance for your help in this matter.

Sincerely,

Michelle Perkins

Michelle Perkins

72   CELLULAR PROBLEMS *(continued)*

1. How long has the purchaser owned the phone? _____

2. What are the problems with the phone? _____

   _____

3. What does *inaudible* mean? _____

4. What does *garbled* mean? _____

5. What does *via* mean? _____

6. What is the purpose of each of the letter's five paragraphs?

   _____

   _____

   _____

   _____

   _____

7. Which words serve as transitions?

   _____

   _____

   _____

   _____

Section Four

READING COMPREHENSION IN MATH AND SCIENCE CLASSES

Reading activities that students would encounter in math and science classes are featured in the twenty-eight activities in Section Four. Vocabulary found in these classes constitute Activities 73, 74, and 78. The three math readings (75, 76, and 77) encompass algebra and probability. The science readings span the science curriculum and tackle topics that students are sure to find intriguing, including ghosts (79), vampires (80), phobias (81), crocodiles (83), snakes (84), salamanders (86), sharks (87), the Milgram experiment (98), the crash test dummy (99), and Ivan

Pavlov (100). Activities focusing on environmental issues, including global warming (89), ecotourism (90), tornadoes (91), the eruption of Krakatoa (96), and the Tunguska event (97), will both fascinate and inform your students. The section also features such diverse topics as anorexia nervosa (82), bats (85), rain forests (88), burns (92), caving (93), friction (94), and the Golden Gate Bridge (95).

The readings in this section have been selected with an eye toward improving your students' reading abilities. In some instances, questions that follow each reading ask students to determine the author's purpose and to look for topic sentences, details, transitions, and summary sentences. In other cases, students will predict outcomes, look for inferences, summarize, and evaluate.

73   HEARING IT IN CLASS

Today is your day to be in five places at the same time! The words found below were spoken in one of the five classes listed here. Write the corresponding letter of the most likely class in which the word was spoken on the line next to the number. When you are done, copy those letters, in order, onto the line below item 25. If your answers are correct, they will spell out four different words.

```
A = English class
D = Math class
E = Social studies class
S = Science or health class
T = Art class
```

1. _____ aorta
2. _____ silhouette
3. _____ preposition
4. _____ easel
5. _____ caucus
6. _____ perpendicular
7. _____ still life
8. _____ phrase
9. _____ corpuscle
10. _____ portrait
11. _____ monarchy
12. _____ corresponding angles
13. _____ apartheid

14. _____ electrode
15. _____ decoupage
16. _____ protagonist
17. _____ studio
18. _____ laissez-faire
19. _____ symbiosis
20. _____ rhombus
21. _____ cartographer
22. _____ watercolors
23. _____ preamble
24. _____ rotator cuff
25. _____ pastels

The consecutive letters are _____.

The four words are _____, _____, _____,

and _____.

74   WHERE HAVE ALL THE VOWELS GONE? (MATH)

Here are twenty terms that you have heard or will hear in your math classes. All of the vowels have been taken out; only the consonants remain. The term's remaining letters are given in the order in which they appear in the complete word. Write the full word in the blank. If the first of the given letters is capitalized, that means it is the first letter in the word. The number in parentheses after the consonants is the number of letters in the complete word. Good luck!

1. _____ ngl (5)

2. _____ Trngl (8)

3. _____ Bsct (6)

4. _____ Rctngl (9)

5. _____ Frml (7)

6. _____ ql (5)

7. _____ Nmrtr (9)

8. _____ Dvd (6)

9. _____ Mltply (8)

10. _____ xpnnt (8)

11. _____ Qtnt (8)

12. _____ Plygn (7)

13. _____ Sqnc (8)

14. _____ Sqr (6)

15. _____ Plynml (10)

16. _____ Zr (4)

17. _____ lgbr (7)

18. _____ Nmbr (6)

19. _____ Dgts (6)

20. _____ Mlln (7)

Reading Comprehension in Math and Science Classes

75 ELEMENTARY ALGEBRA COMPREHENSION

The following article deals with algebra, a field of mathematics. Algebra is useful in solving many types of math problems. Knowing it will help you succeed in math classes. Read the article, and then answer the ten questions that follow it.

Elementary algebra is the most basic form of algebra, taught to students who are presumed to have no knowledge of mathematics beyond the basic principles of arithmetic. Whereas in arithmetic only numbers and their arithmetical operations (such as +, −, ×, ÷) occur, algebra also uses symbols (such as a, x, and y) to denote numbers. This is useful for several reasons:

- It allows the general formulation of arithmetical laws (such as $a + b = b + a$ for all a and b) and thus is the first step to a systematic exploration of the properties of the real number system.
- It allows the reference to "unknown" numbers, the formulation of equations, and the study of how to solve these (for instance, "Find a number x such that $3x + 2 = 10$).
- It allows the formulation of functional relationships (such as "If you sell x tickets, your profit will be $3x − 10$ dollars").

These are the three main strands of *elementary algebra,* which should be distinguished from *abstract algebra,* a much more advanced topic generally taught to college seniors.

In algebra, an *expression* may contain numbers, variables, and arithmetical operations; examples are $a + 3$ and $x^2 − 3$. An *equation* is the claim that two expressions are equal. Some equations are true for all values of the variables involved—for example, $a + (b + c) = (a + b) + c$; these are also known as *identities.* Other equations contain symbols for unknown values, and we are then interested in finding the specific values for which the equation becomes true: $x^2 − 1 = 4$. These answers ($x = 2$ and $x = −2$) are the *solutions* of the equation.

As in arithmetic, it is important in algebra to know precisely how mathematical expressions are to be interpreted. This is determined by the rules governing the order in which operations are to be performed.

It is often necessary to simplify algebraic expressions. For example, the expression $−4(2a + 3) − a$ can be written in the equivalent form $−9a − 12$.

The simplest equations to solve are the *linear* ones, such as $2x + 3 = 10$. The central technique is to add, subtract, multiply, or divide both sides of the equation by the same number and by repeating this process eventually arrive at the value of the unknown x. For the example of $2x + 3 = 10$, if we subtract 3 from both sides, we obtain $2x = 7$, and if we then divide both sides by 2, we get our solution, $x = 7/2 = 3.5$.

75 ELEMENTARY ALGEBRA COMPREHENSION *(continued)*

Equations like $x^2 + 3x = 5$ are known as *quadratic* equations and can be solved using the *quadratic formula.* Expressions or statements may contain many variables, from which you may or may not be able to deduce the values for some of the variables. An example would be the expression $(x - 1)^2 = 0y$. After some algebraic steps not covered here, we can deduce that $x = 1$; however, we cannot deduce the value of y. Try some values of x and y (which may lead to either true or false statements) to get a feel for this.

However, if we had another equation in which the values for x and y were the same, we could deduce the answer in a process known as *systems of equations.* For example, assume that x and y have the same values in both of the following equations:

$4x + 2y = 14$

$2x - y = 1$

Multiply the second one by 2, and you have the following equations:

$4x + 2y = 14$

$4x - 2y = 2$

Because we multiplied both sides of the equation by 2, it still represents the same relationship. Now we can combine the two equations by adding them together to obtain

$8x = 16$

This effectively cancels out y, which allows us to solve for x, which is $16 \div 8 = 2$. Note that you can multiply by negative numbers or multiply both equations to reach a point where a variable cancels out (you could instead have canceled out x, for example).

Now let's take one of our equations:

$4x + 2y = 14$

First we substitute 2 for x:

$4(2) + 2y = 14$

Then we can simplify:

$8 + 2y = 14$

$2y = 14 - 8$

$2y = 6$

We can then solve for y, which equals 3. The answer to this problem is therefore $x = 2$ and $y = 3$, which can also be expressed in the form (2, 3).

75 ELEMENTARY ALGEBRA COMPREHENSION (continued)

1. _____ According to the article, algebra is different from arithmetic in that algebra
   (a) is more difficult for all students **(b)** is easier than arithmetic for most students
   (c) uses symbols to represent numbers **(d)** none of these.

2. _____ Which is an arithmetical operation?
   (a) $x + y$ **(b)** An acute angle measures less than 90 degrees.
   (c) There are several mathematical properties. **(d)** None of these.

3. _____ Which is an example of an equation?
   (a) One branch of math is algebra. **(b)** Angles are acute, right, or obtuse.
   (c) A right angle measures 90 degrees. **(d)** $4x - 3 = 17$

4. _____ Which is an advantage of algebra's employing symbols?
   (a) Algebra allows an exploration of the real number system's properties.
   (b) Algebra allows the formation of functional relationships.
   (c) Users work with unknown numbers and equations. **(d)** All of these.

5. _____ According to the article, which are the simplest equations to solve?
   (a) formulation **(b)** equivalent **(c)** linear **(d)** None of these.

6. _____ Which is not included in an expression?
   (a) variables **(b)** mathematical operations **(c)** numbers **(d)** None of these.

7. _____ Which is correct?
   (a) $-2(2b + 1) - b = -3b - 2$ **(b)** $3(c + 4) + c = 4c + 2c$
   (c) $c(3 + c) - c = 4c + 2c$ **(d)** None of these.

8. _____ What is the term for a claim that two expressions are equal?
   (a) formula **(b)** reference **(c)** equation **(d)** substitution

9. _____ In the equation $3x = 9$, x equals
   (a) 8 **(b)** 1 **(c)** 3 **(d)** none of these.

10. _____ The symbol for an unknown value in the equation $3x = 9$ is
    (a) 3 **(b)** x **(c)** 9 **(d)** none of these.

76 WORD PROBLEMS

Understanding word problems is an important part of your success in mathematics. Here are ten problems to test your skill at solving word problems. Write the solution to each word problem on the line that follows it. Use scrap paper or the back of this page to figure out your answers.

1. Reggie is four years older that Molly. In four years, Molly will be two-thirds Reggie's age. How old are Reggie and Molly?

_____

2. Ted owns 25 percent of the land owned by Shawna. If Shawna owns 400 acres, how many acres does Ted own?

_____

3. The six coins that Junior has in his hand add up to 58 cents. He has two of one coin, three of another, and one of a third coin. What six coins is Junior holding?

_____

4. The Reds, the Eagles, and the Sharks have all played twenty games each. The Reds have won 90 percent of their games. The Eagles have won 80 percent of their games. The Sharks have won 40 percent of their games. How many games have the Eagles won?

_____

5. Eduardo won the mile race with a time of six minutes. It took Ricardo 1.5 times longer to complete the same distance. What was Ricardo's time for the mile race?

_____

6. If Gabriella can read four books in five weeks, how long will it take her to read sixteen books?

_____

7. Captain Bob's boat can hold a maximum of fifty fishermen. If the boat is filled to 40 percent of its capacity, how many fishermen are on the boat?

_____

8. Coach Mullens has won 60 percent of the games he has coached at East High School. If he has coached five hundred games, how many games has he won?

_____

9. If it takes two landscapers, working at their usual pace, six hours to mow Mr. Lynn's lawn, how long will it take them to mow the lawn of an estate triple the size of Mr. Lynn's?

_____

10. Your boss gives you the following choice: She will (a) pay you $100 for working Monday through Friday or (b) give you $10 on Monday and increase your pay by 40 percent each day including Friday. Which would give you more money? _____

77   THE LAW OF AVERAGES

Is it true that if you flip a two-headed coin one hundred times, heads should come up fifty times and tails should come up fifty times? Is it true that if you roll a die six times, each of the numbers 1 through 6 will appear once? These questions deal with the law of averages. Read the passage below, and then answer the ten questions that follow it.

The *law of averages* is a term used to express the view that "everything evens out eventually." For example, two very similar people who drive similar cars in similar circumstances over a long period of time will have roughly the same number of accidents; the more children you have, the more likely you will have an equal division of boys and girls; and the longer you flip a coin, the more likely the number of heads and tails will equalize.

While the general belief in the law of averages is why people gamble in Las Vegas in the belief that they will "sooner or later break even," the *law of large numbers* is why casinos in Las Vegas make billions of dollars.

The law of large numbers states that a large sample of a particular probabilistic event will tend to reflect the underlying probabilities. For example, after tossing a fair coin one thousand times, we would expect the result to be approximately five hundred heads because this would reflect the underlying 0.5 chance of a heads result for any given flip.

However, it is important to recognize that although the *average* will move closer to the underlying probability, in absolute terms *deviation from the expected value* will increase. For example, after a thousand coin flips, we might see 520 heads. After ten thousand flips, we might then see 5,096 heads. The average has now moved closer to the underlying 0.5, from 0.52 to 0.5096. However, the absolute deviation from the expected number of heads has gone up from 20 to 96.

There are common ways to misunderstand and misapply the law of large numbers:

- "If I flip this coin a thousand times, I will get five hundred heads results."

This is false. Whereas we expect *approximately* five hundred heads results, we will not always get *exactly* five hundred heads results (in fact, although five hundred is the most likely outcome, it is quite unlikely). If the coin is fair, the chance of getting exactly five hundred heads is about 2.52 percent. Similarly, getting 520 heads results is not conclusive proof that the coin's true probability of getting heads on a single flip is 0.52.

- "I just got five tails in a row. My chances of getting heads must be very good now."

This too is false. Many probabilistic events are independent of one another, which means that the result of one event does not in any way influence the outcome of another. Coin flips are independent events. The coin does not "remember" what it has flipped previously and self-adjust to

77   THE LAW OF AVERAGES *(continued)*

get an overall average result. The coin is not "due" for heads to come up. The probability remains 0.5 for every individual flip. A belief in this fallacy can be devastating for amateur gamblers. The thought that "I have to win soon now because I've been losing and it has to even out" can encourage a gambler to continue to bet more.

1. _____ The expression "evens out" means that the ultimate result will be
   (a) equal **(b)** unequal.

2. _____ The chances of the same number of heads and the same number of tails coming up if you flip a coin will most likely occur if you flip the same coin
   (a) ten times **(b)** one hundred times **(c)** one thousand times **(d)** ten thousand times.

3. _____ Las Vegas casinos owners **(a)** like **(b)** do not like the law of large numbers.

4. _____ Roberto flips a coin one thousand times. Christina flips a coin ten thousand times. Which person has a greater chance of having a bigger margin or difference between the number of heads and the number of tails that come up? **(a)** Roberto **(b)** Christina

5. _____ If David flips a coin six hundred times, he will most probably get exactly three hundred heads and three hundred tails. Is this statement **(a)** true or **(b)** false?

6. _____ Marcia flipped a coin four hundred times. Heads came up 220 times, or 55 percent of the time. This means that the probability of getting heads on a single flip is 55 percent. Is this statement **(a)** true or **(b)** false?

7. _____ Cesar flips the same two-headed coin four times. Tails comes up all four times. The chance of Cesar's next flip coming up heads is 50–50, or 1 out of 2. Is this statement **(a)** true or **(b)** false?

8. _____ Shawnique's chance of successfully completing a foul shot is 50–50, or 1 out of 2. Is this statement **(a)** true or **(b)** false?

9. _____ Mr. Jones drives a total of 100 miles to and from work each day. Mrs. Smith drives her car a total of 20 miles to and from work each day. Both drivers work the same number of days each year. Both have the same two weeks of vacation. Which driver has the greater chance of being involved in an accident according to the laws of probability? **(a)** Mr. Jones **(b)** Mrs. Smith

10. _____ Mr. Liu just rolled a 6 on his die at the casino table. The chance of his rolling a 6 again on the next roll is **(a)** 1 out of 6 **(b)** 1 out of 2 **(c)** 1 out of 5 **(d)** 1 out of 4.

78 WHERE HAVE ALL THE VOWELS GONE? (SCIENCE)

Here are twenty terms that you might hear in your science classes. All of the vowels have been taken out; only the consonants remain. The remaining letters are in the order in which they appear in the complete word. Write the full word in the blank. If the first of the given letters is capitalized, that means that is the first letter in the term. The number in parentheses indicates the number of letters in the entire word. Good luck!

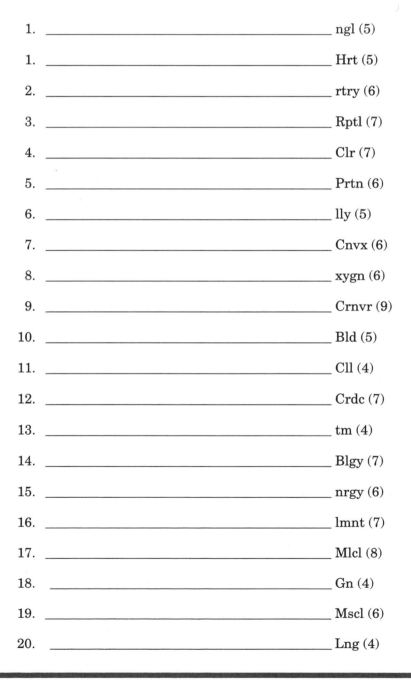

1. _____ ngl (5)

1. _____ Hrt (5)

2. _____ rtry (6)

3. _____ Rptl (7)

4. _____ Clr (7)

5. _____ Prtn (6)

6. _____ lly (5)

7. _____ Cnvx (6)

8. _____ xygn (6)

9. _____ Crnvr (9)

10. _____ Bld (5)

11. _____ Cll (4)

12. _____ Crdc (7)

13. _____ tm (4)

14. _____ Blgy (7)

15. _____ nrgy (6)

16. _____ lmnt (7)

17. _____ Mlcl (8)

18. _____ Gn (4)

19. _____ Mscl (6)

20. _____ Lng (4)

79 GHOSTS

Do you believe in ghosts? Have you heard or read stories about ghosts that frightened you? Ghosts are interesting in many ways. The story below is all about ghosts. Read the paragraphs below to learn more about ghosts and whether or not they truly exist. Then fill in the correct word from Column A in the appropriate space in Column B, and complete the magic square (three answers have already been provided). If your answers are correct, the rows, the columns, and the two diagonals will each add up to the same magic number. Have fun, and do not get spooked out!

Ghosts are the supposed apparitions of the dead. A ghost is often thought to be the spirit or soul of a person who has remained on earth after death. Every culture in the world has stories about ghosts, but beliefs vary substantially regarding what ghosts are and whether such things actually exist.

Ghosts are often depicted of human size and shape but are typically described as "silvery," "shadowy," "semitransparent," or "foglike." Sometimes they manifest themselves not visually but rather in terms of other phenomena, such as the movement of an object, the spontaneous throwing of a light switch, or noises, that supposedly have no natural explanation.

In the West, believers in ghosts sometimes hold them to be souls that could not find rest after death and so linger on earth. The inability to find rest is often explained by unfinished business, such as a victim seeking justice or revenge after death. Criminals sometimes supposedly linger to avoid purgatory or hell. It is sometimes held that ghosts reside in limbo, a place, according to Catholic doctrine, between heaven and hell where the souls of unbaptized infants go.

In Asian cultures, many people believe in reincarnation. Ghosts are thought to be souls that refused to be "recycled" because they have unfinished business on earth, a belief similar to that in the West. Exorcists can either help a ghost be reincarnated or blow it out of existence. In Chinese belief, a ghost can be reincarnated, but it can also become immortal and become a demigod, or it can go to hell and suffer for eternity, or it can die again and become the "ghost of a ghost."

Both the West and the East share some fundamental beliefs about ghosts. They are said to wander around places they frequented when alive or the place where they died. Such places are known as "haunted," and the rounds the ghosts go on are known as "hauntings." Ghosts are presumed not to have a physical body like human beings, but they are often seen wearing the sort of clothing they would have worn when alive.

A = 4	B =	C =	D =
E =	F =	G =	H = 8
I =	J =	K =	L =
M =	N = 1	O =	P =

Magic Number: _____

Name: _____ Date: _____ Period: _____

79   GHOSTS (continued)

Column A

A. shadowy

B. clothing

C. visible

D. recycled

E. died

F. Western

G. immortal

H. reincarnation

I. haunted

J. exorcists

K. natural

L. eternally

M. human

N. dead

O. Criminals

P. revenge

Column B

1. Ghosts are supposed apparitions of the _____.

2. The Chinese believe that a ghost can become _____ and become a demigod.

3. The Chinese also believe that a ghost can suffer _____ in hell.

4. A ghost is often described as _____.

5. Ghosts may manifest themselves without any _____ explanation.

6. Though both the Western and Eastern cultures believe that a ghost does not have a physical body, they believe that a ghost will often wear the type of _____ the person wore while alive on earth.

7. Most ghosts are depicted to be the size of a _____.

8. In Asian cultures, many people believe in _____, the rebirth of the soul in another body.

9. To be considered a ghost, the person must have already _____.

10. Some cultures believe that ghosts seek _____ after death.

11. An apparition is a _____ appearance.

12. A ghost can be reincarnated with the help of _____.

13. In Asian cultures, ghosts are souls who have not been _____ because they have unfinished business to do.

14. Places that ghosts frequent are said to be _____.

15. _____ cultures believe that ghosts are souls that could not find rest after death and so they linger on earth.

16. _____ supposedly linger on earth to avoid purgatory or hell.

80   VAMPIRES

How much do you know about vampires, creatures that are said to thrive on human blood? Here is an article that will tell you a lot more about them. Read it through, and then answer the ten questions that follow it by writing the correct letter on the appropriate line. The paragraphs have been numbered for your convenience.

(1) A vampire is a mythical or folkloric creature said to subsist on human or animal blood. Usually the vampire is the corpse of a dead person, reanimated or made undead by one means or another. Some cultures have myths of nonhuman vampires, such as demons or animals like bats, dogs, and spiders. Vampires are often described as having a wide variety of additional powers and character traits, extremely variable in different traditions, and are frequent subjects of folklore, cinema, and contemporary fiction.

(2) Vampirism is the practice of drinking blood. In folklore and popular culture, the term generally refers to a belief that one can gain supernatural powers by drinking human blood. The historical practice of vampirism can generally be considered a more specific and less commonly occurring form of cannibalism. The consumption of another person's blood has been used as a tactic of psychological warfare intended to terrorize the enemy, and it can be used to reflect various spiritual beliefs.

(3) In zoology, the term *vampirism* is used to refer to leeches, mosquitoes, mistletoe, vampire bats, and other organisms that survive on the bodily fluids of other creatures. The term also applies to fictional animals of the same nature, including the chupacabra or goatsucker.

(4) Tales of the dead craving blood are ancient. In Homer's *Odyssey,* for example, the shades (ghosts) that Odysseus meets on his journey to the underworld are lured to the blood of freshly sacrificed rams, a fact that Odysseus uses to his advantage to summon the shade of Tiresias.

(5) Some Slavic peoples believed in vampires as early as the fourth century. In their mythology, a vampire drank blood, feared silver (but could not be killed by it), and could be destroyed by cutting off its head and putting it between the corpse's legs or by driving a wooden stake into its heart.

(6) In popular Western culture, vampires are depicted as unaging, intelligent, and mystically endowed in many ways. The vampire typically has a variety of notable abilities. These include great strength and immunity to the lasting effect of any injury inflicted by mundane means, with specific exceptions. Vampires can also change into a mist, a wolf, or a bat, and some can control the minds of others. They typically have extended canines or fangs.

(7) It is believed that vampires have no reflection, as it was traditionally thought that mirrors reflected the soul and creatures of evil have no soul. Fiction has extended this belief to an actual aversion to mirrors, as depicted in Bram Stoker's novel *Dracula,* in which the vampire casts Harker's shaving mirror out the window.

80   VAMPIRES *(continued)*

(8) A Western vampire (which is not alive in the classical sense and is therefore referred to as "undead") can be destroyed using several methods, which vary among vampire types and mythologies:

- Ramming a wooden stake through a vampire's heart. Traditionally, the stake is made from ash or hawthorn, and the vampire should be impaled with a single blow. In some traditions, a red-hot iron was preferred. In many Western stories and films, impalement with a wooden stake only subdues a vampire, and further measures must be taken to destroy the body or else the monster will quickly recover once the stake is removed. Destruction can be done by decapitating the body and burying the head separately, burning the body, burying the body at a crossroads, or moving the body to a place where it would be exposed to sunlight. Some stories extend the idea with vampire hunters using arrows or crossbow bolts made completely of wood to attempt to strike the monster's heart from a distance.
- Exposing a vampire to sunlight. This varies from culture to culture. Vampires that are active from sunset to sunrise often avoid sunlight, as they can be weakened or even destroyed by it. Many species of vampires are active from noon to midnight or the converse, and consequently to them sunlight is harmless. The idea of Western vampires' being vulnerable to sunlight began with Stoker's novel and was reinforced by the 1922 film *Nosferatu,* and it has come to be seen as the surest way to completely destroy a vampire.
- Removing internal organs and burning them.
- Pouring boiling water into a hole beside the vampire's grave.

(9) Vampires will be burned or badly hurt if they come into contact with a cross. Other typical weaknesses of the vampire include the following:

- Garlic or holy water, both of which repel vampires.
- Objects made of silver, which can keep a vampire away or harm them if they are in physical contact. A popular American addition to the folklore is the idea of fashioning bullets made of silver so that mortal vampire hunters can use firearms against the monster.
- Small items such as rice, poppy seeds, or grains of salt, which can be strewn in a vampire's path. This common feature of many vampire myths may have originated in the belief that vampires suffer from obsessive-compulsive disorder and are therefore easily distracted. Thus the hanging of many cloves of garlic or the scattering of small objects is said to sidetrack the vampire into counting the exact number of such objects before moving on, thereby keeping them out of mischief until morning, when they must retreat to avoid the sun.
- Running water, which vampires cannot cross. This varies by tradition; some stories have vampires simply turn into bats and fly over when faced with this obstacle.

80 VAMPIRES (continued)

- Crosses and Bibles, which can keep vampires away. Simply holding the object in front of the vampire keeps the monster at a distance. Other stories hold that any religious symbol used by a sincere believer is effective. For example, in some stories, a Jew can use the Star of David to ward off a vampire. However, in many stories, the monster can use its mind control powers to force the wielder to put the object down.
- Requiring an invitation to enter a home. Western vampires are thought to be unable to enter a residence unless they are invited inside. After that invitation, they can enter the location freely.

1. _____ Which paragraph covers the topic "Vampires in literature and culture"?
   (a) paragraph 1 (b) paragraph 2 (c) paragraph 3 (d) paragraph 4 (e) paragraph 7

2. _____ Which paragraph explains what vampirism is?
   (a) paragraph 1 (b) paragraph 2 (c) paragraph 3 (d) paragraph 5 (e) paragraph 8

3. _____ Which paragraph discusses the abilities of vampires?
   (a) paragraph 1 (b) paragraph 2 (c) paragraph 3 (d) paragraph 4 (e) paragraph 6

4. _____ Which paragraph provides a general description of a vampire?
   (a) paragraph 1 (b) paragraph 2 (c) paragraph 3 (d) paragraph 6 (e) paragraph 7

5. _____ Which paragraph explains how to destroy a vampire?
   (a) paragraph 1 (b) paragraph 2 (c) paragraph 3 (d) paragraph 6 (e) paragraph 8

6. _____ Which is *not* a characteristic of a vampire?
   (a) It can become an animal. (b) It is strong.
   (c) It is smart. (d) It can become a meteorite.

7. _____ Vampirism is nearly the same as which of these?
   (a) cannibalism (b) bats' behaviors (c) the underworld (d) Western literary culture

8. _____ Which is thought to be the most effective way to destroy a vampire?
   (a) Read Homer's *Odyssey* to it. (b) Take the vampire with you for a walk on a sunny day. (c) Introduce it to another vampire. (d) Give it human blood.

9. _____ Which can a vampire do?
   (a) drink blood (b) become a mist (c) bite with its long fangs (d) all of these

10. _____ Which word means "brought back to life"?
    (a) vampirism (b) folklore (c) reanimation (d) notable

81   PHOBIAS

Many of us have different things that we fear. Some people fear snakes, crocodiles, the dark, or speaking in front of a large group of people. Such fears or phobias can be harmful to a person's mental and physical well-being. Read this article to learn more about phobias. Then fill in the answers to the crossword puzzle. The first letter of each answer is provided. Now don't be afraid to attempt this puzzle!

Psychologists apply the term *phobia,* which comes from the Greek word for "fear," to a number of psychological conditions that can seriously disable their carriers.

Phobias are the most common form of anxiety disorder. An American study by the National Institute of Mental Health (NIMH) found that between 5.1 and 21.5 percent of Americans suffer from phobias. Broken down by age and gender, the study found that phobias were the most common mental illness among women in all age groups and the second most common illness among men older than twenty-five.

Most psychologists divide phobias into three categories:

- Social phobias—fears having to do with other people and social relationships, such as performance anxiety or fears of speaking in public
- Specific phobias—fears of a single specific panic trigger, like dogs, flying, or running water
- Agoraphobia—a generalized fear of leaving home or one's small, familiar "safe" area and of the panic attacks that will inevitable follow (Agoraphobia is the only phobia regularly treated as a medical condition.)

Many specific phobias, such as fears of dogs, heights, and spider bites, are extensions of fears that everyone has. People with these phobias treat them by avoiding the things they fear.

Many specific phobias can be traced back to a specific triggering event, usually a traumatic experience at an early age. Social phobias and agoraphobia have more complex causes that are not entirely understood. It is believed that heredity, genetics, and brain chemistry combine with life experiences in the development of anxiety disorders and phobias.

Phobias vary in severity among individuals, with some phobics simply disliking or avoiding the subjects of their fear and suffering mild anxiety. Others suffer full-blown panic attacks, with all the associated disabling symptoms.

It is possible for a person to become phobic about virtually anything. The name of a phobia is generally formed from the Greek word for whatever the patient fears plus the suffix *-phobia.* Coining these terms is something of a word game. Few of these terms are found in medical literature.

81 PHOBIAS *(continued)*

81   PHOBIAS *(continued)*

Across

4. The word *phobia* comes from the _____ language.

6. Some people treat phobias by _____ the things they fear.

7. Agoraphobia is a fear of leaving a familiar _____ area.

8. A person's fear of speaking before a group is an example of a _____ fear.

9. A severe phobia can be devastating to one's _____ health.

11. Phobias are the most common mental illness among _____ in all age groups.

13. Acrophobia is the fear of _____.

16. Perhaps as many as one-_____ of all Americans suffer from phobias.

17. The word *phobia* means _____.

18. A medical _____ can help a person overcome a phobia.

Down

1. Agoraphobia is the only phobia regularly _____ as a medical condition.

2. People suffering from phobias experience _____ attacks.

3. Some who suffer from phobias experience only _____ anxiety.

5. Many phobias started because of a traumatic or frightening _____.

8. The article classifies fear of flying as a _____ phobia.

10. Phobia is a type of _____ disorder.

11. If a hydroplane is an airplane that can land on water, hydrophobia is most probably a fear of _____.

12. Superstitious people who suffer from triskadekaphobia do not look forward to the thirteenth day of the month because they fear the number _____.

14. _____ and genetics can also contribute to phobias.

15. Phobias are the _____ most common illness among American men over twenty-five years of age.

82   ANOREXIA NERVOSA

Here is an essay on anorexia nervosa, the eating disorder, followed by twelve statements about the disorder that may or may not be accurate. Read the essay; then determine which statements are true and which are false. For each statement, circle the two-letter answer code in the appropriate answer column. If your answers are correct, your answers to the true items, read from the top down, will spell out the name of one sort of person who helps anorexics deal with their problems, and your answers to the false answers will spell out the name of another such person.

Anorexia nervosa is an eating disorder characterized by voluntary starvation and exercise stress. It is a complex disease, involving psychological, sociological, and physiological components. A person who is suffering from anorexia is known as an anorexic.

Anorexia warps an individual's body image to the point that she—for indeed, the great majority of anorexics are female—may regard herself as being fat and even repulsive regardless of her actual size and shape. This distorted body image is a source of considerable anxiety, and losing weight is considered the solution. However, even when the anorexic reaches her weight-loss goal, she still feels that she is overweight and in need of further weight loss.

Losing weight is typically viewed as a victory, and gaining weight is a bitter defeat. *Control* is a factor strongly associated with anorexia, and anorexics typically feel out of control of their life. However, the role of such psychological factors is complex and not fully understood.

Other psychological difficulties and mental illnesses often coexist with anorexia. Mild to severe manifestations of depression are common, partly because an inadequate calorie intake is a well-known trigger for depression in susceptible individuals. Other afflictions may include self-harm and obsessive-compulsive thinking. However, not all anorexics have any problems beyond their eating disorder.

Many anorexics reach such a low body weight that hospitalization and forced feeding become necessary on a long-term or recurring basis in order to keep them from starving to death. Prolonged starvation causes the body's systems progressively to shut down, eventually leading to death, and this is the major danger factor of anorexia, in addition to the patient's mental suffering and the risk of suicide due to depression.

Some anorexics may adopt bulimic behavior: binge-eating and then purging themselves of food (that is, forcing themselves to vomit). Some individuals actually evolve from anorexia to bulimia. Although bulimia poses less of a mortal danger than anorexia, many individuals who have suffered both say that bulimia involves more mental suffering, and bulimics may develop serious problems of the throat, mouth, and gums due to their frequent exposure to caustic stomach acids.

Anorexia alters one's body image so that one does not see the truth about oneself even when one looks in the mirror. To the anorexic, there is no such thing as being too thin. Anorexics acknowledge their condition to different degrees—at one extreme, they do not regard their

82 ANOREXIA NERVOSA *(continued)*

"disease" as dangerous and resent being labeled as psychologically ill; at the other, they understand and accept that they have a problem but cannot overcome the anorexic mind-set. In ways not too dissimilar from people who have had cult programming or posttraumatic stress disorder, an anorexic may be "triggered" into disordered thinking by being exposed to certain words or conditions.

Some people eat unusually small amounts of food for reasons other than their own perceived obesity. Examples include those who fast for religious reasons, embark on a hunger strike as a political statement, or seek to lengthen their life span through caloric restriction. Such individuals are not ordinarily considered anorexic, although some modern critics of religious asceticism have likened habitual fasting to anorexia.

		True	False
1.	Individuals who suffer from anorexia nervosa choose to do so of their own free will.	(ps)	(do)
2.	More often than not, the anorexic suffers from both physiological and psychological difficulties.	(yc)	(lt)
3.	Depression cannot be caused by inadequate caloric intake.	(ma)	(ph)
4.	Some anorexics also do other types of physical damage to their bodies.	(hi)	(nu)
5.	Unfortunately, some anorexics starve themselves to death.	(at)	(al)
6.	Binge eating and purging are characteristics of anorexia.	(ly)	(ys)
7.	Bulimia is more likely to cause death than anorexia.	(fo)	(io)
8.	Anorexics almost never become bulimics.	(re)	(lo)
9.	Anorexics do not think of themselves as ever being "too thin."	(ri)	(ig)
10.	Anorexics do not appreciate being told they have a behavioral problem.	(st)	(ne)
11.	A comment like "Looks like you're putting on a little weight" would be pleasing to a person with anorexia.	(rs)	(gi)
12.	People who fast for religious reasons but eat normally at all other times are nevertheless considered anorexic.	(gh)	(st)

The true answers spell out _____.

The false answers spell out _____.

83   CROCODILES

Many people are deathly afraid of crocodiles. Are you? Those big teeth and quick reflexes are enough to frighten most of us! Read the article below. Then, without looking back at the article and using the word bank on the next page, fill in the correct word for each blank. Each word is used only once.

Contrary to popular belief, only three species of crocodile (the saltwater, the mugger, and the Nile) and one species of alligator (the nearly extinct black caiman) have been known to stalk or attack human beings for food. Large specimens of these four are extremely dangerous. Saltwater crocodiles in northern Australia dine on careless tourists once every few years.

Crocodiles are very fast over short distances, even out of water. They have extremely powerful jaws and razor-sharp teeth for tearing flesh, but they cannot open their mouth if it is held closed; this lends credence to the stories told of people escaping from the long-snouted Nile crocodile by holding its jaws shut. All large crocodiles also have sharp and powerful claws. Crocodiles are ambush hunters, waiting for fish or land animals to come close and then attacking with a rush. As cold-blooded predators, they can go long periods without food and rarely need to go actively hunting. Despite their slow appearance, crocodiles are top-level predators in their chosen environment, and various species have been observed attacking and killing lions, large hoofed mammals, and even sharks.

Name: _____ Date: _____ Period: _____

83 CROCODILES (continued)

ambush	escaping	predators	species
appearance	fast	razor-sharp	stalk
careless	food	rush	tearing
dangerous	killing	sharks	top-level
environment	powerful	shut	years

Contrary to popular belief, only three (1) _____ of crocodile (the saltwater, the mugger, and the Nile) and one species of alligator (the nearly extinct black caiman) have been known to (2) _____ or attack human beings for food. Large specimens of these four are extremely (3) _____. Saltwater crocodiles in northern Australia dine on (4) _____ tourists once every few (5) _____.

Crocodiles are very (6) _____ over short distances, even out of water. They have extremely (7) _____ jaws and (8) _____ teeth for (9) _____ flesh, but they cannot open their mouth if it is held closed; this lends credence to the stories told of people (10) _____ from the long-snouted Nile crocodile by holding its jaws (11) _____. All large crocodiles also have sharp and powerful claws. Crocodiles are (12) _____ hunters, waiting for fish or land animals to come close and then attacking with a (13) _____. As cold-blooded (14) _____, they can go long periods without (15) _____ and rarely need to go actively hunting. Despite their slow (16) _____, crocodiles are (17) _____ predators in their chosen (18) _____, and various species have been observed attacking and (19) _____ lions, large hoofed mammals, and even (20) _____.

84   THE TRUTH ABOUT SNAKES

Are you afraid of snakes? Does even the thought of them creep you out? How powerful and deadly are snakes? Do all of them spew venom? This article will tell you a great deal about snakes. After you have completed reading the article, answer the fifteen questions by writing T (for true) or F (for false) in each blank.

Snakes are cold-blooded, legless reptiles closely related to lizards; in fact, both belong to the order Squamata. There are also several species of legless lizards that superficially resemble snakes but are not otherwise related to them. A love of snakes is called *ophiophilia.*

All snakes are carnivorous, eating small animals (including lizards and other snakes), birds, eggs, or insects. Some snakes have a venomous bite that they use to kill their prey before eating it. Other snakes kill their prey by constriction, resulting in death by strangulation. Snakes do not chew their food; they have a very flexible lower jaw, the two halves of which are not rigidly attached, and numerous other joints in their skull, all of which allow them to open their mouths wide enough to swallow their prey whole, even if it is larger in diameter than the snake itself. Contrary to the popular myth, at no point do they "unhinge" their jaws; their mandibular joints are distended but remain attached. After eating, snakes enter a state known as torpor while the process of digestion takes place. Digestion is an intensive activity, requiring vast amounts of metabolic energy, especially after the consumption of very large prey. Consequently, a snake disturbed after a recent meal will often regurgitate the prey in order to be able to muster the energy to escape the perceived threat. However, the digestive process, when undisturbed, is highly efficient, dissolving and absorbing everything but hair and claws, which are excreted along with uric acid waste.

The skin of a snake is covered in scales. For locomotion, most snakes use specialized belly scales that help them grip surfaces. The body scales may be smooth, keeled (ridged), or granular (grainy). Snakes' eyelids are transparent scales that remain permanently closed. Snakes shed their skin periodically. Unlike other reptiles, it is stripped off in one piece, like pulling off a sock. It is thought that the primary purpose of shedding is to remove external parasites. This periodic renewal has led to the snake's becoming a symbol of healing and medicine.

Although snakes are not believed to see very well, detection of movement is based on more than just vision. Some snakes (including pit vipers, boas, and pythons) have infrared sensitive receptors in deep grooves between the nostril and eye that allow them to "see" the heat radiated by living beings. Snakes have no external ears; their hearing is restricted to the sensing of vibrations, but this sense is extremely well developed. A snake smells by using its forked tongue to collect airborne particles and passing them to a specialized organ in the mouth for examination and identification. The forked tongue gives the snake a sort of directional sense of smell. The left lung is very small or sometimes even absent, as snakes' tubular bodies require that their organs be long and thin, and to accommodate them all, only one lung is functional. Many other organs that are paired, such as kidneys or reproductive organs, are staggered within the body, with one located ahead of the other.

84   THE TRUTH ABOUT SNAKES (continued)

1. _____ All snakes shed their skin periodically.

2. _____ Digestion is an intensive activity for snakes.

3. _____ All snakes are carnivorous.

4. _____ Snakes do not chew their food.

5. _____ Snakes do not unhinge their jaws.

6. _____ Snakes are reptiles.

7. _____ Many snakes use their belly scales for gripping purposes.

8. _____ If threatened, snakes may regurgitate what they are eating.

9. _____ A snake smells by using its tongue.

10. _____ A snake can survive with only one lung.

11. _____ The snake is a symbol of healing and medicine.

12. _____ A snake's eyelids are never opened.

13. _____ Snakes are cold-blooded.

14. _____ Snakes have no external ears.

15. _____ Some snakes have infrared sensitive receptors between the nostril and the eye.

85   BATS

Read these paragraphs about bats. You will learn a great deal about these interesting creatures. Then without looking back at the article, fill in the blanks in the ten sentences on the next page. The first letter of each answer is given to you. Try not to go batty doing this activity!

Bats are usually divided into two groups: megabats and microbats. Most megabats have large eyes and short, round ears and eat fruit. Microbats are generally smaller than megabats. They have large ears and small eyes and eat insects.

All bats are active at night or at twilight, so the eyesight of most species is not highly developed. The senses of smell and hearing, however, are excellent. By emitting high-pitched sounds and listening for the echoes, microbats locate prey and other nearby objects. This is known as *echolocation,* a skill they share with dolphins and whales. Bats' teeth are very sharp in order to bite through the chitin armor of insects or the skin of fruits.

Newborn bats cling to the fur of their mother and are transported, although they soon grow too large for this. It would be difficult for an adult bat to carry more than one young bat, so normally only one offspring is born at a time. Two mammary glands are situated between the chest and the shoulders. Only the mother cares for the young, and there is no continuous partnership with the father. Bats often form nursery roosts, with many females giving birth in the same area, which might be a cave, a hole in a tree, or a cavity in a building.

The ability to fly is inborn, but at birth the wings are too small to support the bat in flight. Microbats become independent at the age of six to eight weeks, but megabats do not leave the roost until they are four months old. Bats can reproduce by the age of two years.

Small bats are sometimes preyed on by owls and falcons, but otherwise, few animals hunt bats. In Asia there is a bird, the bat hawk, that specializes in hunting bats. The domestic cat is a regular predator in urban areas; cats may catch bats as they enter or leave a roost or on the ground. Bats land on the ground for feeding, in bad weather, or due to accidents while learning to fly.

Bats' worst enemies are parasites. The wing membranes, rife with blood vessels, are ideal food sources for fleas, ticks, and mites. Some groups of insects, such as the bat fly, live exclusively on bat blood. In their caves, the bats hang close together, so it is easy for parasites to infest new hosts.

Of the very few cases of rabies reported in the United States every year, most are caused by bat bites. Although most bats do not have rabies, those that do may be clumsy, disoriented, and unable to fly, which makes it more likely that they will come into contact with humans. Although one should not have an unreasonable fear of bats, one should avoid handling them or having them in one's living space, as with any wild animal. If a bat is found in living quarters near a child, a mentally handicapped person, an intoxicated person, a sleeping person, or a pet, the person or pet should receive immediate medical attention for rabies. Bats have very small teeth and can bite a sleeping person without the bite necessarily being felt.

85   BATS (continued)

If a bat is found in a house and the possibility of exposure cannot be ruled out, the bat should be sequestered and an animal control officer called immediately so that the bat can be analyzed. This also applies if the bat is found dead. If it is certain that nobody has been exposed to the bat, it should be removed from the house. The best way to do this is to close all the doors and windows to the room except one to the outside. The bat should soon leave of its own accord. Due to the risk of rabies and also due to health problems related to their guano (feces), bats should be excluded from inhabited parts of houses.

Where rabies is not endemic, small bats can be considered harmless. Larger bats can give a nasty bite. Treat them with the respect due to any wild animal.

1. There are _f_____ cases of rabies reported in the United States every year.

2. Most cases of rabies are caused by bat _b_____.

3. Bats that are clumsy, disoriented, and unable to fly will more likely come into contact with

   _h_____.

4. No one should have an _u_____ fear of bats.

5. Bats have very small, sharp _t_____.

6. A bat can bite a sleeping person without its being _f_____.

7. If a bat is in a house, try to _s_____ it.

8. One should call an animal _c_____ officer if a bat is in the house.

9. Even a dead bat should be _a_____ to detect if it is diseased.

10. The best way to remove a living bat from the house is to close all the windows and doors to the rooms except one to the _o_____.

86 SALAMANDERS

Read this article about salamanders. Then without looking back at the article, fill in the blanks on the next page, using the words in the word bank. Use each word only once.

The name *salamander* is applied to approximately 350 amphibian vertebrates with slender bodies, short legs, and long tails. The moist skin of the amphibians limits them to habitats either near water or under some protection on moist ground, usually in a forest. Some species are aquatic throughout life, some take to the water intermittently, and some are entirely terrestrial as adults. Salamanders superficially resemble lizards but are easily distinguished by their lack of scales. They are capable of regenerating lost limbs. The known salamanders fall into ten families belonging to the order Urodela, divided into three suborders.

Species of salamanders are numerous and are found in most moist or aqueous habitats, such as brooks and ponds, in the Northern Hemisphere. Most salamanders are small, but some can grow to several feet in length. Northern America has the hellbender and the mudpuppy, which can reach the length of a foot. Japan has the giant salamander, which reaches 5 feet and can weigh as much as 55 pounds.

Reading Comprehension in Math and Science Classes

86 SALAMANDERS *(continued)*

amphibian	limbs	ponds
aquatic	lizards	scales
feet	long	short
forest	moist	slender
habitats	northern	weigh

The name *salamander* is applied to approximately 350 (1) _____ vertebrates

with (2) _____ bodies, (3) _____ legs, and

(4) _____ tails. The (5) _____ skin of the amphibians

limits them to (6) _____ either near water or under some protection

on moist ground, usually in a (7) _____. Some species are

(8) _____ throughout life, some take to the water intermittently,

and some are entirely terrestrial as adults. Salamanders superficially resemble

(9) _____ but are easily distinguished by their lack of

(10) _____. They are capable of regenerating lost

(11) _____. The known salamanders fall into ten families belonging to the

order Urodela, divided into three suborders.

Species of salamanders are numerous and are found in most moist or aqueous habitats,

such as brooks and (12) _____, in the (13) _____

Hemisphere. Most salamanders are small, but some can grow to several

(14) _____ in length. Northern America has the hellbender and the

mudpuppy, which can reach the length of a foot. Japan has the giant salamander, which reaches

5 feet and can (15) _____ as much as 55 pounds.

87 SHARKS

The shark is both very dangerous and very interesting. Many people are so afraid of sharks that they will not go into the water fearing that a shark might attack them. Today you will learn more about sharks. Read the article; then without looking at it again, use the words in the word bank to complete the ten sentences that follow it. Each word is used only once.

Sharks have such a keen olfactory sense that they can smell one part blood in one million parts seawater. Some species have even protrusions known as barbels near the mouth that aid even more in sensing prey. Sharks' eyes are much like those of other vertebrates, with similar lenses, corneas, and retinas, but their eyesight is well adapted to their marine environment. Some sharks have adaptations that allow them to see in dark environs. They have a sort of eyelid known as a nictitating membrane to protect the eye during hunting. More than sight, sharks rely on their superior sense of smell to find prey. They also have receptors along their sides that sense electrical pulses sent out by wounded or dying fish. Sharks' teeth are not attached to the jaw but are instead embedded in the flesh of the mouth. The lower teeth are used primarily for holding prey, while the top teeth are used for cutting into it.

Not all sharks are "large," "marine," and "predatory." They range from the hand-sized pygmy shark, a deep-sea species, to the whale shark, the largest known fish (although sharks are not closely related to bony fish), which is believed to grow to a maximum length of around 60 feet and which, like the great whales, feeds only on plankton. The bull shark is unique in that it can swim in both saltwater ocean and freshwater rivers. A few of the larger species, including the mako shark and the white shark, are mildly homeothermic, which means they are able to maintain their body temperature at a level slightly above that of the ocean.

If a shark is swimming near you, immediately move into shallow waters to limit its mobility. If a shark bites you, beat and claw its eyes, nose, and gills. If you hurt these sensitive regions, it will most likely release you and retreat. If available, surfboards or other flotation devices can be shoved into a shark's mouth to confuse or distract it. If you are wounded, get out of the water immediately, as the blood will attract more sharks quickly. If for some reason a shark has to be pulled ashore (perhaps to retrieve a severed limb), grasp it around the tail and pull it ashore backward; this is effective because most of the shark's strength is derived from its tail motions, so grabbing it there makes it much weaker. If you are forced to grapple with a shark in this manner, be wary of its skin, which has the texture of sandpaper and can tear flesh from your body as easily as its teeth can.

The best way to survive a shark attack is to avoid one. Do not swim when you are bleeding or in areas that are known to harbor sharks.

87   SHARKS (continued)

> barbels   olfactory   shallow
>
> blood   plankton   smell
>
> dark   retreat
>
> electrical   sandpaper

1. Sharks have such a keen _____ sense that they can smell one part blood in one million parts seawater.

2. Some species have even protrusions known as _____ near the mouth that aid even more in sensing prey.

3. Some sharks have adaptations that allow them to see in _____ environs.

4. More than sight, sharks rely on their superior sense of _____ to find prey.

5. They also have receptors along their sides that sense _____ pulses sent out by wounded or dying fish.

6. Sharks range from the hand-sized pygmy shark to the whale shark, which is believed to grow

   to a maximum length of around 60 feet and which feeds only on _____.

7. If a shark is swimming near you, immediately move into _____ waters to limit its mobility.

8. If you harm its sensitive regions, the shark will most likely release you and

   _____.

9. If you are wounded, get out of the water immediately, as the _____ will attract more sharks quickly.

10. If you are forced to grapple with a shark, be wary of its skin, which has the texture of

    _____ and can tear flesh from your body as easily as its teeth can.

88   RAIN FORESTS

The elimination of the world's rain forests has become a major problem. What exactly is a rain forest? Why are the rain forests disappearing? Is there any hope that some will not be eliminated? This article will answer these and other questions about rain forests. Read the article; then answer the ten questions that follow. Write the letter corresponding to the correct answer in the blank for each question. The paragraphs have been numbered for your convenience.

(1) A rain forest is a forested biome (ecological community) with high annual rainfall. Some authorities set a minimum normal annual rainfall of about 100 inches and normal rainfall at least 2.5 inches in each of the twelve months of the year. Others set the minimum annual rainfall qualifier as low as 67 inches. The soil can be poor because high rainfall tends to leach out soluble nutrients. This type of biome is found in both temperate and tropical climates. In addition to prodigious rainfall, many rain forests are characterized by a large number of resident species and tremendous biodiversity.

(2) The undergrowth in a rain forest is restricted in many areas by the lack of sunlight at ground level. This makes it possible for humans and other animals to walk through the forest. If the leaf canopy is destroyed or thinned for any reason, the ground beneath is soon colonized by a dense tangled growth of vines, shrubs, and small trees called jungle.

(3) It is estimated that rain forests provide as much as 40 percent of the oxygen currently found in the atmosphere. Nevertheless, tropical and temperate rain forests have been subjected to heavy logging and agricultural clearance for more than a century, meaning that the portion of the earth that is covered by rain forest has been rapidly shrinking. It is estimated that the rain forest was reduced by about 22,620 square miles annually in the 1990s. Rain forests used to cover 14 percent of the earth's surface. This figure is now down to 6 percent, and it is estimated that the remaining rain forests could disappear within forty years at the present rate of logging. Many scientists dispute these estimates in light of the rapid growth of new tropical rain forests in cleared areas. Biologists have estimated that large numbers of species are being driven to extinction—possibly more than fifty thousand a year—due to the loss of habitat resulting from the destruction of the rain forests.

(4) The largest tropical rain forests exist in the Amazon basin in South America, in the equatorial portions of the Democratic Republic of Congo, and in much of Indonesia. Temperate rain forests are found along the Pacific coast of North America from Alaska down to Washington state and in parts of Japan. Most temperate rain forests result from a prevailing upslope air flow along a mountain range.

Reading Comprehension in Math and Science Classes

88 RAIN FORESTS *(continued)*

1. _____ Which paragraph describes the rain forest's floor?
   (a) paragraph 1 **(b)** paragraph 2 **(c)** paragraph 3 **(d)** paragraph 4

2. _____ Which paragraph gives the locations of rain forests?
   (a) paragraph 1 **(b)** paragraph 2 **(c)** paragraph 3 **(d)** paragraph 4

3. _____ Which paragraph discusses problems within the rain forest?
   (a) paragraph 1 **(b)** paragraph 2 **(c)** paragraph 3 **(d)** paragraph 4

4. _____ Which paragraph details the rain forest's characteristics?
   (a) paragraph 1 **(b)** paragraph 2 **(c)** paragraph 3 **(d)** paragraph 4

5. _____ What portion of the earth's surface is covered by rain forests?
   (a) 22,620 square miles **(b)** 6 percent **(c)** 40 percent **(d)** 100 percent

6. _____ Approximately how many years might it take for all the rain forests to disappear?
   (a) fifty thousand **(b)** six **(c)** forty **(d)** one hundred

7. _____ Approximately how many species are driven to extinction each year due to the
   destruction of the rain forest? **(a)** fifty thousand **(b)** six **(c)** forty **(d)** one hundred

8. _____ What is the rain forest's annual rainfall, in inches? **(a)** 50,000 **(b)** 6 **(c)** 40 **(d)** 100

9. _____ *Leach* means **(a)** improve **(b)** drain out **(c)** fix **(d)** add to.

10. _____ If the rain forests disappear, what could be the result?
    (a) less oxygen in the air **(b)** fewer trees **(c)** both *a* and *b* **(d)** neither *a* nor *b*

89 GLOBAL WARMING

Is the earth's temperature rising? In another five hundred years, will the planet's average temperature be higher or lower than it is today? Why? This article will help you understand some of the components that contribute to global warming. After completing your reading, answer the ten questions. Write the letter corresponding to the correct answer in the blank next to each question.

Global warming is the name applied to an increase over time in the average temperature of the earth's atmosphere and oceans. These temperatures have risen since the late nineteenth century, and global warming theory holds that the rise has been caused by human activity (this is known as anthropogenic global warming).

Experts in the field dislike the expression "global warming." They contend that "climate change" is a more accurate characterization because whereas human-induced change is predicted to lead to increases in global mean average temperatures, temperature change at the regional level can be in any direction. Moreover, "climate change" implies changes in more than just temperature: precipitation, cloudiness, weather, and all the other elements of our atmospheric system will be affected by human-induced changes in atmospheric gas concentrations.

In the 1970s, it was unclear whether warming or cooling was more likely in the next hundred years. By the late 1980s, however, the prospect that the earth's surface might become dangerously overheated captured public attention, and it has been a vigorously debated topic ever since.

Leaving the realm of scientific journals, the debate has spilled out into the public arena, with some politicians making the issue a component of their campaigns for high office.

Much about global warming theory is controversial, particularly the issue as to whether there exists a scientific consensus sufficient to justify radical action to ameliorate its effects.

Proponents of global warming theory express a wide range of opinions. Some merely accept that an increase in temperature has occurred. Others support measures such as the Kyoto Protocol, intended to have minor climatic effects but lead to further measures. Still others believe that the resulting environmental damage will have such a severe impact that immediate steps must be taken to reduce CO_2 emissions, regardless of the economic costs to advanced nations such as the United States (the United States has the largest emissions of greenhouse gases of any country in absolute terms and the second largest per capita emissions after Australia).

Critics of global warming theory, who constitute a very small minority of atmospheric scientists, similarly offer a wide spectrum of opinions. Some, such as Patrick Michaels, propose that human influence has warmed the atmosphere yet dispute the contention that most of the warming observed over the past fifty years is attributable to human activities. Others conclude that observations of global temperatures over much larger time spans—of thousands of years rather than decades—show global temperatures fluctuated wildly long before the introduction of human industrial activity. An additional assertion of many critics is that it is impossible to identify any definitive trend from the limited temperature record we have, considering the vast age of the earth. And certain scientists feel it is most likely that global temperature change is the result of natural causes, such as volcanism and solar activity.

89   GLOBAL WARMING *(continued)*

1. _____ Which is unrelated to the concept of global warming?
   (a) the earth's atmosphere **(b)** time **(c)** average rainfall **(d)** none of these

2. _____ Global warming theory states that most responsible for the rise in temperature
   are **(a)** polar ice caps **(b)** human activities **(c)** both *a* and *b* **(d)** neither *a* nor *b*.

3. _____ Experts in the field prefer the term "climate change" rather than "global warming"
   because **(a)** temperature change can be in any direction at a regional level
   (b) changes are also occurring in atmospheric conditions other than temperature
   (c) both *a* and *b* **(d)** neither *a* nor *b*.

4. _____ "Climate change" implies changes in **(a)** weather **(b)** precipitation **(c)** cloudiness
   (d) all of these.

5. _____ Which expression illustrates how important global warming has become with the
   world's population? **(a)** "a vigorously debated topic" **(b)** "scientific consensus"
   (c) "next hundred years" **(d)** "greenhouse gases of any country"

6. _____ Who has focused attention on the effects of global warming?
   (a) the general population **(b)** scientists **(c)** politicians **(d)** all of these

7. _____ Which country has the largest emissions of greenhouse gases per person?
   (a) the United States **(b)** Argentina **(c)** Australia **(d)** none of these

8. _____ A consensus justifying radical action to lessen the damaging effects of global warming
   has been reached. Is this statement **(a)** true or **(b)** false?

9. _____ Wild global temperature changes have occurred long before the current global warming concern began. Is this statement **(a)** true or **(b)** false?

10. _____ Some scientists believe that global temperature changes could be caused by the sun's
    actions. Is this statement **(a)** true or **(b)** false?

90 ECOTOURISM

Travel is a major financial resource for many countries. So are natural resources. How do these countries allow tourism and still keep the environment healthy? Read this article to find out. When you have finished your reading, answer the questions by filling in the blank in each sentence. The first letter of each word is given to you. Finally, select a country you have visited or would like to visit, and discuss with the class how it is dealing with ecotourism.

Ecotourism is shorthand for *ecological tourism,* and the *ecological* aspect has both environmental and social connotations. Ecotourism is defined both as a tourism movement and as a tourism sector. Born in its current form in the late 1980s, ecotourism came of age in 2002 when the United Nations celebrated the "International Year of Ecotourism." The World Conservation Union defines it as "environmentally responsible travel and visitation to relatively undisturbed areas, in order to enjoy and appreciate nature (and any accompanying cultural features, both past and present), [in a manner] that promotes conservation, has low visitor impact, and provides for beneficially active socioeconomic involvement of local populations." However, this is a new and vibrant movement, and definitions are still evolving.

Many global environmental organizations and aid agencies favor ecotourism as a vehicle to sustainable development.

Ideally, ecotourism must focus on several goals, including the following:

- Conserving biological diversity and cultural diversity through ecosystems protection
- Sharing socioeconomic benefits with local communities and indigenous peoples by obtaining their informed consent and their participation in the management of ecotourism-related businesses
- Increasing environmental and cultural knowledge
- Minimizing the environmental impact of tourism
- Maintaining affordability and avoiding waste and needless luxury

For many countries, ecotourism has evolved from being a marginal activity intended to finance protection of the environment to being a major sector of the national economy and a means of obtaining foreign exchange. For example, in such countries as Kenya, Ecuador, Nepal, Costa Rica, and Madagascar, ecotourism provides a significant stream of foreign revenue.

Critics claim that ecotourism, abusively practiced, often consists of plunking a hotel in a splendid landscape, to the detriment of the ecosystem. According to them, ecotourism must above all sensitize people to the beauty and the fragility of nature. They condemn some operators as "greenwashing" their operations—using the labels "ecotourism" and "green-friendly" while behaving in environmentally irresponsible ways.

90 ECOTOURISM (continued)

Although academics argue about who can be classified as an ecotourist and statistical data are virtually nonexistent, some observers estimate the number of ecotourists at more than five million worldwide; the majority come from the United States and the others from Europe, Canada, and Australia.

Countries where ecotourism has been championed by the government include Costa Rica and Australia. Currently, moves are under way to create national and international ecotourism certification programs, although the process is causing controversy.

1. Ecotourism is defined as ecological tourism, where *ecological* has both e_____ and social connotations.

2. As used in the text, the word *evolve* means to develop g_____.

3. Ecotourism took on its current form in the late t_____ century.

4. Ecotourism includes environmentally r_____ travel.

5. Ecotourism should have a low visitor i_____ on the environment.

6. Ecotourism should provide for the active i_____ of local populations.

7. Ecotourism is a new and v_____ movement.

8. Above all, ecotourism must s_____ people to the beauty and the fragility of nature.

9. Most ecotourists come from the U_____.

10. In such countries as Kenya, Ecuador, and Madagascar, ecotourism is now a m_____ sector of the national economy.

11. "Greenwashing" implies that certain people are environmentally i_____.

12. The word *indigenous* means n_____ or existing naturally in a region or country.

13. The southernmost country in which ecotourism is supported is A_____.

14. Some c_____ surrounds national and international ecotourism certification programs.

15. Placing a hotel in the middle of a beautiful landscape could h_____ the ecosystem.

91 TORNADOES

Talk about violence! That's exactly what a powerful tornado brings with it. People who have experienced a tornado will attest to its power and furor. Read the article about tornadoes. Then complete each sentence in Column A with the correct word or words from Column B. (Each item is used only once.) Copy the two-letter answer code from Column B into the blank in Column A. One is done to help you get started. Then write them, in order, on the line below the columns. If your answers are correct, they will spell out a three-word phrase associated with tornadoes.

A tornado is a violent windstorm characterized by a twisting, funnel-shaped cloud. The word *tornado* comes from the Spanish or Portuguese verb *tornar,* meaning "turn." Tornadoes appear in storms all around the world; they are especially frequent in a broad swath of the American Midwest and South known as Tornado Alley, but some other countries see the storms occur in even higher densities.

Tornadoes develop from severe thunderstorms, usually spawned from squall lines and supercell thunderstorms, though they sometimes happen as a result of a hurricane. They are believed to be produced when cool air overrides a layer of warm air, forcing the warm air to rise rapidly, though tornadoes over water (waterspouts) are frequently observed forming in the absence of convection or apparent strong surface temperature differences. Tornadoes are inextricably associated with lightning, and they exhibit enormous electromagnetic fields that are inexplicable by convection models. (This trait is shared by their whirling windstorm cousins known as dust devils.)

The damage from a tornado is a result of the high wind velocity and windblown debris, as well as from electromagnetic effects, which frequently cause "freak" occurrences such as wood impaling metal or stone, dried grasses (straw) impaling wood or animals, and other events that cannot be explained by fluid dynamics alone. Tornado winds range from a slow 40 miles per hour at the low end to a possible 300 miles per hour in the strongest storms. Some computer models have suggested that certain storms can produce supersonic wind speeds in excess of around 750 miles per hour. Tornado season in North America is generally March through August, although tornadoes can occur at any time of the year. They tend to occur in the afternoons and evenings. Over 80 percent of all tornadoes strike between noon and midnight.

91 TORNADOES *(continued)*

Column A

1. _____ A tornado's cloud is _____ -shaped.

2. _____ The verb *tornar* means _____.

3. _¹re_ Tornados develop from severe ___*thunderstorms*___.

4. _____ Tornados develop when _____ air over-rides a layer of warm air.

5. _____ As a tornado forms, warm air will _____.

6. _____ Tornadoes are associated with _____.

7. _____ The damage from a tornado is a result of high wind _____.

8. _____ A tornado can generate a lot of dangerous windblown _____.

9. _____ The winds from some tornadoes may reach _____ speeds.

10. _____ Tornados most often occur in the _____ _____.

11. _____ Most tornadoes strike between noon and _____.

12. _____ Tornadoes are most common in the American South and _____.

13. _____ The word _____ means "piercing" or "stabbing."

14. _____ The word _____ means "produced from" or "started from."

15. _____ Tornado season in North America is generally from _____ to August.

The thirty letters are _____.

The three-word phrase associated with tornadoes is _____

_____.

Column B

ap. funnel

at. debris

ed. afternoon and evening

er. velocity

es. March

fe. Midwest

if. midnight

mp. lightning

nc. spawned

nt. cool

pa. turn

¹re. thunderstorms

²re. impaling

te. rise

ur. supersonic

92 BURNS

Read the following short article about burns and how to treat them. Then fill in the nineteen answers in the crossword puzzle. The first letter of each answer has been provided. Stay alert, and don't get burned!

In medicine, a burn is a type of injury to the skin caused by heat, electricity, chemicals, or radiation (sunburn is an example of a radiation burn).

Immediate first aid for burns consists of immersing the injured area in cool, clean water to soothe the injured tissues.

There are three degrees of burns. First-degree burns are usually limited to redness and pain at the site. Second-degree burns also have blistering of the skin. Third-degree burns exhibit charring of the skin (or scab formation). Burns that injure the tissues underlying the skin, such as muscles or bones, are sometimes characterized as "fourth-degree burns."

Serious burns, especially if they cover large areas of the body, can cause death.

Any hint of burn injury to the lungs, as through smoke inhalation, is a medical emergency.

The chances of survival after severe burn injuries is markedly improved if the patient is treated in a specialized burn center rather than a hospital.

Scalding is a specific type of burning that is caused by nonsolid hot material (liquid or steam), usually water and vapor or sometimes oil (especially for cooks). Damage is usually localized and ordinarily does not cause death.

Copyright © 2005 by John Wiley & Sons, Inc.

92   BURNS *(continued)*

Across

1. one cause of burns

4. type of burn caused by nonsolid hot material

5. one cause of burns

11. the best place to be treated for severe burn injuries

14. A burn limited to redness and pain at the site is a _____-degree burn.

16. one cause of burns

17. a raised area of the skin containing watery liquid

Down

2. possible consequence of a serious burn

3. serious, painful

5. One should immerse the injured, burned area in _____ water.

6. one cause of burns

7. Smoke inhalation can cause damage to the _____.

8. Burns should be given _____ treatment.

9. A burn that blisters the skin is a _____-degree burn.

10. noticeably

12. To cool the injured _____, one should immerse the wound in clean water.

13. one symptom of a burn

14. A burn that injures the tissues underlying the skin, such as muscles and bones, is sometimes called a _____-degree burn.

15. A burn that chars the skin is a _____-degree burn.

93   CAVING

If you have ever had dreams or plans of exploring caves, this article is for you. This informative piece explains much about the art of working your way through caves, including what equipment you should use and what tactics cave explorers should use. Read the article. Then answer the ten questions that follow it. Write the letter corresponding to the correct answer in the blank next to the number.

Caving is the recreational sport of exploring caves.

The challenges of the sport depend on the cave being visited but often include the negotiation of pitches (steep slopes), squeezes (narrow passages), and water. Climbing or crawling is often necessary, and ropes are used extensively.

Caving is often undertaken solely for the enjoyment of the activity or for physical exercise, but original exploration is an important goal for many cavers. Unexplored cave systems comprise some of the last unexplored regions on earth, and much effort is put into trying to locate and enter them. In well-explored regions (such as most industrialized countries), the most accessible caves have already been explored, and finding new caves often requires digging or diving.

Caves have been explored out of necessity for thousands of years, but only in the past century or two has the activity become a sport. In recent decades, caving has changed considerably due to the availability of modern protective wear and equipment. It has recently come to be known as an "extreme sport" by some (though not commonly by its practitioners). Many of the skills of caving can also be used in the sports of mining and urban exploration.

Clay Perry wrote in 1939 about a group of men and boys who explored and studied caves throughout New England and referred to themselves as *spelunkers.* Throughout the 1950s, *spelunking* was the general term used in American English for exploring caves.

In the 1960s, the term *spelunking* began to become associated with inexperienced cavers, using unreliable light sources and wearing cotton clothing. In 1985, Steve Knutson, editor of *American Caving Accidents,* made the following distinction: "I use the term *spelunker* to denote someone untrained and unknowledgeable in current exploration techniques," reserving the term *caver* for a trained and knowledgeable cave explorer.

Potholing refers to exploring *potholes,* a term applied in northern England to a predominantly vertical cave. Today, *potholing* is often used as a synonym for *caving,* and outside the caving world, there is a general impression that potholing is a more "extreme" version of caving.

Helmets are worn to protect the head from bumps and falling rocks. The caver's primary light source is usually mounted on the helmet in order to keep the hands free. Electric lights are most common; halogen lamps are standard, and white LEDs are a more recent technology. Carbide-based systems are still popular, especially on expeditions.

93   CAVING *(continued)*

The type of clothing worn underground varies according to the environment of the cave being explored and the local culture. Typically, the caver will wear a warm base layer that retains its insulating properties when wet, such as a fleece suit, and an oversuit of hard-wearing waterproof material. Wetsuits are worn if the cave is particularly wet, and lighter clothing may be worn in warm countries if the cave is dry.

On the feet, knee boots are standard, often paired with "wetsocks" made of neoprene (synthetic rubber). Knee pads and sometimes elbow pads are useful for protection while crawling.

Ropes are used for descending or ascending pitches or for protection. Knots commonly used in caving are the figure-eight (or figure-nine) loop, bowline, alpine butterfly, and Italian hitch. Ropes are usually rigged using bolts, slings, and carabiners (hinged rings).

Perhaps the best way to find equipment is to attend a caver gathering and talk to a specialist caving supplier. Several of these have retail stores and sites on the Internet. The novice caver should first consult more seasoned cavers before making investments in gear that might not be best suited for them.

Caves can be dangerous places; hypothermia, falling, flooding, and physical exhaustion are the main risks. Rescue from underground is difficult and time-consuming.

Some commonsense rules apply:

- Always check to be sure there is no danger of flooding during the time you plan to be in the cave.
- Teams of at least three, or preferably four, cavers are safest. Caving alone is particularly risky.
- Always make sure someone on the surface knows where you are caving, when you expect to return, and how to contact cave rescue services in the event you do not return.
- Carry backup light sources.

The cave environment is more fragile than most people realize. And since water that flows through a cave eventually comes out in streams and rivers, any pollution will wind up in someone's drinking water and can seriously affect the surface environment as well.

These are the caver's commandments: Take nothing but pictures. Leave nothing behind—not even footprints, if you can avoid them. And kill nothing but time.

93 CAVING *(continued)*

1. _____ Steve Knutson notes that the difference between cavers and spelunkers is one of
   (a) equipment and family background **(b)** knowledge and training **(c)** friends and
   cave size.

2. _____ Which two words does the author treat as synonyms?
   (a) *original* and *common* **(b)** *time-consuming* and *difficult* **(c)** *unexplored* and *original*

3. _____ Digging and diving probably take place more frequently in caves found in
   (a) explored regions **(b)** unexplored regions.

4. _____ Was caving considered a sport in 1725? **(a)** yes **(b)** no

5. _____ Most practicing cavers consider caving an extreme sport. Is this statement
   (a) true or **(b)** false?

6. _____ The sports whose participants use many of the same skills as participants in caving
   are **(a)** football and mountain climbing **(b)** mining and gymnastics **(c)** mining and
   urban exploration.

7. _____ The caver's primary light source is mounted on the **(a)** helmet **(b)** belt **(c)** shoulder.

8. _____ Do cavers use the words *potholing* and *caving* as synonyms? **(a)** yes **(b)** no

9. _____ Helmets serve which two primary purposes? **(a)** protection and conversation
   (b) protection and illumination **(c)** enjoyment and illumination

10. _____ Carabiners are used with the caver's **(a)** ropes **(b)** helmet **(c)** boots.

94 FRICTION

Read the following article about the resistive force called friction. Then, without referring to the article again, fill in the fifteen blanks on the following page, using the words in the word bank. Each word will be used only once.

In physics, friction is the resistive force that occurs when two surfaces travel along each other while forced together. It causes physical deformation and heat buildup.

The force of friction is always exerted in a direction that opposes movement. For example, a chair sliding to the right across a floor experiences the force of friction in the left direction.

The coefficient of friction also depends on the type of friction. There are three general types:

- Static friction occurs when the two objects are not moving relative to each other (like a desk on the ground). The initial force to get an object moving is often dominated by static friction, sometimes called "stiction."
- Kinetic friction occurs when the two objects are moving relative to each other and rub together (like a sled on the ground).
- Rolling friction occurs when the two objects are moving relative to each other and one "rolls" on the other (like a shopping cart on the ground).

Physical deformation is associated with friction. While this can be beneficial, as in polishing, it is often a problem, as the materials are worn away.

The work done by friction is released in the form of heat. This can translate into deformation and heat that in the long run may affect the material's specification. Friction can in some cases cause solid materials to melt.

A common way to reduce friction is by using a lubricant between the two surfaces.

Lubricants to overcome friction need not always be thin, turbulent fluids; acoustic lubrication occurs when sound (measurable in a vacuum by placing a microphone on one element of the sliding system) permits vibration to introduce separation between the sliding faces. World War II Panzer tank treads lubricated by their own squeak are the most famous example.

94 FRICTION (continued)

acoustic	left	resistive	together
deformation	lubricant	rolling	vibration
heat	melt	static	worn
kinetic	opposes	tank	

In physics, friction is the (1) _____ force that occurs when two surfaces travel along each other while forced (2) _____ . It causes physical (3) _____ and (4) _____ buildup.

The force of friction is always exerted in a direction that (5) _____ movement. For example, a chair sliding to the right across a floor experiences the force of friction in the (6) _____ direction.

The coefficient of friction also depends on the type of friction. There are three general types:

- (7) _____ friction occurs when the two objects are not moving relative to each other (like a desk on the ground). The initial force to get an object moving is often dominated by static friction, sometimes called "stiction."

- (8) _____ friction occurs when the two objects are moving relative to each other and rub together (like a sled on the ground).

- (9) _____ friction occurs when the two objects are moving relative to each other and one "rolls" on the other (like a shopping cart on the ground).

Physical deformation is associated with friction. While this can be beneficial, as in polishing, it is often a problem, as the materials are (10) _____ away.

The work done by friction is released in the form of heat. This can translate into deformation and heat that in the long run may affect the material's specification. Friction can in some cases cause solid materials to (11) _____ .

A common way to reduce friction is by using a (12) _____ between the two surfaces.

Lubricants to overcome friction need not always be thin, turbulent fluids; (13) _____ lubrication occurs when sound (measurable in a vacuum by placing a microphone on one element of the sliding system) permits (14) _____ to introduce separation between the sliding faces. World War II Panzer (15) _____ treads lubricated by their own squeak are the most famous example.

Copyright © 2005 by John Wiley & Sons, Inc.

95   THE GOLDEN GATE BRIDGE

Here is the story behind the Golden Gate Bridge, a magnificent modern wonder on America's West Coast. Read the article; then use the sixteen words in Column A to complete the sentences in Column B. First, write the correct word in each blank in the sentence. Then write the number for each word in Column B in the appropriate box in the magic square. (Three answers are already provided.) If your answers are correct, the rows, the columns, and the two diagonals will each add up to the same magic number. Good luck!

The Golden Gate Bridge is a suspension bridge spanning the Golden Gate, the opening from the Pacific Ocean into San Francisco Bay. The bridge connects the city of San Francisco, on the northern tip of the San Francisco peninsula, with Sausalito, on the south-facing Marin County headlands. Completed in 1937, it has ever since been hailed as a beautiful and graceful example of bridge engineering.

The bridge was the brainchild of Joseph Strauss, an engineer who had constructed more than four hundred drawbridges, all of them far smaller than this project and mostly inland. Strauss spent over a decade drumming up support in Northern California. His initial proposal for the bridge was not at all pretty, consisting of a massive cantilever on each side connected with a central suspension segment. Other key figures in the bridge's construction include architect Irving Morrow, responsible for the Art Deco touches and the choice of color—known as international orange—and engineer Charles Alton Ellis and bridge designer Leon Moisseiff, who collaborated on the complicated mathematics.

Construction of the bridge began on January 5, 1933, in the depth of the Great Depression. Many experts thought it foolhardy to undertake such an ambitious project at such an economically unstable time. Nevertheless, it was completed in April 1937 and opened to pedestrians on May 27 of that year. The next day, President Roosevelt pushed a button in Washington, D.C., signaling the start of vehicle traffic over the bridge. The cost to build it was $35 million. A unique aspect of the construction of this bridge was that a safety net was strung beneath it, significantly reducing the number of deaths that were typical for a construction project such as this in the early 1900s. Eleven men were killed in falls during construction, and nineteen more were saved by the safety net. Most of the deaths occurred toward the end of the project when the net itself failed after a scaffold fell into it.

The bridge is 1.22 miles long, the distance between the towers ("main span") is 4,200 feet, and the towers rise to 746 feet above the water.

The bridge has been declared one of the Seven Wonders of the Modern World by the American Society of Civil Engineers. It was for thirty-seven years the suspension bridge with the longest main span in the world, superseded in 1964 (by about 60 feet) by the Verrazano-Narrows Bridge in New York City; several even longer spans have been constructed since. It also had the world's tallest suspension towers at the time of construction and held that record until quite recently.

95 THE GOLDEN GATE BRIDGE (continued)

Why isn't the bridge gold, as its name might suggest? As noted earlier, the Golden Gate is in fact the strait that the bridge crosses, and this name predated the bridge by more than a century. The actual paint color, international orange, was chosen for its visibility in fog—a frequent phenomenon for which the San Francisco Bay Area is famous.

Bearing the only road to exit San Francisco to the north, the bridge is part of both U.S. Highway 101 and California State Route 1. The bridge has six total lanes of vehicle traffic, and walkways line both sides of the roadway. The median markers between the lanes are moved to conform to traffic. On weekday mornings, most traffic flows into the city, so four of the six lanes run southbound. Conversely, on weekday afternoons, four lanes run northbound. Although installation of a movable barrier has been discussed for decades, no satisfactory solution has yet been found. Ordinarily, the eastern walkway is reserved for pedestrians and the western walkway for bicyclists. Both walkways are closed to pedestrian traffic during the evening and at night.

A =	B = 6	C =	D =
E =	F =	G =	H =
I = 14	J =	K =	L =
M =	N =	O = 16	P =

Magic Number: _____

95 THE GOLDEN GATE BRIDGE *(continued)*

Column A

A. twentieth

B. ten

C. Pacific

D. 1,500

E. bicyclists

F. suspension

G. Depression

H. strait

I. evening

J. twenty-seven

K. fog

L. one mile

M. orange

N. markers

O. double

P. net

Column B

1. Median _____ are used to conform to traffic.

2. The bridge was built during the Great _____.

3. The bridge is a little over _____ long.

4. The bridge was completed in the _____ century.

5. The bridge's color was chosen primarily because of _____ in the Bay Area.

6. Joseph Strauss spent at least _____ years trying to drum up support for the bridge's construction.

7. The bridge is painted international _____.

8. Golden Gate is the name of the _____ that the bridge crosses.

9. One walkway is used by pedestrians, and the other is used by _____.

10. During the bridge's construction, workers set up a safety _____ to catch falling workers.

11. San Francisco Bay is directly connected to the _____ Ocean.

12. The Golden Gate Bridge held the record as the longest bridge of its kind for _____ years.

13. The combined height of the two towers is approximately _____ feet.

14. Both walkways are closed to pedestrian traffic during the _____ and at night.

15. The Golden Gate Bridge is a _____ bridge.

16. The number of workers saved by safety measures was nearly _____ the number of workers killed during the bridge's construction.

96 KRAKATOA

When the volcano known as Krakatoa erupted on the Indonesian island of Rakata in 1883, the blast was heard as far as 3,000 miles away, and the tsunami it caused killed some thirty-six thousand people. Read the article about this volcano. Then use the words in Column A to complete the sentences in Column B by writing the correct word in each blank; then complete the magic square by writing each number from Column B in the corresponding box. (Two answers are already provided.) If your answers are correct, the rows, the columns, and the two diagonals will each add up to the same magic number. Have a blast!

Krakatoa (known locally as Krakatau) was a volcano on the island of Rakata in the Sunda Strait in what is now Indonesia. It erupted massively and with disastrous consequences on August 26, 1883. Although no one was killed directly by the explosion, the tsunami it generated killed more than thirty-six thousand people. Settlements were wiped out on Sumatra and Java, and ships as far away as South Africa rocked as the tsunami hit them. The bodies of victims could be found floating in the ocean for weeks after the event. An additional thousand or so people died from the effects of volcanic fumes and ash.

Four eruptions occurred that day, at 5:30, 6:42, 8:20, and 10:02 A.M. local time. The last was the loudest and most destructive, and could be heard in Australia, 2,200 miles away, and even on the island of Rodrigues, near Mauritius, 3,000 miles distant.

These were the most severe volcanic explosions recorded on earth in modern times, with a force equivalent to 200 megatons of TNT. Concussive air waves from the explosions traveled seven times around the world, and the sky remained darkened for days afterward. The island of Rakata itself largely ceased to exist; more than two-thirds of its exposed land area was blown to dust, and its surrounding ocean floor was drastically altered. Two nearby islands, Verlaten and Lang, increased in landmass due to deposits of volcanic ash, which continues to be a significant part of their geological makeup today. The dust from the explosions produced many exotic sunsets around the world for many months, the result of sunlight reflected from suspended dust particles.

Volcanic and seismic activity on the island had begun earlier that year, when an earthquake occurred. On May 20, 1883, the hitherto dormant volcano erupted. By August 11, three separate vents were regularly spewing lava. Tides were unusually high, and phenomena such as windows suddenly shattering were commonplace. Ships at anchor sometimes had to be tied down with chains.

Since the 1883 eruption, a new island volcano, called Anak Krakatau ("Child of Krakatoa"), has formed in the caldera (crater) of the original volcano. The island has been studied extensively since 1960, not only by volcanologists but also by ecologists fascinated by its ecosystem, regenerated from zero, as no macroscopic life survived the 1883 explosion. The island is still active, growing at the rate of 5 inches a week.

96   KRAKATOA *(continued)*

A = 7	B =	C =	D =
E =	F =	G =	H =
I =	J =	K = 9	L =
M =	N =	O =	P =

Magic Number: _____

Column A

A. seven

B. volcanic

C. five

D. earthquake

E. sunsets

F. Indonesia

G. windows

H. tsunami

I. macroscopic

J. four

K. zero

L. one thousand

M. two-thirds

N. 1960

O. three

P. 3,000

Column B

1. What portion of the island of Rakata was blown to dust?

   _____

2. Krakatoa is located in the country known today as _____.

3. A massive wave called a _____ resulted from Krakatoa's explosion.

4. Two weeks before Krakatoa erupted, _____ vents were regularly erupting on the volcano.

5. Approximately _____ people died from fumes and ash.

6. The island that contains Anak Krakatau ("Child of Krakatoa") is growing at the rate of _____ inches each week.

7. Concussive air waves from the explosions traveled _____ times around the world.

8. Krakatoa erupted _____ times on August 26, 1883.

9. The number of people that died from Krakatoa's direct explosion was _____.

10. What natural event occurred the same year as the eruption of Krakatoa? _____

11. The eruption of Krakatoa remains the strongest _____ explosion ever recorded.

12. No _____ life survived the Krakatoa explosion.

13. The "Child of Krakatoa" has been studied since _____.

14. The dust from the explosions caused exotic _____ for many months.

15. Krakatoa caused _____ to shatter.

16. People on the island of Rodrigues near Mauritius, _____ miles away, heard Krakatoa erupt.

97   THE TUNGUSKA EVENT

In 1908, a fireball exploded near the ground in Siberia, a densely forested region of Russia. Approximately sixty million trees were knocked over in what is known as the Tunguska event, which caused destruction over a radius of nearly 400 miles away. Few natural disasters have fascinated both scientists and ordinary people as this puzzling explosion. Read the story of the Tunguska event, and then match the effects in Column A with their appropriate causes in Column B by writing the two-letter answer code from Column B in the appropriate blank in Column A. Copy these answers, in order, onto the line below the list of causes. If your answers are correct, the letters will spell out three words found in this story.

The Tunguska event was an aerial explosion that occurred near the Tunguska River in what is now Evenkia, in Siberia, at 7:17 A.M. on June 30, 1908. The blast felled an estimated sixty million trees over about 840 square miles. A few minutes earlier, Tungus natives and Russian settlers in the hills northwest of Lake Baykal observed a huge fireball, almost as bright as the sun, moving across the sky. Suddenly, there was a flash that lit up half the sky, followed by a shock wave that knocked people off their feet and broke windows as far as 400 miles away. The explosion registered on seismic stations across Eurasia and produced fluctuations in atmospheric pressure strong enough to be detected by recently invented barographs set up in Britain. Over the next few weeks, night skies over Europe and western Russia glowed brightly enough for people to read by. In the United States, the Smithsonian Astrophysical Observatory and the Mount Wilson Observatory observed a decrease in atmospheric transparency that lasted for several months.

The size of the blast was later estimated to be between 10 and 15 megatons. Had the object responsible for the explosion hit the earth a few hours later, it would have exploded over Europe instead of the sparsely populated Tunguska region, causing massive loss of human life.

Surprisingly, there was little scientific curiosity about the impact at the time, possibly due to the isolation of the Tunguska region. Any records of expeditions to the site were destroyed during the unrest of those years—World War I, the Russian Revolution, and the Russian Civil War. It took until the 1920s for the next expedition to arrive.

In 1921, the Russian mineralogist Leonid Kulik visited the Podkamennaya Tunguska River basin as part of a survey for the Soviet Academy of Sciences. After studying local accounts, he reasoned that the explosion was caused by a giant meteorite impact and persuaded the Soviet government to fund an expedition to the Tunguska region, based on the prospect of meteoric iron that could be salvaged for Soviet industry.

Kulik's expedition reached the site in 1927. To their surprise, no crater was to be found. There was instead a region of scorched trees about 30 miles across. A few near ground zero were still strangely standing upright, their branches and bark stripped off. Those farther away had been knocked down in a direction away from the center.

Over the next ten years, there were three more expeditions to the area, and none of them discovered anything different from what Kulik and his people had found. Kulik found a little

97 THE TUNGUSKA EVENT *(continued)*

"pothole" bog that he thought might be the crater, but after the laborious exercise of draining the bog, he found old stumps on the bottom, ruling out the possibility that it was a crater.

Kulik did manage to arrange an aerial photographic survey of the area in 1938 that revealed that the event had knocked over trees in a huge butterfly-shaped pattern, thereby providing information on the direction of the object's motion. It found no crater, despite the large amount of devastation. Expeditions sent to the area in the 1950s and 1960s found microscopic glass spheres in siftings of the soil. Chemical analysis showed that the spheres contained high proportions of nickel and iridium, which are found in high concentrations in meteorites, and indicated that they were of extraterrestrial origin.

Column A: Effects

1. _____ Sixty million trees fell over an area of 840 square miles.

2. _____ The meteorite would have landed in Europe.

3. _____ There was little scientific curiosity about the impact when it occurred in 1908.

4. _____ Records of expeditions to the Tunguska region were destroyed.

5. _____ A few trees near ground zero were standing upright, their branches and bark stripped off.

6. _____ High proportions of nickel and iridium were contained in the microscopic glass spheres found at Tunguska, which helped prove that a meteorite had caused the destruction.

7. _____ The number of human fatalities was not high.

8. _____ Even today people are amazed by what happened that morning in Russia.

9. _____ Trees were knocked over in a huge butterfly-shaped pattern.

10. _____ The Soviet government funded an expedition to the Tunguska region.

Column B: Causes

as. World War I, the Russian Revolution, and the Russian Civil War were occurring.

el. The meteorite fell in Siberia, a region where few people lived.

eu. An aerial explosion occurred in Siberia.

ke. The Russian mineralogist Leonid Kulic visited the Podkamcnnaya River basin as part of a survey.

pa. The meteorite's impact destroyed trees away from the impact's direct location.

ra. If the object had hit the earth a few hours later.

ro. The meteorite's direction of motion influenced its impact.

rs. Meteorites contain these elements.

si. The event occurred in an isolated and sparsely populated region.

yb. The Tunguska event was quite unusual.

The twenty letters are _____.

The three words found in the article are _____, _____, and _____.

98   THE MILGRAM EXPERIMENT

Are most people willing to inflict pain on others when a third party is urging them to do so? That was the question that researchers wanted to answer in the Milgram experiment. Read this article about the experiment, and then answer the fifteen true-or-false questions that follow. Write T for true or F for false in the blank next to each statement.

The Milgram experiment was a scientific experiment of social psychology described by Yale University psychologist Stanley Milgram in his 1974 book *Obedience to Authority: An Experimental View.* It was intended to measure the willingness of a subject to obey an authority who instructs the subject to do something that may conflict with the subject's personal conscience.

The method of one experiment was as follows. The subject and an actor pretending to be another subject are told by the experimenter that they will be participating in an experiment to test the effectiveness of punishment on learning behavior. Two slips of paper marked "teacher" are handed to the subject and actor; the actor claims, however, that his says "learner," so the subject is led to believe that his role has been chosen randomly. Both are then given a sample 45-volt electric shock from an apparatus attached to a chair into which the actor is strapped. The "teacher" is then given simple memory tasks to give to the "learner" and instructed to administer a shock by pressing a button each time the learner makes a mistake.

The "teacher" is then told that the voltage is to be raised by 15 volts after each mistake. He is not told that there are no actual shocks being given to the actor, who feigns discomfort. At "150 volts," the actor requests that the experiment be terminated and is told by the experimenter, "The experiment requires that you continue. Please go on" or words to that effect. He continues, and the actor at first indicates greater discomfort, then cries out in considerable pain, and finally screams for the experiment to stop as the simulated shocks continue. If the "teacher" becomes reluctant, he is instructed that the experimenter takes all responsibility for the results of the experiment and the safety of the learner and that the experiment requires that he continue.

Before the experiment was conducted, Milgram polled fellow psychiatrists as to what the results would be. They unanimously believed that only a few sadists would be prepared to give the maximum voltage.

In Milgram's first set of experiments, 65 percent of experimental subjects administered the experiment's final "450-volt shock," though many were quite uncomfortable in doing so. No subject stopped before the "300 volt" level. The experiment has been repeated by other psychologists around the world with similar results. Variations have been performed to test for variables in the experimental setup. For example, subjects are much more likely to be obedient when the experimenter is physically present than when the instructions are given over the telephone.

The experiment raised questions about the ethics of scientific experimentation itself because of the extreme emotional stress suffered by the subjects (even though it could be said that this stress was brought on by their own free actions). Most modern scientists would consider the experiment unethical today, though it resulted in valuable insights into human psychology.

98 THE MILGRAM EXPERIMENT (continued)

1. _____ At least three people are needed to conduct the experiment.

2. _____ One of the participants is called the experimenter.

3. _____ One of the participants instructs the subject to do something that may conflict with the subject's personal conscience.

4. _____ One of the participants will fake reactions.

5. _____ One of the participants lies about what his slip of paper says.

6. _____ Both the "teacher" and the "subject" are given a sample 45-volt electric shock.

7. _____ No electric shocks are actually administered to the "learner."

8. _____ The "teacher" is instructed to administer a shock by pressing a button each time the "learner" makes a mistake.

9. _____ The "teacher" is told that the strength of the shock is to be raised by 15 volts after each mistake.

10. _____ The actor requests that the experiment be terminated at "150 volts."

11. _____ The experimenter, not the "teacher," says that the experiment must continue regardless of the amount of pain.

12. _____ The experimenter says that he will take all responsibility for both the results of the experiment and the safety of the "learner."

13. _____ Before the experiment was conducted, most psychiatrists believed that most people would be against giving the maximum voltage.

14. _____ More than half of the "teachers" in Milgram's first set of experiments administered the highest voltage.

15. _____ The extreme emotional stress of the subjects has raised questions about the ethics of the experiment itself.

99 THE FUTURE OF THE CRASH TEST DUMMY

No one wants to be in a motor vehicle accident. What is the best way to prevent such accidents? Who will serve as accident victims in the tests that must be conducted to prevent accidents? For years, the crash test dummy has been the stand-in. But are his days numbered? Read this article and find out about the dummy's future. Then answer each of the ten questions by writing the letter for the correct answer in the blank next to the question number. Be confident—you're no dummy!

Crash test dummies have provided valuable data on how human bodies react in crashes and have contributed greatly to improved vehicle design. Although they have saved millions of lives, their use, like that of cadavers and animals, has reached a point of reduced data return.

The largest problem with acquiring data from cadavers, other than their availability, was that an essential element of standardized testing, repeatability, was impossible. No matter how many elements from a previous test could be reused, the cadaver had to be different each time. Although modern test dummies have overcome this, testers still face essentially the same problem when it comes to testing the vehicle. A vehicle can be crashed only once; no matter how carefully the test is done, it cannot be repeated exactly.

A second problem with dummies is that they are only approximately human. Forty-four data channels on a Hybrid III is not even a remote representation of the number of data channels in a living person. The mimicking of internal organs is crude at best, a fact that means that even though cadavers and animals are no longer the primary sources of accident data, they must still be employed in the study of soft-tissue injury.

The future of crash testing has begun at the same place it all started: Wayne State University in Michigan. King H. Yang is one of Wayne State's researchers involved in creating detailed computer models of human systems. Currently, computers are not fast enough and programmers are not skilled enough to create full-body simulations, but injury analysis of individual body systems is producing reliable and encouraging results.

The advantage of the computer is that it is unbound by physical laws. A virtual vehicle crashed once can be uncrashed and then crashed again in a slightly different manner. A virtual back broken can be unbroken, the seat belt configuration changed, and the back rebroken. When every variable is controllable and every event is repeatable, the need for physical experimentation is greatly reduced.

At present, legal certification of new car models still requires the use of physical dummies in actual vehicles. However, soon neither skin and bone nor plastic and steel will determine the shape of vehicles to come. The next generation of crash test dummies will perform their tasks entirely on a computer screen.

99   THE FUTURE OF THE CRASH TEST DUMMY *(continued)*

1. _____ Dummies have reached a point of "reduced data return." This means that dummies **(a)** are valuable for giving us more future information about crashes **(b)** cannot give researchers much more information in the future **(c)** cannot talk **(d)** are humorous.

2. _____ The thesis statement of this article is **(a)** "The advantage of the computer is that it is unbound by physical laws." **(b)** "At present, legal certification of new car models still requires the use of physical dummies in actual vehicles." **(c)** "When every variable is controllable and every event is repeatable, the need for physical experimentation is greatly reduced." **(d)** Although they have saved millions of lives, they [crash test dummies], like cadavers and animals, have reached a point of reduced data return."

3. _____ Crash test dummies and cadavers are alike in which of these ways? **(a)** Both are expensive to use. **(b)** Both can be used only once in a crash. **(c)** It is illegal to use both. **(d)** None of these.

4. _____ A problem with using a dummy in a crash test situation is that the dummy **(a)** is not exactly like a human being **(b)** is a primary source of accident data **(c)** can be crashed several times **(d)** all of these.

5. _____ The number of data channels in a dummy is **(a)** much greater than **(b)** less than **(c)** equal to **(d)** unrelated to the number of data channels in a living person.

6. _____ Which of the following is true? **(a)** The computer cannot help us learn about accidents. **(b)** Computers are quick enough to create full-body simulations. **(c)** Seat belt configuration cannot be changed. **(d)** The analysis of body systems is more than adequate for researchers' purposes.

7. _____ The crash test dummy will be replaced by **(a)** a scientist's drawing **(b)** King H. Yang **(c)** a computer simulation **(d)** skin and bones.

8. _____ Which word in the article means "a dead body," especially that of a person? **(a)** data **(b)** virtual **(c)** mimicking **(d)** cadaver

9. _____ The article's author predicts that **(a)** the number of motor vehicle accidents will increase **(b)** the number of motor vehicle accidents will be reduced **(c)** computerized images will replace dummies in simulating automobile crashes **(d)** computer programmers will be paid more for their efforts.

10. _____ The main purpose of the final paragraph is to **(a)** introduce the reader to the world of the future **(b)** illustrate the strengths of the crash test dummy **(c)** illustrate the work of the cadavers **(d)** all of these.

Name: _____ Date: _____ Period: _____

100   IVAN PAVLOV

The following article is about Ivan Pavlov, the Russian scientist known for his experiments regarding conditioning. His work taught us much about how humans and animals respond to certain stimuli. Read the article. Then use the word bank to fill in the blanks in the sixteen sentences that follow. Each word is used only once.

Ivan Petrovich Pavlov (1849–1936) was a Russian physiologist who first described the phenomenon now known as *conditioning* in experiments with dogs. He was awarded the Nobel Prize in Physiology or Medicine in 1904 for his work.

Pavlov was investigating the gastric function of dogs by externalizing a salivary gland so that he could collect, measure, and analyze the saliva produced in response to food under different conditions. He noticed that the dogs tended to salivate before food was actually delivered to their mouths, and so he set out to investigate this "psychic secretion," as he called it. He decided that this was more interesting than the chemistry of saliva and changed the focus of his research, carrying out a long series of experiments in which he manipulated the stimuli occurring before the presentation of food. He thereby established the basic laws for the establishment and extinction of what he called "conditional reflexes," reflex (instinctive) responses like salivation that nevertheless seemed to be based on the animals' specific previous experiences. These experiments were carried out in the 1890s and 1900s and were known to Western scientists through translations of individual accounts but were not fully available in English until published in book form in 1927.

Pavlov's phrase "conditional reflex" was mistranslated from the Russian as "conditioned reflex," and other scientists reading his work concluded that since such reflexes were "conditioned," they must be produced by a process called "conditioning." As Pavlov's work became known in the West, particularly through the writings of John B. Watson, the idea of "conditioning" as an automatic form of learning became a key concept in the developing field of comparative psychology and the general approach to psychology that underlay it, behaviorism. Bertrand Russell was an enthusiastic advocate of the importance of Pavlov's work for the philosophy of the mind.

Unlike many scientists who had been active before the 1918 Russian Revolution, Pavlov was highly regarded by the Soviet government and was allowed to continue his research. In later life, he was particularly interested in trying to use conditioning to establish an experimental model of the induction of neurosis.

It is popularly believed that Pavlov always signaled the occurrence of food by ringing a bell. His laboratory in Moscow has been carefully preserved. In fact, his writings record the use of a wide variety of auditory stimuli, including whistles, metronomes, tuning forks, and the bubbling of air through water, in addition to a range of visual stimuli. When in the 1990s it became easier for Western scientists to visit Pavlov's laboratory in Moscow, no trace of a bell could be found.

100   IVAN PAVLOV (continued)

bell	eye	Nobel	saliva
dogs	food	psychology	stimuli
ear	mistranslated	reflex	Watson
English	Moscow	Russian	whistles

1. Pavlov sought to collect, measure, and analyze the animals' _____.

2. *Auditory* refers to the _____.

3. In 1904, Pavlov was awarded the _____ Prize.

4. Pavlov's laboratory was located in _____.

5. Pavlov used _____ as auditory stimuli.

6. Pavlov was a _____ scientist.

7. Pavlov's phrase "conditional reflex" was _____.

8. Pavlov manipulated the _____ occurring before the presentation of food.

9. A book of Pavlov's experiments was finally published in _____ in 1927.

10. No _____ was found in Pavlov's laboratory in the 1990s.

11. *Visual* refers to the _____.

12. Pavlov conducted experiments on _____.

13. The animals were responding to _____ under different conditions.

14. Salivation is a _____ response.

15. Pavlov's work became a key concept in comparative _____.

16. _____ and Russell helped spread the word of Pavlov's work.

Section Five

READING COMPREHENSION IN SOCIAL STUDIES CLASSES

The sixteen activities in Section Five feature readings from social studies classes. Here students will improve their comparison-and-contrast skills (Activity 102), and they will also read and ponder memorable American speeches (103, 108, 109, and 110). This section also tackles the topic of civil disobedience (104 and 105) and reviews the life of a famous American aviator, Amelia Earhart (106 and 107). Students will read about world events (111), famous places (112, 115, and 116), and interesting people (113 and 114).

The questions that follow these readings test the students' abilities in identifying topic sentences, recalling details, using inferences, summarizing ideas, and evaluating what they have read.

101   WHERE HAVE ALL THE VOWELS GONE?
(SOCIAL STUDIES)

Twenty terms that you will hear in your social studies class are listed below. But all the vowels are missing! The consonants appear in the order in which they occur in the complete word. If the first letter is capitalized, that is the first letter in the term. The number in parentheses after the consonants indicates the total number of letters in the word. Write the term in the blank next to its number. Have fun!

1. _____ Plt (7)

2. _____ Rcll (6)

3. _____ mndmnt (9)

4. _____ Prsdnt (9)

5. _____ Snt (6)

6. _____ Cngrss (8)

7. _____ slnd (6)

8. _____ Mnply (8)

9. _____ Rcssn (9)

10. _____ Dmcrcy 9)

11. _____ Prmbl (8)

12. _____ Cnstttn (12)

13. _____ Vt (4)

14. _____ Rpblc (8)

15. _____ mpr (6)

16. _____ Gvrn (6)

17. _____ Ldr (6)

18. _____ Mnrchy (8)

19. _____ Frgn (7)

20. _____ cnmy (7)

Name: _____ Date: _____ Period: _____

102   COMPARING LINCOLN AND KENNEDY

The numerous coincidences that can be found between U.S. Presidents Abraham Lincoln and John Fitzgerald Kennedy are very interesting! Read the list of parallel facts below. Then answer the ten questions in the blanks.

Abraham Lincoln was elected to Congress in 1846.

John F. Kennedy was elected to Congress in 1946.

Abraham Lincoln was elected president in 1860.

John F. Kennedy was elected president in 1960.

The validity of each president's election was contested.

The names *Lincoln* and *Kennedy* each contain seven letters.

Both men were particularly concerned with civil rights.

Both presidents' wives lost children while living in the White House.

Lincoln's close associate (possibly his secretary) was named Kennedy.

Kennedy's secretary was named Lincoln.

Lincoln's secretary, Kennedy, warned him not to go to Ford's Theater.

Kennedy's secretary, Lincoln, warned him not to go to Dallas.

Both their successors were named Johnson.

Andrew Johnson, who succeeded Lincoln, was born in 1808.

Lyndon Johnson, who succeeded Kennedy, was born in 1908.

Both presidents were shot in the head on a Friday and in the presence of their wives.

Both were assassinated by southerners.

Both assassins were known by three names, John Wilkes Booth and Lee Harvey Oswald.

The names of the assassins each contain fifteen letters.

John Wilkes Booth was born in 1839.

Lee Harvey Oswald was born in 1939.

Booth shot Lincoln in a theater and was caught in a warehouse.

Oswald shot Kennedy from a warehouse and was caught in a theater.

Both Booth and Oswald were assassinated before they could be brought to trial.

102   COMPARING LINCOLN AND KENNEDY (continued)

1. _____ What was the last name of the men who succeeded both Lincoln and Kennedy?

2. _____ What aspect of both Lincoln's and Kennedy's presidency was contested?

3. _____ What was the last name of Abraham Lincoln's close associate or secretary?

4. _____ On what day of the week were both men shot?

5. _____ Both men were assassinated by men from what part of the United States?

6. _____ How many years apart were Lincoln and Kennedy born, elected to Congress, and elected to the presidency?

7. _____ How many years apart were their assassins born?

8. _____ In what body part were both shot?

9. _____ Both assassins were known by how many names?

10. _____ What kind of building was Lincoln in when he was assassinated?

Name: _____ Date: _____ Period: _____

103 LINCOLN'S GETTYSBURG ADDRESS

Abraham Lincoln, the sixteenth president of the United States, delivered this memorable speech on November 19, 1863, on the battlefield near Gettysburg, Pennsylvania, at the dedication of the military cemetery there. His brief and poetic speech has been studied and praised ever since.

Read the speech carefully, perhaps several times. Then answer the questions that follow it by writing the code letter for the correct answer in the blank. Discuss your answers—and the content of the speech—with your classmates.

Fourscore and seven years ago our fathers brought forth on this continent a new nation, conceived in liberty and dedicated to the proposition that all men are created equal.

Now we are engaged in a great civil war, testing whether that nation or any nation so conceived and so dedicated can long endure. We are met on a great battlefield of that war. We have come to dedicate a portion of it as a final resting place for those who died here that the nation might live. It is altogether fitting and proper that we should do this.

But in a larger sense, we can not dedicate, we can not consecrate, we can not hallow this ground. The brave men, living and dead, who struggled here, have consecrated it far above our poor power to add or detract. The world will little note, nor long remember, what we say here, but it can never forget what they did here.

It is for us the living, rather, to be dedicated here to the unfinished work which they who fought here have thus far so nobly advanced. It is rather for us to be here dedicated to the great task remaining before us—that from these honored dead we take increased devotion to that cause for which they gave the last full measure of devotion—that we here highly resolve that these dead shall not have died in vain—that this nation, under God, shall have a new birth of freedom—and that government of the people, by the people, for the people, shall not perish from the earth.

103 LINCOLN'S GETTYSBURG ADDRESS *(continued)*

1. _____ If a score is twenty, how many years is "fourscore and seven"? **(a)** 47 **(b)** 87 **(c)** 107

2. _____ Which two concepts did America's founders have in creating this country?
   (a) equality and capitalism **(b)** freedom and capitalism **(c)** freedom and equality

3. _____ What phrase makes references to a cemetery?
   (a) "can long endure" **(b)** "final resting place" **(c)** "have consecrated it far above"

4. _____ Why does Lincoln feel that he and the other Americans present at Gettysburg that
   day cannot consecrate the Gettysburg field? **(a)** The brave men who fought and are
   still living or who have died there have already blessed it. **(b)** Religious officials have
   already blessed it. **(c)** It would be sacrilegious to bless this bloody battlefield.

5. _____ The word *hallow* most nearly means **(a)** "empty" **(b)** "forget" **(c)** "make sacred."

6. _____ Which does Lincoln think will be remembered longest?
   (a) his speech **(b)** the soldiers' actions **(c)** "us the living"

7. _____ Lincoln urges the people to **(a)** keep in mind what the soldiers fought and died for
   (b) forget about the deaths that occurred at Gettysburg **(c)** both *a* and *b* **(d)** neither *a*
   nor *b*.

8. _____ Which is an example of parallel structure, an important device in both writing and
   speechmaking that Lincoln uses quite effectively? **(a)** "the last full measure of devotion" **(b)** "of the people, by the people, for the people" **(c)** "but it can never forget what
   they did here"

9. _____ What is the noun form of the verb *resolve* in the last paragraph?
   (a) resolute **(b)** resolvement **(c)** resolution

10. _____ Who or what "shall not perish from the earth"?
    (a) Lincoln **(b)** government **(c)** soldiers

104 CIVIL DISOBEDIENCE

People who refuse to obey certain laws, demands, or commands of a controlling authority, such as a government, without resorting to physical violence are engaging in an activity known as civil disobedience. Mohandas Gandhi of India and Americans Henry David Thoreau and Martin Luther King Jr. are probably the individuals most closely associated with civil disobedience in the contemporary mind. Read the article below, and then answer the questions that follow it by writing the code letter for the answer in the blank.

Civil disobedience is characterized by the active refusal to obey certain laws, demands, or commands of a government or of an occupying power without resorting to physical violence.

Civil disobedience has been used in struggles in India in the fight against British colonization, in South Africa in the fight against apartheid, and in civil rights movements in the United States and Europe.

The American author Henry David Thoreau pioneered the modern theory behind this practice in an 1849 essay originally titled "Resistance to Civil Government" and later retitled "Civil Disobedience." The driving idea behind the essay was self-reliance and the fact that you are in morally good standing as long as you "get off the other man's back"; thus you don't have to physically fight the government, but you must not support it or have it support you if you are against it. Thoreau's reason for writing was to explain his refusal to pay taxes as an act of protest against slavery and the Mexican War. His essay has had an important influence on practitioners of civil disobedience ever since.

As noted, civil disobedience was a major tactic of nationalist movements in former colonies in Africa and Asia prior to their gaining independence. Most notably, Mohandas ("Mahatma") Gandhi pursued civil disobedience as an anticolonialist tool. Martin Luther King Jr., a leader of the civil rights movement in the United States in the 1950s and 1960s, also employed civil disobedience techniques, and antiwar activists both during and after the Vietnam War have done likewise. More recently, people have used civil disobedience to protest the legalization of abortion, Communist governments in Eastern Europe, world trade agreements, and the U.S. invasion of Iraq.

Many people who practice civil disobedience do so out of religious faith, and clergy often participate in or lead such protests. The Berrigan brothers in the United States, for example, both priests, were arrested dozens of times in acts of civil disobedience in antiwar protests.

In seeking an active form of resistance, practitioners of civil disobedience may choose to deliberately break certain laws, as by forming a peaceful but illegal blockade or occupying a facility without permission. Protesters act with the expectation that they will be arrested or even attacked or beaten by the authorities. Protesters often receive advance training in how to react to being arrested or attacked so that they will resist and defend themselves without threatening the authorities or being drawn into violence.

104   CIVIL DISOBEDIENCE *(continued)*

1. _____ Which of the following is *not* an aspect of civil disobedience?
   (a) violence **(b)** calm resistance **(c)** protest **(d)** refusal to obey laws

2. _____ In which country was civil disobedience *not* identified as a major tactic employed to induce political change? **(a)** Canada **(b)** United States **(c)** India **(d)** South Africa

3. _____ An example of civil disobedience is **(a)** paying your taxes on time **(b)** fighting in a war in which your country is involved **(c)** refusing to fight in a war for moral reasons **(d)** giving money to a politician's campaign fund.

4. _____ The Mexican War took place closest to what year? **(a)** 1776 **(b)** 1850 **(c)** 1910 **(d)** 1960

5. _____ According to this article, who has *not* been involved in civil disobedience?
   (a) Martin Luther King Jr. **(b)** the Berrigan brothers **(c)** antiabortion groups
   (d) none of these

6. _____ Which would Thoreau consider an act of civil disobedience? **(a)** dropping a bomb on a country **(b)** demolishing a politician's campaign headquarters **(c)** peacefully protesting outside a politician's campaign headquarters **(d)** kidnapping enemy soldiers

7. _____ According to this article, which of these did *not* involve civil disobedience?
   (a) the American colonists' breaking away from Great Britain in the late 1700s
   (b) the U.S. civil rights movement in the mid-1900s **(c)** antiwar activists during the Vietnam War **(d)** Polish opponents of the Communists

8. _____ Civil disobedience practitioners **(a)** often undergo training on how to react to arrest or attack **(b)** often form a blockade **(c)** often act out of religious convictions **(d)** all of these

9. _____ Who originated the concept of civil disobedience? **(a)** Henry David Thoreau **(b)** Mohandas Gandhi **(c)** the Berrigan brothers **(d)** Martin Luther King Jr.

10. _____ In the term *civil disobedience,* the word *civil* means **(a)** peaceful **(b)** national **(c)** violent **(d)** sneaky.

105 GANDHI'S RULES FOR CIVIL DISOBEDIENCE

Civil disobedience advocate Mohandas Gandhi established the following rules for individuals participating in civil disobedience activities. Read them all. Then decide whether each statement below the article is true or false. Write T for true or F for false in the blank.

---

1. A satyagrahi [a civil resister] will harbor no anger.
2. He will suffer the anger of the opponent.
3. In so doing, he will put up with assaults from the opponent and never retaliate; but he will not submit, out of fear of punishment or the like, to any order given in anger.
4. When any person in authority seeks to arrest a civil resister, he will voluntarily submit to the arrest, and he will not resist the attachment or removal of his own property, if any, when it is sought to be confiscated by authorities.
5. If a civil resister has any property in his possession as a trustee, he will refuse to surrender it, even though in defending it he might lose his life. He will, however, never retaliate.
6. Nonretaliation includes not swearing and not cursing. Therefore, a civil resister will never insult his opponent and also not take part in any of the newly coined cries that are contrary to the spirit of ahimsa [refraining from harming any living thing].
7. A civil resister will not salute the Union Jack [the British flag]; neither will he insult it or officials, English or Indian.
8. In the course of the struggle, if anyone insults an official or commits an assault on him, a civil resister will protect such official from the insult or attack even at the risk of his life.

---

1. _____ A civil resister or demonstrator must voluntarily submit to arrest by an opponent.

2. _____ When appropriate, a civil resister is urged to verbally insult an opponent.

3. _____ The civil resister should allow an opponent to confiscate possessions sought or demanded by authorities.

4. _____ A satyagrahi is a civil resister.

5. _____ Nonretaliation includes not swearing and not cursing.

6. _____ A civil resister should protect an official or officials from the insult or attack even at the risk of the resister's own life.

7. _____ A civil resister will not insult either Indian or English officials.

8. _____ A civil resister should suffer the anger of his opponent without reacting.

9. _____ A civil resister should obey all orders given by an opponent.

10. _____ A resister must never retaliate under any conditions.

106   AMELIA EARHART, LOST FOREVER (PART ONE)

Amelia Earhart (1897–1937) was a famous American aviator. You will read the story of her career in this activity and of her fateful final year in the next one. After you have completed the reading on this page, answer the true-or-false questions that follow it. Write T for true or F for false in the blank.

Born in Atchinson, Kansas, Amelia Mary Earhart worked as a nurse's aide in a military hospital in Canada during World War I. Her career began in Los Angeles in 1921 when, at age twenty-four, she took flying lessons from Neta Snook and bought her first airplane, a Kinner. Due to family problems, she sold the plane in 1924 and moved back east, where she was employed as a social worker.

One afternoon in April 1928, a man she did not know phoned her and asked, "Would you like to fly the Atlantic?" The offer was too tempting to resist; the first successful transatlantic flight had taken place just a few years earlier. She interviewed with the project coordinators, including a book publisher and publicist named George Putnam, and was invited to fly with the pilot, Wilmer Stultz, and his copilot and mechanic, Louis Gordon. The team left Trepassey Harbor, Newfoundland, in a Fokker F7 on June 17, 1928, and arrived at Burry Point, Wales, approximately twenty-one hours later. When the crew returned to the States, they were greeted with a ticker-tape parade in New York City and a reception hosted by President Calvin Coolidge at the White House. From then on, flying was the focus of Earhart's life. She placed third at the Cleveland Women's Air Derby (nicknamed the "Powder Puff Derby" by humorist Will Rogers). Her life also began to include Putnam. The two developed a friendship during preparation for the Atlantic crossing. They were married on February 7, 1931. Earhart referred to the marriage as a "partnership" with "dual control."

On May 20, 1932, she took off from Harbour Grace, Newfoundland, in a Lockheed Vega, intending to fly to Paris, duplicating Charles Lindbergh's 1927 solo flight. However, strong north winds, icy conditions, and mechanical problems forced her to land in a pasture near Londonderry, Ireland. She received the Distinguished Flying Cross from Congress, a similar honor from the French government, and the Gold Medal of the National Geographic Society, presented by President Herbert Hoover.

On January 11, 1935, Earhart became the first person to fly solo from Honolulu, Hawaii, to Oakland, California. Later that year, she soloed from Los Angeles to Mexico City and then to Newark, New Jersey.

106 AMELIA EARHART, LOST FOREVER (PART ONE) *(continued)*

1. _____ Amelia Earhart did not live to celebrate her fiftieth birthday.

2. _____ Amelia Earhart was employed in the airplane industry throughout her adult life.

3. _____ Earhart made her first transatlantic trip with two men.

4. _____ Her initial transatlantic trip took several days.

5. _____ Earhart was greeted by people speaking Welsh at the end of her first transatlantic trip.

6. _____ President Calvin Coolidge congratulated Earhart after the transatlantic venture.

7. _____ Amelia Earhart married a man who was a friend, a publicist, and a publisher.

8. _____ There were no other people in Earhart's plane when she landed in Ireland in 1932.

9. _____ After her 1932 flight, Earhart was given honors from the French, American, and Portuguese governments.

10. _____ Earhart was the first person to fly solo across the Atlantic Ocean.

107 AMELIA EARHART, LOST FOREVER (PART TWO)

This is the conclusion of the tale of the famous aviator, Amelia Earhart. Read the text; then answer the ten true-or-false questions that follow it. Write T for true or F for false in the blank.

In July 1936, Earhart took delivery of a Lockheed Electra 10E and started planning a round-the-world flight, with the financial backing of Purdue University.

Her flight would not be the first to circle the globe, but it would be the longest, at 29,000 miles, following an equatorial route. Fred Noonan was chosen as the navigator. A licensed ship's captain as well as a pilot, he had vast experience in both marine and flight navigation. He had recently left PanAmerican World Airways, where he helped establish the company's seaplane routes across the Pacific. He hoped that the publicity resulting from the flight would help him establish his own navigation school in Florida.

On March 17, 1937, Earhart and Noonan flew the first leg, westward from Oakland, California, to Honolulu, Hawaii. The flight resumed three days later, but a tire blew during takeoff, causing the plane to spin on the runway. Severely damaged, the aircraft had to be shipped to California for repairs, and the flight was called off. The second attempt would begin at Miami, this time flying from west to east. Earhart and Noonan departed on June 1, and after numerous stops in South America, Africa, the Indian subcontinent, and Southeast Asia, they arrived at Lae, New Guinea, on June 29. About 22,000 miles of the journey was completed; the remaining 7,000 miles would all be over the Pacific.

On July 2, 1937, around 10:00 A.M., Earhart and Noonan took off from Lae. Their intended destination was Howland Island, a flat sliver of land $1\frac{1}{4}$ miles long, $\frac{1}{3}$ mile wide, 10 feet high, and 2,556 miles away. Their last positive position report and sighting placed them over the Nukumanu Islands, about 800 miles into the flight. The U.S. Coast Guard cutter *Itasca* was waiting at Howland, assigned to communicate with Earhart's plane and guide her to the island once she arrived in the vicinity.

Through a series of misunderstandings or errors, the details of which are still unclear, the final approach to Howland using radio navigation was never accomplished, although vocal transmissions by Earhart indicated that she and Noonan believed they had reached Howland's charted position (which was off by about 5 nautical miles on their map) over scattered clouds. After several hours of frustrating attempts at two-way communications, contact was lost, although subsequent transmissions from the downed Electra may have been received by operators elsewhere in the Pacific.

107 AMELIA EARHART, LOST FOREVER (PART TWO) *(continued)*

The United States government spent $4 million looking for Earhart, which made it the most costly and most intensive air and sea search in history at that time, organized by the Navy and the Coast Guard. Many researchers believe that the plane ran out of fuel and Earhart and Noonan ditched at sea; however, one group, the International Group for Historic Aircraft Recovery, suggests that they may have flown along a standard line of position, which Earhart specified in her last transmission received at Howland, to Nikumaroro (then known as Gardner) Island in what is now Kiribati, landed there, and ultimately perished. The group has accumulated an array of archaeological and anecdotal evidence—but no proof—supporting this theory.

1. _____ Earhart's flight circling the globe would be the first to circle the globe.

2. _____ For a number of reasons, including experience in marine and flight navigation, Fred Noonan was a good choice as Earhart's navigator for her circle-the-globe trip.

3. _____ Noonan had left from PanAm before he was chosen to navigate Earhart's circle-the-globe trip.

4. _____ Earhart and Noonan never landed in Hawaii on their first attempt to circle the globe.

5. _____ Earhart and Noonan completed more than 20,000 miles of their journey.

6. _____ A major reason that Earhart and Noonan never completed their journey was ineffective radio navigation.

7. _____ The Army, Navy, and Coast Guard assisted in the attempt to find Earhart and Noonan.

8. _____ One group believes that Earhart's incompetence as a pilot was the reason that the plane went down.

9. _____ The $4 million that the United States government spent attempting to find Earhart and Noonan was the largest amount ever spent on an air and sea search up to that time in history.

10. _____ Some people believe that Earhart died at Nikumaroro.

108   JOHN F. KENNEDY'S INAUGURAL ADDRESS
(PART ONE)

On a cold January day in 1961, John Fitzgerald Kennedy took the oath of office as the thirty-fifth president of the United States. Here is the first of three parts of his inaugural address. As you can see from his speech, he came into the office of the presidency at a time of world crisis. Read his words, and then answer the questions that follow them. Write the letter of the correct answer in the blank next to each question.

We observe today not a victory of party but a celebration of freedom—symbolizing an end as well as a beginning—signifying renewal as well as change. For I have sworn before you and Almighty God the same solemn oath our forebears prescribed nearly a century and three-quarters ago.

The world is very different now. For man holds in his mortal hands the power to abolish all forms of human poverty and all forms of human life. And yet the same revolutionary beliefs for which our forebears fought are still at issue around the globe—the belief that the rights of man come not from the generosity of the state, but from the hand of God.

We dare not forget today that we are the heirs of that first revolution. Let the word go forth from this time and place, to friend and foe alike, that the torch has been passed to a new generation of Americans—born in this century, tempered by war, disciplined by a hard and bitter peace, proud of our ancient heritage—and unwilling to witness or permit the slow undoing of those human rights to which this Nation has always been committed, and to which we are committed today at home and around the world.

Let every nation know, whether it wishes us well or ill, that we shall pay any price, bear any burden, meet any hardship, support any friend, oppose any foe, in order to assure the survival and the success of liberty.

This much we pledge—and more.

To those old allies whose cultural and spiritual origins we share, we pledge the loyalty of faithful friends. United, there is little we cannot do in a host of cooperative ventures. Divided, there is little we can do—for we dare not meet a powerful challenge at odds and split asunder.

To those new States whom we welcome to the ranks of the free, we pledge our word that one form of colonial control shall not have passed away merely to be replaced by a far more iron tyranny. We shall not always expect to find them supporting our view. But we shall always hope to find them strongly supporting their own freedom—and to remember that, in the past, those who foolishly sought power by riding the back of the tiger ended up inside.

To those people in the huts and villages across the globe struggling to break the bonds of mass misery, we pledge our best efforts to help them help themselves, for whatever period is required—not because the Communists may be doing it, not because we seek their votes, but because it is right. If a free society cannot help the many who are poor, it cannot save the few who are rich.

108   JOHN F. KENNEDY'S INAUGURAL ADDRESS (PART ONE) *(continued)*

To our sister republics south of our border, we offer a special pledge—to convert our good words into good deeds—in a new alliance for progress—to assist free men and free governments in casting off the chains of poverty. But this peaceful revolution of hope cannot become the prey of hostile powers. Let all our neighbors know that we shall join with them to oppose aggression or subversion anywhere in the Americas. And let every other power know that this Hemisphere intends to remain the master of its own house.

1. _____ Kennedy's speech begins with a series of **(a)** dates and opinions **(b)** contrasts and parallel structures **(c)** random ideas **(d)** none of these.

2. _____ The "forebears" to whom Kennedy refers **(a)** founded the nation **(b)** are yet to be born **(c)** lived during prehistoric times **(d)** elected him to office.

3. _____ This speech was given **(a)** in the 1920s **(b)** in the 1960s **(c)** in the 1980s **(d)** last year.

4. _____ According to Kennedy, most people believe that our rights as citizens come from **(a)** God **(b)** the state **(c)** neither.

5. _____ Heirs are people who **(a)** give things to others **(b)** inherit things from others **(c)** discover things **(d)** hide things.

6. _____ The paragraph that begins "Let every nation know . . ." makes use of **(a)** contrasts **(b)** difficult vocabulary for most adults **(c)** verb phrases **(d)** warnings to world leaders.

7. _____ *Asunder* means **(a)** together **(b)** apart **(c)** calmly **(d)** violently.

8. _____ "Iron tyranny" is used as a parallel idea to **(a)** "supporting their own freedom" **(b)** "riding the back of the tiger" **(c)** colonial control **(d)** all of these.

9. _____ Kennedy's main reason for helping the poor is **(a)** to counter the threat of communism **(b)** that it is the moral thing to do **(c)** so that the rich can profit financially from it **(d)** to win their votes.

10. _____ By "sister republics south of our border," Kennedy is referring to **(a)** Canada **(b)** Greenland **(c)** Latin America **(d)** Russia.

109   JOHN F. KENNEDY'S INAUGURAL ADDRESS (PART TWO)

Being the president of the United States is not an easy job. Here in the second part of John F. Kennedy's 1961 inaugural speech, Kennedy acknowledges the task in front of him and addresses U.S. citizens and the citizens of the world's other nations. Read this portion of his speech, and then answer the questions that follow it. Write the letter of the correct answer in the blank next to the question.

To that world assembly of sovereign states, the United Nations, our last best hope in an age where the instruments of war have far outpaced the instruments of peace, we renew our pledge of support—to prevent it from becoming merely a forum for invective—to strengthen its shield of the new and the weak—and to enlarge the area in which its writ may run.

Finally, to those nations who would make themselves our adversary, we offer not a pledge but a request: that both sides begin anew the quest for peace, before the dark powers of destruction unleashed by science engulf all humanity in planned or accidental self-destruction.

We dare not tempt them with weakness. For only when our arms are sufficient beyond doubt can we be certain beyond doubt that they will never be employed. But neither can two great and powerful groups of nations take comfort from our present course—both sides overburdened by the cost of modern weapons, both rightly alarmed by the steady spread of the deadly atom, yet both racing to alter that uncertain balance of terror that stays the hand of mankind's final war.

So let us begin anew—remembering on both sides that civility is not a sign of weakness, and sincerity is always subject to proof. Let us never negotiate out of fear. But let us never fear to negotiate.

Let both sides explore what problems unite us instead of belaboring those problems which divide us.

Let both sides, for the first time, formulate serious and precise proposals for the inspection and control of arms—and bring the absolute power to destroy other nations under the absolute control of all nations.

Let both sides seek to invoke the wonders of science instead of its terrors. Together let us explore the stars, conquer the deserts, eradicate disease, tap the ocean depths, and encourage the arts and commerce.

Let both sides unite to heed in all corners of the earth the command of Isaiah—to "undo the heavy burdens . . . and to let the oppressed go free." And if a beachhead of cooperation may push back the jungle of suspicion, let both sides join in creating a new endeavor, not a new balance of power, but a new world of law, where the strong are just and the weak secure and the peace preserved.

All this will not be finished in the first 100 days. Nor will it be finished in the first 1,000 days, nor in the life of this Administration, nor even perhaps in our lifetime on this planet. But let us begin.

109 JOHN F. KENNEDY'S INAUGURAL ADDRESS (PART TWO) *(continued)*

1. _____ How many reasons does Kennedy cite for supporting the United Nations?
   (a) one **(b)** two **(c)** three **(d)** four

2. _____ To explain his United Nations support, Kennedy uses **(a)** parallel structures
   (b) infinitives **(c)** both *a* and *b* **(d)** neither *a* nor *b*.

3. _____ To what does "the dark powers of destruction unleashed by science" refer?
   (a) communism **(b)** volcanic eruptions **(c)** atomic weapons **(d)** dictatorships

4. _____ Throughout his speech, Kennedy supports **(a)** war **(b)** peace **(c)** bombing enemies
   (d) none of these.

5. _____ By "arms," Kennedy means **(a)** weapons **(b)** limbs **(c)** soldiers **(d)** all of these.

6. _____ Which of the "wonders of science" Kennedy cites is an allusion to the space
   program? **(a)** "encourage the arts and commerce" **(b)** "eradicate disease"
   (c) "tap the ocean depths" **(d)** "explore the stars"

7. _____ The reference to "the command of Isaiah" is **(a)** a literary illusion to the Bible
   (b) a quotation from one of Kennedy's political friends **(c)** a great military hero
   (d) none of these.

8. _____ When does Kennedy believe his plans will be completed?
   (a) in 100 days **(b)** in 1,000 days **(c)** by the end of his term of office
   (d) perhaps not even in this generation

9. _____ In the next-to-last paragraph, what is Kennedy's attitude regarding the possibility of
   peace? **(a)** optimistic **(b)** pessimistic **(c)** neutral **(d)** dismissive.

10. _____ Kennedy wants the weak people to be **(a)** angry **(b)** secure **(c)** kept in their place
   (d) ignored.

110 JOHN F. KENNEDY'S INAUGURAL ADDRESS (PART THREE)

This is the conclusion of President John F. Kennedy's inaugural address, in which he explains the world's condition at the time that he took office. What is his purpose? How does he try to convince his listeners? Read this portion of his speech, and then answer the questions that follow it. Write the letter of the correct answer in the blank for each question.

In your hands, my fellow citizens, more than in mine, will rest the final success or failure of our course. Since this country was founded, each generation of Americans has been summoned to give testimony to its national loyalty. The graves of young Americans who answered the call to service surround the globe.

Now the trumpet summons us again—not as a call to bear arms, though arms we need; not as a call to battle, though embattled we are—but a call to bear the burden of a long twilight struggle, year in and year out, "rejoicing in hope, patient in tribulation"—a struggle against the common enemies of man: tyranny, poverty, disease, and war itself.

Can we forge against these enemies a grand and global alliance, North and South, East and West, that can assure a more fruitful life for all mankind? Will you join in that historic effort?

In the long history of the world, only a few generations have been granted the role of defending freedom in its hour of maximum danger. I do not shrink from this responsibility—I welcome it. I do not believe that any of us would exchange places with any other people or any other generation. The energy, the faith, the devotion which we bring to this endeavor will light our country and all who serve it—and the glow from that fire can truly light the world.

And so, my fellow Americans: ask not what your country can do for you—ask what you can do for your country.

My fellow citizens of the world: ask not what America will do for you, but what together we can do for the freedom of man.

Finally, whether you are citizens of America or citizens of the world, ask of us the same high standards of strength and sacrifice which we ask of you. With a good conscience our only sure reward, with history the final judge of our deeds, let us go forth to lead the land we love, asking His blessing and His help, but knowing that here on earth God's work must truly be our own.

110   JOHN F. KENNEDY'S INAUGURAL ADDRESS (PART THREE) *(continued)*

1. _____ Who does Kennedy feel will be most responsible for the chance for peace?
   (a) American politicians **(b)** religious leaders **(c)** foreign leaders **(d)** none of these

2. _____ What is the prevalent tone of the paragraph that begins "Now the trumpet summons us again . . ."? **(a)** hopeful **(b)** patient **(c)** both *a* and *b* **(d)** neither *a* nor *b*

3. _____ *Tyranny* means **(a)** friendliness **(b)** patience **(c)** oppressive rule **(d)** stormy weather.

4. _____ How might you summarize the paragraph that ends "Will you join in that historic effort?" **(a)** Today could be worse than tomorrow. **(b)** Let's all join hands and work together. **(c)** The violent will be victorious. **(d)** See for yourself.

5. _____ Where are "the graves of young Americans who answered the call to service" located? **(a)** in national military cemeteries **(b)** in France **(c)** all over the world **(d)** at the bottom of the sea

6. _____ What "fire" does Kennedy believe can light the world?
   (a) the eternal flame **(b)** religion **(c)** voting rights **(d)** the defense of freedom

7. _____ Kennedy's speech is intended primarily for **(a)** citizens of the United States **(b)** political leaders around the world **(c)** some citizens of all the world's countries **(d)** the British people.

8. _____ Kennedy feels that Americans alone are responsible for the planet's future course. Is this statement **(a)** true or **(b)** false?

9. _____ The only reward for working toward the betterment of the planet that one is assured of receiving is **(a)** fewer weapons **(b)** fewer casualties **(c)** a clear conscience **(d)** none of these.

10. _____ According to Kennedy, who or what will assess the deeds of the people of the world? **(a)** God **(b)** history **(c)** other nations **(d)** college professors

111   THE BLACK DEATH

Imagine one-third of a continent's population wiped out by a disease. Such was the case with the Black Death in the fourteenth century. How did the disease start? What did people do to try to eliminate the disease and its deadly effects? Read the article below, and then match the sentence beginnings in Column A with their logical endings in Column B. Write the three-letter answer code from Column B in the blank next to the appropriate number in Column A. Then copy the thirty answer letters onto the line below the columns. If your answers are correct, they will spell out the names of four things that spread the Black Death.

The Black Death was a devastating epidemic in Europe in the fourteenth century that is estimated to have killed about a third of the population. Most scientists believe that the Black Death was an outbreak of bubonic plague, a dreaded disease that has spread in pandemic form several times through history. In 1896, a scientist named Alexander Yersin determined that the plague is caused by the bacterium *Yersinia pestis,* which is spread by fleas with the help of animals like the black rat (*Rattus rattus*)—what we would call today the sewer rat. Sometimes, the name Black Death is used for all outbreaks of plague and epidemics. But the fourteenth-century outbreak was the worst of them all.

It is not entirely clear where this major epidemic started, but it has been traced back to northern India or, even more likely, the steppes of Central Asia near the Gobi Desert. We do know that it was carried west by Mongol armies. It was imported to Europe by way of the Crimea, where the Genoese colony known as Kaffa (modern Feodosiya) was besieged by the Mongols. It is said that the Mongols catapulted their infected corpses into the city, and the bodies poisoned the water in the wells. Refugees from Kaffa took the plague to Messina, Genoa, and Venice toward the end of 1347. From Italy, the disease spread clockwise around Europe over the next four years, moving into France, Spain, England (in June 1348) and the rest of Britain, Germany, Scandinavia, and finally northwestern Russia. As the death tolls mounted, whole villages were abandoned, the few survivors fleeing and spreading the disease further. There were even reports of ships running aground without a single passenger or crew member alive.

Estimates of the death toll vary from source to source, but the consensus is that about a third of the population of Europe died from the outbreak in the mid-1300s—a total of 25 million deaths on that continent alone, with many others occurring in Africa and Asia.

The great population loss brought economic changes as depopulation further eroded the peasants' obligations to remain on their traditional holdings, where most worked as indentured servants to the landowners. The sudden scarcity of cheap labor provided an incentive for innovation and social mobility that broke the stagnation of the Dark Ages and, some experts argue, lay the groundwork for the cultural and intellectual rebirth known as the Renaissance.

111   THE BLACK DEATH *(continued)*

Column One

1. _____ The Black Death

2. _____ One-third of the continent's population

3. _____ The cause, Bubonic plague,

4. _____ *Yersinia pestis*

5. _____ The name Black Death

6. _____ Mongol armies most likely

7. _____ In 1896, Alexander Yersin

8. _____ The few survivors of this disease

9. _____ Depopulation caused

10. _____ Some experts believe that the Black Death

Column Two

asp. was wiped out by disease.

dwe. is sometimes used for all breakouts of plague and epidemics.

ees. lay the groundwork for the Renaissance.

fle. was a devastating disease in fourteenth-century Europe.

fug. an increase in innovation and social mobility.

lls. carried the plague west from the steppes of Central Asia.

ois. was a disease that has spread several times in history.

one. is spread by fleas with the help of animals like the black rat.

rat. determined that the plague was caused by a bacterium.

sre. fled their villages and spread the disease further.

The thirty letters are _____

_____ .

Four things responsible for the spread of the Black Death were _____ ,

_____ , _____ ,

and _____ .

112   THE TOWER OF LONDON

The Tower of London has served many purposes. It has been a palace, a fort, a prison, and a zoo—interesting! Read this article about the Tower of London, and then answer the fifteen true-or-false questions that follow it. Write T for true or F for false in the blank next to each statement.

The Tower of London is officially Her Majesty's Palace and Fortress, although the last ruler to reside in it as a palace was King James I (1566–1625). The White Tower, the square building with turrets on each corner that gave it its name, is actually in the middle of a complex of several buildings along the River Thames in London that have served as fortress, armory, treasury, mint, palace, place of execution, public records office, observatory, refuge, and prison, particularly for "upper-class" prisoners. This last use led to the phrase "sent to the Tower," meaning "imprisoned." Queen Elizabeth I (1533–1603) was imprisoned for a time in the Tower during the reign of her cousin, Mary, Queen of Scots (1542–1587); the last known use of the Tower as a prison was during World War II, for Rudolf Hess (1894–1987), a leader of the Nazi party in Germany during the 1930s.

In 1078, the Norman invader William the Conqueror (c. 1027–1087) ordered the White Tower to be built—as much to protect the Normans from the people of the city of London as to protect London from anyone else. Earlier forts there, including the Roman one, had been primarily wooden buildings, but William ordered his tower to be of stone. It was King Richard the Lion-hearted (1157–1199) who had the moat dug around the surrounding wall and filled with water from the Thames. The moat did not hold water very well until Henry III (1207–1272) redesigned it using a Dutch moat-building technique. (It was drained in 1830, and human bones were in the refuse found at its bottom.)

A royal menagerie was established at the Tower in the thirteenth century, possibly as early as 1204, in the reign of King John, and possibly stocked with animals from an earlier menagerie started in 1125 by Henry I at his palace in Woodstock, near Oxford. Its year of origin is often stated as 1235, when Henry III received a wedding gift of three leopards (so recorded, although they may have been lions) from Frederick II, the Holy Roman emperor. In 1264, the menagerie was moved to the Bulwark, which was duly renamed the Lion Tower, near the main western entrance. It was opened as an occasional public spectacle in the reign of Elizabeth I. By 1804, the menagerie was regularly open to the public. This was where William Blake saw the tiger that inspired his poem "Tiger, Tiger, Burning Bright." The menagerie's last director, Alfred Cops, who took over in 1822, found the collection in a dismal state but restocked it and issued an illustrated scientific catalogue. Unfortunately for him, the menagerie was not to last. The new London Zoo was due to open in Regent's Park, and partly for commercial reasons and partly for animal welfare, the animals were moved to the zoo. The last of the animals left in 1835, and most of the Lion Tower was demolished soon after, although Lion Gate remains.

112   THE TOWER OF LONDON *(continued)*

1. _____ The last known use of the Tower of London as a prison was during World War II.

2. _____ The White Tower is square.

3. _____ A menagerie is a place primarily used to store trophies and medals.

4. _____ William the Conqueror ordered that the White Tower be made of stone.

5. _____ Executions took place in the vicinity of the White Tower.

6. _____ The White Tower was the first fort built on that site in London.

7. _____ The river that flows through London is the Vistula.

8. _____ The prison served mostly lower-class prisoners.

9. _____ Most of the Lion Tower has been demolished.

10. _____ The phrase "sent to the Tower" means "imprisoned."

11. _____ The year 1204 was in the twelfth century.

12. _____ Henry III received animals as a wedding gift.

13. _____ Human bones were found at the bottom of the moat surrounding the White Tower.

14. _____ The White Tower has served as a public records office, an observatory, and a treasury.

15. _____ William Blake was a building architect.

113 GLADIATORS: ANCIENT WARRIORS (PART ONE)

Did you ever think about what it was like to be a gladiator, one of the Roman professional fighters of so many years ago? How ferocious were these fighters? Who were selected to be gladiators? Read the following article to find out. Then fill in the blanks and transfer your answers to the crossword puzzle. The first letter of each answer is provided. Let the games begin!

Gladiators were professional fighters in ancient Rome who fought against each other and against wild animals, sometimes to the death, for the entertainment of spectators. These fights took place in arenas in many cities during the Roman Republic (which was founded in 509 B.C.) and the Roman Empire (which lasted until A.D. 395).

The word *gladiator* comes from *gladius,* the Latin name for a short sword used by legionnaires and some gladiators.

Gladiator fights probably originated in the Etruscan custom of ritual human sacrifices to honor the dead. The first Roman fights took place in 264 B.C. in the Forum Boarium, organized by Marcus and Decimus Brutus at the funeral of their father.

Gladiator games (called *munera,* the plural of *munus*) took place in amphitheaters (like the Colosseum) and took the latter half of the day, after the fights against animals (*venationes*) and public executions (*noxii*). Initially, rich private individuals organized these, often to gain political favor with the public. The person who organized the show was called the *editor, munerator,* or *dominus* and was honored with the official signs of a magistrate. Later the emperors would exert a near complete monopoly on staging the *ludi circenses,* "games" that included hunts of wild animals, public executions, and gladiator fights. Musical accompaniment was usually provided.

Gladiators were typically picked from prisoners of war, slaves, and sentenced criminals. There were also occasional volunteers. They were trained in special gladiator schools (*ludi*). One of the largest schools was in Ravenna. There were four schools in Rome itself, the largest of which was called the Ludus Magnus. The Ludus Magnus was connected to the Colosseum by an underground tunnel. Gladiators often belonged to a troupe (*familia*) that traveled from town to town. A trainer of gladiators or the manager of a team of gladiators was known as a *lanista.* The troupe's owner rented gladiators to whoever wanted to stage games. A gladiator would typically fight no more than three times per year.

A gladiator could also be the property of a rich individual, who would hire a *lanista* to train him. Several senators and emperors acquired their own favorites.

Criminals were expected to die within a year, but if they survived three years, they could earn their release.

113 GLADIATORS: ANCIENT WARRIORS (PART ONE) *(continued)*

113   GLADIATORS: ANCIENT WARRIORS (PART ONE) (continued)

Across

2. Criminals were expected to _____ within a year of service as a gladiator.

4. Gladiators fought in the ancient city of _____.

6. Gladiator fights were held in outdoor _____.

9. A gladiator could be the _____ of a wealthy individual.

10. _____ often accompanied gladiator fights.

12. Roman _____ eventually monopolized the staging of gladiator fights.

14. Usually a gladiator would fight no more than _____ times each year.

15. *Gladiator* comes from the Latin name for a type of _____.

17. Gladiators were usually prisoners of war, _____, or sentenced criminals.

18. Gladiator fights took place in structures called _____.

Down

1. Some people would _____ to become gladiators.

2. Gladiator fights most likely began as contests to honor the _____.

3. Public _____ were held the morning of gladiator fights.

5. _____ watched the gladiator fights.

7. Gladiators fought other gladiators or wild _____.

8. Gladiators belonged to a _____ that traveled from town to town.

11. Criminals could earn their release from being a gladiator after three _____ of service.

13. Ravenna was the site of a large gladiator _____.

16. Initially, gladiator fights were organized by _____ individuals who sought to gain public favor and approval.

114 GLADIATORS: ANCIENT WARRIORS (PART TWO)

In this part of the article about gladiators, you will learn how the gladiators were matched up to fight and what part the audience played in the outcome of the fights. After you have read the article, answer the questions that follow it on the lines provided or on a separate sheet of paper.

Gladiators usually fought in pairs, one gladiator against another. However, a sponsor or the audience could request other combinations, such as several gladiators fighting together or specific gladiators against each other, even from outside the established troupe. If a requested gladiator was dead or incapacitated, the *lanista* sometimes had to rely on substitutes. Emperors could request participation by their own gladiators.

At the end of a fight, when one gladiator acknowledged defeat by raising a finger, the audience could decide whether the loser should live or die. It is known that the audience (or sponsor or emperor) indicated with the thumb if they wanted the loser to be killed, but the exact gesture remains unclear. It is possible that they pointed the thumb upward if they wanted the loser to live and downward if they wanted him to die; or it may have been the other way around. Another possibility is that they raised their fist but kept their thumb inside it if they wanted the loser to live and pointed downward to signify death. A gladiator did not have to die after every match—if the audience felt that both men fought admirably, they would likely want both to live and fight for their amusement in the future. A gladiator who won several fights was allowed to retire, often to train other fighters. Gladiators who managed to win their freedom—often by request of the audience or sponsor—were given a wooden sword as a memento.

The attitude of Romans toward the gladiators was ambivalent: socially, they were considered lower than slaves, yet some successful gladiators rose to celebrity status. Gladiators often developed large followings of women, who apparently found them sexually attractive. This may be one reason that many gladiators fought bare-chested. It was socially unacceptable for citizen women to have sexual contact with a gladiator, but Faustina, the mother of the emperor Commodus, was said to have conceived Commodus with a gladiator (Commodus likely invented this story himself).

Despite the extreme dangers and hardships of the profession, some gladiators were volunteers who fought for money; effectively, this career was a sort of last chance for people who had gotten into financial trouble. Their oath (which Seneca describes as particularly shameful) conveyed their acceptance of slave status and of the worst consideration in the public mind.

Some emperors, among them Hadrian, Caligula, Titus Flavius, and Commodus, also entered the arena for (presumably) rigged combats. Emperor Trajan organized as many as five thousand gladiator fighting pairs. Gladiator contests could take months to complete.

Female gladiators also existed; Emperor Commodus liked to stage fights between dwarfs and women.

One of the most famous gladiators was Spartacus, who became the leader of a group of escaped gladiators and slaves. His revolt, which began in 73 B.C., was crushed by Marcus Licinius Crassus two years later. After this, gladiators were deported from Rome and other cities during times of social disturbances for fear that they might organize and rebel again.

The Greek physician Galen worked for a while as a gladiator's physician in Pergamon.

Gladiator fights were first outlawed by Emperor Constantine I in 325 but continued sporadically until about 450. The last known gladiator competition in the city of Rome occurred on January 1, 404.

114   GLADIATORS: ANCIENT WARRIORS (PART TWO) *(continued)*

1. Explain how gladiators were matched up to do battle.

   _____

   _____

2. How would audience members indicate that they wanted a gladiator killed?

   _____

   _____

3. What would the reward be for the gladiator who won several fights?

   _____

   _____

4. In what ways were the Romans' attitudes toward gladiators ambivalent?

   _____

   _____

5. Considering the many dangers involved, why would individuals volunteer to become gladiators?

   _____

   _____

6. What did the oath taken by the gladiators imply?

   _____

   _____

7. Did a gladiator have to die after every match?

   _____

   _____

8. Emperor Commodus pitted women gladiators against whom?

   _____

   _____

9. What rules were put into effect in the aftermath of Spartacus's revolt?

   _____

   _____

10. Approximately how many centuries ago did the final gladiator competition take place in Rome?

   _____

   _____

115   LEARNING ABOUT MEXICO

A student took notes while reading an article about Mexico. He organized his notes into neat categories; unfortunately, he dropped his folders and all the notes fell out. So help him place each of the fifteen notes below back into its proper category by writing the corresponding letter in the blank next to each note. A letter can be used more than once.

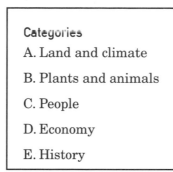

Categories

A. Land and climate

B. Plants and animals

C. People

D. Economy

E. History

1. _____ Mexico was a colony of Spain for three hundred years.

2. _____ Mexico fought the United States over disputed territory between 1846 and 1848.

3. _____ Oil is Mexico's largest export.

4. _____ Mexico City's temperatures are pleasant year-round.

5. _____ *Mestizos* make up most of the population.

6. _____ Mexico is the southernmost country in North America.

7. _____ Mexico's coastal plains receive much rainfall.

8. _____ Seven out of ten Mexicans have at least some European ancestry.

9. _____ Many valuable minerals are found in Mexico.

10. _____ Mexico is the world's largest producer of silver.

11. _____ Nearly 25 percent of the country is covered with forests.

12. _____ Volcanoes are found in the Sierra Madre Occidental.

13. _____ The country was ruled by the Aztecs for two hundred years.

14. _____ Monkeys, jaguars, and parrots are found throughout the country.

15. _____ The rectangular plateau called the Mexican Plateau is where most of the country's important cities are located.

116 ALL ABOUT FRANCE

Here are fifteen facts about France. A word is missing from each sentence. Select the most appropriate word from the word bank, and insert it in its proper space in one of the sentences. Each word is used only once. *Bonne chance!*

account	conflict	holiday	republic
alliance	economy	mob	symbol
bankruptcy	empire	mountains	topography
capital	guillotine	palace	

1. The Bastille was a fortress that was a _____ of the ruling French monarchy.

2. A _____ of revolutionaries stormed this fortress.

3. There was a _____ between the Catholics and the Protestants in the sixteenth century.

4. France's _____ features the Alps, including Mont Blanc, the Jura and Vosges Mountains, and the famous Pyrenees.

5. Charlemagne's _____ included much of Europe at the time.

6. The high _____ of France are snow-capped throughout the year.

7. Before World War II, France's _____ was primarily agricultural.

8. The French national _____ is Bastille Day, July 14.

9. People were executed using the _____ during the French Revolution.

10. One _____ of the French Revolution is *A Tale of Two Cities* by Charles Dickens.

11. A(n) _____ of European powers defeated Napoleon Bonaparte.

12. After Napoleon's 1870 defeat, France became a _____ again.

13. One of the French leaders, Louis XIV, built a magnificent _____ at Versailles.

14. Paris is the _____ of France.

15. King Louis XVI lost his subjects' confidence by driving the country to the brink of _____.

Reading Comprehension in Social Studies Classes

Section Six

READING COMPREHENSION IN BIOGRAPHY AND CURRENT AFFAIRS

Students will find plenty to like in the twenty-three activities in Section Six. They will encounter childhood heroes, including Superman (Activity 117) and Walt Disney (120). Athletes, past and present, including Jackie Robinson (121 and 122), David Beckham (123), Muhammad Ali (124), Lance Armstrong (125), and Barry Bonds (126), are also featured, along with an amateur named Jose (139). Students will read about interesting human beings such as firefighter Red Adair (118), escape artist Harry Houdini (119), and entertainer Sir Elton John (127). Debatable issues such as observations about life (128) and the death penalty (130), video games (133), photojournalism ethics (136), and pyramid schemes (138) are also tackled in this section. Fun topics such as fashion (132), skateboarding (134), and hip-hop music (135) will stimulate your students' reading interests. Your students will also read about the world of work (129), a Long Island town (131), and the 2004 tsunami (137).

The questions feature organization by topic, summarizing, details, cause and effect, and opinions. Answer keys to the magic square, crossword puzzle, multiple-choice, and matching-column activities provide students with immediate feedback.

117 SUPERMAN: THE GREATEST HERO

Superman is one of the all-time great superheroes. Here you will read about his awesome powers and some of his weaknesses. After reading the article, complete the crossword puzzle with the words missing from the clues. The first letter of each answer is provided to get you going faster than a speeding bullet!

Superman made his debut as an action hero in the first issue of *Action Comics*, published in June 1938. It took many installments of the comic to establish his persona, his backstory, and his powers. But right from the start, Superman possessed a number of extraordinary powers, the most widely known being that he is "faster than a speeding bullet." His powers were rather limited in 1940s and '50s stories but grew to godlike proportions in the 1960s, '70s, and early '80s. In 1986, in a major effort undertaken to reconcile the various story lines over the years, his powers were scaled back somewhat.

One was almost complete invulnerability. In the 1940s, a bursting artillery shell could harm him but not kill him. By the 1970s, he could fly through a star and shrug off a nuclear blast. Today, Superman is still extremely resilient and can withstand the assault of dozens of artillery shells, lasers, and explosives, but he would be killed if he flew into a star or was close to the center of a nuclear explosion. In addition, his superhuman immune system makes him impervious to most toxins and diseases.

His vision-related powers evolved in the 1950s and 1960s. X-ray vision gives him the ability to see through nearly any substance except lead. The selective application of this power allows him to see through walls but not through the people on the other side. His telescopic vision affords him the ability to see at a considerable distance, such as several miles away. When these two senses are used in combination, it is called Super Vision. Superman can also see the entire electromagnetic spectrum if he wishes, including infrared and ultraviolet, which thus allows him to see in the dark. His microscopic vision allows him to see extremely small objects and images.

Another of Superman's powers is heat vision, the ability to apply heat to any target he can see, much like a laser. The beams are also normally invisible to normal vision, which allows Superman to work with subtlety when called for. He also possesses superhearing, allowing him to hear any sound regardless of volume or pitch.

The power of flight by force of will allows Superman to maneuver easily and precisely in any direction; he can hover as well. Superman originally could jump up to one-eighth of a mile but not fly; that ability developed only in the late 1940s.

Superman's superbreath can create hurricane-force winds by simply blowing. He can also chill his breath to freeze a target he cannot reach. His superspeed allows him to move incredibly fast, much like another comic book hero, The Flash. This includes running, but flying is more versatile and less strenuous for him. At first, his running speed was a mere 30 miles per hour, but it got much faster in the 1950s and thereafter.

117 SUPERMAN: THE GREATEST HERO *(continued)*

From the 1950s through the 1980s, Superman's strength, speed, and abilities were literally unlimited: at the height of his power, he could travel millions of light-years across the span of the universe in brief periods of time; he could dive into the hearts of stars and survive unharmed; he could easily travel through time by moving at speeds faster than light; and he could move planets and lift any weight. When Superman's character was re-created in 1986, he became much more "vulnerable" and no longer omnipotent. He can no longer fly faster than light, and he can no longer shrug off nuclear blasts. He has survived nearby nuclear explosions, but attacks of that magnitude have left him wounded and seriously weakened. They are generally seen as reaching the limits of Superman's power. Likewise, while Superman could move a mountain if he pushed his strength to the limit, he can no longer affect the orbit of the earth, as he used to do. Nonetheless, he is still one of the strongest and most powerful of all superheroes.

Superman has had his power levels increased over the past decade or so since coming back to life in 1986. Superman can now survive nuclear blasts and has survived plunging into the sun itself, which in fact provided a temporary increase in his power. Superman's strength is again increased, and he is capable of moving far more weight than he could in 1986.

Yet Superman also has some weaknesses. Originally, Superman's powers were simply typical of all adult Kryptonians, but this was well before powers like flight and utter invulnerability were invented for him. The origin of Superman's powers then became the radiation of the sun, which differs from the radiation of the star around which Superman's native planet, Krypton, orbits. The yellow sun of our solar system grants him powers he would not have under Krypton's red sun. Numerous stories have had Superman's enemies take advantage of that fact and expose him to synthesized red solar radiation to neutralize his powers as long as they can maintain the exposure. The older version of his story had the weakness that his powers could vary, depending on the color of the closest star. For instance, a yellow sun gives him maximum power, an orange one only half strength.

Another source of his strength is that Krypton has much higher gravity and so his muscles are adapted to higher gravity. His strength is then dependent on the lower gravity of the earth. As noted, in early comics, Superman did not have the ability to fly and only used the lower gravity of the earth for long jumps. The jumps then evolved into flying.

The remains of his shattered home planet spread throughout the universe as a green crystalline or metallic substance known as kryptonite, which is harmful to Superman and robs him of his powers when it comes near him. A variant form of kryptonite is "red kryptonite," which does not usually harm him directly but has highly unpredictable effects on his psyche and powers (for example, red kryptonite exposure once transformed Superman's head into that of a giant ant). Gold kryptonite removes Superman's powers under the influence of the earth's yellow sun, but fortunately, it is rare in the extreme. There have been a number of other rare variants of kryptonite, introduced sporadically over the years whenever a particular plotline required them and

117 SUPERMAN: THE GREATEST HERO (continued)

then forgotten, but in the 1986 reinvention of the Superman story, they no longer exist. Kryptonite was invented specifically for the *Superman* radio serial, to permit the star who played Superman to take a vacation!

The comics have also established that Superman and other Kryptonians are highly vulnerable to magic. This means that any wizard, magic-based monster, or ordinary person with a magic object can be extremely dangerous. (In the fictional universe of the comics, "magic" is a type of energy that can be harnessed and controlled. It differs from the definition of magic as applied to the everyday world.)

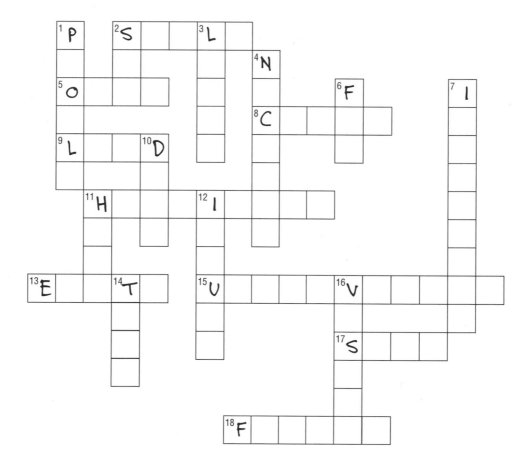

117   SUPERMAN: THE GREATEST HERO (continued)

Across

2. Superman's microscopic vision allows him to see _____ objects.

5. Superman is no longer _____ potent.

8. Superman's breath can _____ a target to freeze it until he gets there.

9. He can see through most surfaces but cannot see through _____.

11. Superman's breath resembles the force of a _____.

13. Superman can no longer affect the orbit of the _____ as he used to.

15. Superman can see the entire electromagnetic spectrum, including infrared and _____ light.

17. Superman would be killed if he flew into a _____.

18. _____ is more versatile and less strenuous than running for Superman.

Down

1. Superman cannot see through _____ on the other side of a wall.

2. Superman survived plunging into the _____.

3. Superman can beam heat toward a target, much like a _____ does.

4. Superman can survive a _____ attack.

6. In the early 1940s, Superman could jump up to one-eighth of a mile but he could not _____.

7. Superman's powers have _____ over the last two decades.

10. Superman can see in the _____.

11. Superman can _____ regardless of volume or pitch.

12. He is _____ to most toxins and diseases.

14. By moving faster than light, Superman can travel through _____.

16. Superman possesses X-ray _____.

Name: _____ Date: _____ Period: _____

118   RED ADAIR: FIREFIGHTER EXTRAORDINAIRE

Red Adair helped extinguish thousands of large and dangerous fires during his lifetime. He specialized in stopping oil well fires on land and on the seas. How did he accomplish these remarkable feats? Read Adair's story; then fill in the crossword puzzle with words found in this article. The clues are synonyms for the answers, and the first letter of each answer has been given to you.

Paul Neal "Red" Adair (June 18, 1915–August 7, 2004) was a famous oil field firefighter. He became known around the world as an innovator in the highly specialized and extremely hazardous profession of extinguishing and capping blazing, erupting oil wells, both on land and offshore.

Adair was born in Houston, Texas. He began fighting oil well fires after returning from serving in a bomb disposal unit during World War II. Adair founded Red Adair Co., Inc., in 1959, and over his long career battled more than two thousand oil well, natural gas well, and other spectacular fires. In 1991, at age seventy-five, Adair helped extinguish the oil well fires in Kuwait set by retreating Iraqi troops after the Persian Gulf War. He officially retired in 1994. Three years later, his company was bought by its competitor, Boots & Coots International Well Control, Inc., which had been founded in 1978 by Adair's top lieutenants, Asger "Boots" Hansen and Ed "Coots" Matthews.

Fire requires fuel, heat, and oxygen to burn. In fighting a fire at a wellhead (the portion of the well at and just above the ground's surface), typically, high explosives such as dynamite are used to "snuff" the flame first. Doing so removes the heat, but the fuel (the natural gas or oil) is still present; indeed, often a huge fountain of oil surrounds the work area, showering fuel on the working crew.

After snuffing, the wellhead must be capped to stop the flow of fuel. During this time, the fuel and oxygen required to create another inferno are present in copious amounts. At this perilous stage, one small spark (perhaps from a steel or iron tool striking a stone) or other heat source might reignite the fuel.

To prevent reignition, brass or bronze tools, which do not strike sparks, are used during the capping process. Meticulous care is used to avoid heat and sparks or any other ignition source. The reignition of a wellhead may take the form of an extremely powerful explosion, possibly even worse than the original blowout.

118   RED ADAIR: FIREFIGHTER EXTRAORDINAIRE (continued)

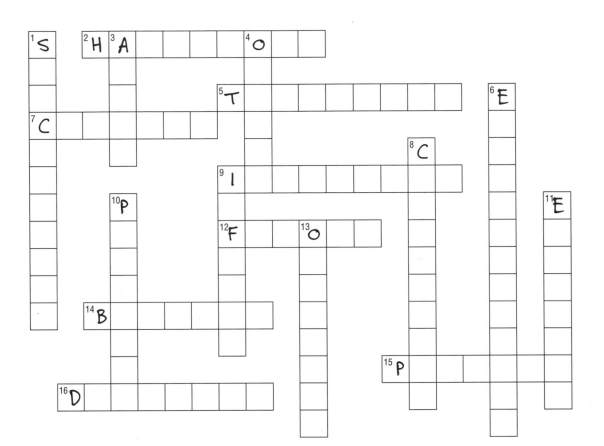

Across

2. dangerous

5. commonly

7. plentiful; abundant

9. one who makes changes

12. well known; renowned

14. on fire

15. share; allotment

16. getting rid of trash or explosives

Down

1. unusual to a striking degree

3. keep away from; evade; shun

4. a colorless, odorless, gaseous chemical element

6. putting out

8. rival

9. very hot place

10. dangerous

11. bursting forth; breaking out

13. first; earliest; new; novel

119 HARRY HOUDINI: SUPREME ESCAPE ARTIST

One of the greatest escape artists and stunt performers of all time was Harry Houdini. Handcuffs, chains, ropes, or straitjackets were no problem for Houdini—he could work his way out of them all. How Houdini died is still a much-talked-about event. Read the following article to see how Houdini lived, performed, and died. Then match the items in Column A with their mates in Column B by writing the two-letter answer code from Column B in the appropriate blank in Column A. Then copy the thirty answer letters, in order, onto the line below the columns. If your answers are correct, they will spell out the names of three terms associated with Houdini. There is no escaping the fun here!

Harry Houdini (March 24, 1874–October 31, 1926) was the stage name of Ehrich Weiss, one of the most famous magicians, escapologists, and stunt performers of all time.

Houdini was born in Budapest, Hungary. In 1878, when he was four, his family emigrated to the United States. At first, they lived in Appleton, Wisconsin, where his father, Mayer Samuel Weiss, served as rabbi of the Zion Reform Jewish Congregation. After losing his tenure, the elder Weiss moved to New York City with Ehrich in 1887, where they lived in a boarding house on East Seventy-Ninth Street. Rabbi Weiss later called for the rest of his family to join him once he found more permanent housing.

In 1891, Ehrich became a professional magician and began calling himself Harry Houdini as a tribute to the French magician Jean-Eugène Robert-Houdin. (Weiss would make Houdini his legal name in 1913.) Initially, his magic career met with little success, although he met fellow performer Wilhelmina Beatrice (Bess) Rahner in 1893 and married her after a three-week courtship. For the rest of his performing career, Bess would work as his stage assistant.

Houdini initially focused on card tricks and other traditional magic acts. At one point, he billed himself as the King of Cards. He soon began experimenting with escape acts, however. Houdini's "big break" came in 1899, when he met the showman Martin Beck. Impressed by Houdini's handcuffs act, Beck advised him to concentrate on escape acts and booked him on the Orpheum vaudeville circuit. Within months, he was performing at the top vaudeville houses in the country. In 1900, Houdini traveled to Europe to perform. By the time he returned in 1904, he had become a sensation.

Throughout the first two decades of the twentieth century, Houdini performed with great success in the United States. He would free himself from handcuffs, chains, ropes, and straitjackets, often while hanging from a rope or suspended in water, sometimes in plain sight of the audience. In 1913, he introduced perhaps his most famous act, the Chinese Water Torture Cell, in which he was suspended upside-down in a locked glass and steel cabinet of water, from which he escaped in full view of the audience.

119 HARRY HOUDINI: SUPREME ESCAPE ARTIST *(continued)*

He explained some of his tricks in books written in the 1920s. Many locks and handcuffs could be opened with properly applied force and others with shoestrings. Sometimes he carried concealed picks or keys. He was able to escape from a milk can that had its top fastened to its collar because, he revealed, the collar could be separated from the rest of the can from the inside. When tied down in ropes or straitjackets, he gained wiggle room by expanding his shoulders and chest, moving his arms slightly away from his body, and then dislocating his shoulders.

His straitjacket escape was originally performed behind curtains, with him popping out free at the end. However, Houdini discovered that audiences were more impressed and entertained when the curtains were eliminated so that they could watch him struggle to get out.

Difficult though it was, Houdini's entire act, including escapes, was also performed on a coordinated but separate tour schedule by his brother, Theo Weiss ("Dash" to the Weiss family), who used the stage name Hardeen. The major difference between the two was in the straitjacket escape; Houdini dislocated both his shoulders to get out, whereas Hardeen could dislocate only one.

In the 1920s, after the death of his beloved mother, Houdini turned his energies toward debunking self-proclaimed psychics and mediums, a pursuit that would inspire and be followed by the latter-day magician and skeptic James Randi. Houdini's magic training allowed him to expose frauds who had successfully fooled many scientists and academics. He was a member of a *Scientific American* committee that offered a cash prize to any medium who could successfully demonstrate supernatural abilities. The prize was never collected. As his fame as a "ghostbuster" grew, Houdini took to attending séances in disguise, accompanied by a reporter and police officer. Possibly the most famous medium whom he debunked was the Boston medium Mina Crandon, also known as Margery.

These activities cost Houdini the friendship of Sir Arthur Conan Doyle, the creator of Sherlock Holmes. Doyle, a firm believer in spiritualism, refused to believe any of Houdini's exposés, and the two men became public antagonists.

Houdini died of peritonitis from a ruptured appendix on Halloween 1926, at the age of fifty-two. He had sustained a blow to his abdomen from a college boxing student in Montreal two weeks earlier. Contrary to popular belief, however, this incident is unlikely to have been the cause of his appendicitis.

Houdini's funeral was held on November 4 in New York, with over two thousand mourners in attendance. He was interred in the Machpelah Cemetery in Queens, New York, with the crest of the Society of American Magicians inscribed on his gravesite. The society holds its Broken Wand ceremony at the gravesite on the anniversary of his death to this day.

Houdini left a final sting for his spiritualist opponents: shortly before his death, he had made a pact with his wife, Bess, to contact her from the other side if possible and deliver a prearranged coded message. Every Halloween for the next ten years, Bess held a séance to test the pact. In 1936, after a last unsuccessful séance on the roof of a hotel, she put out the candle that she had kept burning beside a photograph of Houdini since his death.

119 HARRY HOUDINI: SUPREME ESCAPE ARTIST *(continued)*

Column A

1. _____ Houdini's wife
2. _____ Houdini's father's occupation
3. _____ The inspiration for Houdini's name
4. _____ Man who suggested that Houdini concentrate on escape acts
5. _____ Where Houdini became a sensation
6. _____ Where some of Houdini's tricks were performed
7. _____ Houdini's stage billing in the early years
8. _____ Prove wrong
9. _____ Houdini's brother could only dislocate one of these
10. _____ Objects Houdini used to aid in his escapes
11. _____ What Houdini expanded to aid in his escape
12. _____ Article of clothing from which Houdini could escape
13. _____ Houdini's brother's stage name
14. _____ Person who can supposedly communicate with the dead
15. _____ Friend lost in a dispute over spiritualism
16. _____ What Houdini eliminated from his act to please the audience
17. _____ Who punched Houdini in the abdomen
18. _____ A session held in an attempt to contact the dead
19. _____ What Houdini's wife used to keep his memory alive
20. _____ The day Houdini died

Column B

an. Martin Beck

ce. burning candle

ci. French magician

cu. the King of Cards

ff. debunk

gi. rabbi

ha. Europe

hi. shoestrings

ll. Halloween

ma. Wilhelmina Rahner

nd. suspended in water

ne. shoulders and chest

or. curtains

re. séance

rt. Sir Arthur Conan Doyle

sc. shoulder

se. straitjacket

te. medium

tu. a college boxing student

wa. Hardeen

The thirty letters are _____.

The three terms associated with Houdini are _____,

_____, and _____

_____.

120   WALT DISNEY: MORE THAN A CARTOONIST

Readers are often impressed with the actions and words of people who have accomplished much in life. The philosophies of successful people can motivate others to try harder and to pursue a cherished dream even when giving up seems like the appropriate thing to do.

Walter Elias Disney (December 5, 1901–December 15, 1966), the American cartoon artist and producer of animated films, created such memorable characters as Mickey Mouse, Donald Duck, and Pluto. He left school when he was sixteen. Wanting to learn to draw, he studied at art schools in Chicago and in Kansas City, Missouri, before beginning to produce animated motion pictures at the age of twenty-two. By the time of his death in 1966, Disney had won twenty-six Academy Awards and had created California's Disneyland and started planning for Walt Disney World in Florida.

Walt Disney's many successes were due to desire and much hard work. Read the passage, and then answer the questions on the lines provided or on a separate sheet of paper. Perhaps his words will inspire you to make your dreams a reality!

Too young to enlist as a soldier in World War I, Disney joined the Red Cross and served as a volunteer providing assistance to the troops in Europe. At the war's end, he moved to Kansas City and started looking for a job. Disney had always wanted to be a filmmaker. He even once applied for a job working for Charlie Chaplin but was turned down. He was also interested in becoming a political cartoonist, but after a time of being unemployed, he had to settle for a job at the Posman-Rubin Commercial Art Studio for $50 a month. In his new job, Disney met and befriended Ubbe Ert Iwerks, later known simply as Ub Iwerks. The two friends were interested in creating their own company, and in January 1920, they formed Iwerks-Disney Commercial Artists. The company soon folded, however, and the duo was hired by the Kansas City Film Ad Company.

Disney wasn't content with the animated ads the company assigned him and started devoting his spare time to making his own short animated films, which he sold to the Newman Theater Company. The films were called Newman Laugh-O-Grams and were shown in movie theaters. They were originally only about a minute long, but they soon gained the attention of the public by focusing on local problems and criticizing the local government. Apparently Disney still wanted to be a political cartoonist.

In 1922, Disney started making longer shorts based on well-known fairy tales like "Cinderella." The next year, Disney also started experimenting with shorts combining live action and animation. Few of the shorts that Disney worked on during these years have survived. They were locally successful at the time, and Disney's ambitions grew.

Disney was now working at his own company again, along with Ub Iwerks, Hugh Harman, Rudolf Ising, and Carmen Maxwell, but the Laugh-O-Grams weren't satisfying him anymore. Though reasonably popular in Kansas, they weren't financially successful.

His next attempt at success would involve the combination of live action and animation. This was already the basis of the moderately successful "Out of the Inkwell" series produced by brothers Max and Dave Fleischer, which had begun in 1918 and was still running. The Fleischer brothers had their animated star, Koko the Clown, interacting with a live-action setting. Disney

120   WALT DISNEY: MORE THAN A CARTOONIST (continued)

wanted to create a series of cartoons, called the "Alice Comedies," in which a live-action little girl would interact with animated characters. The idea would be used successfully much later in the Disney Studio's Roger Rabbit cartoons but was quite original for its time.

Disney and his team put all their efforts into creating a film they called *Alice's Wonderland.* The young actress playing Alice was Virginia Davis, who had worked for the Kansas City Film Ad Company. Unfortunately for them, the profits from Laugh-O-Grams weren't enough to cover their expenses, and the company went bankrupt in July 1923. But Disney had his finished project in hand and set off for Hollywood in the hope of finding interested distributors. Reportedly, he had only $40 to his name at this point. Iwerks followed him, but Ising, Harman, and Maxwell decided to follow their own separate path. They would form the Arabian Nights Cartoon Studio and later Harman-Ising Studio.

1. Before Disney teamed up with Ub Iwerks in 1920, what two careers did he dream of having?

   _____

2. Why did Disney start making his own animated films in his spare time?

   _____

3. Beyond the fact that Disney's animated ads for the Newman Theater Company were skillfully made, what two reasons accounted for their popularity?

   _____

4. What approaches did Disney combine in his short films in 1923?

   _____

5. Why was Disney unhappy with the Laugh-O-Grams?

   _____

6. What animated character did the Fleischer brothers create?

   _____

7. How are Disney's Alice Comedies and Roger Rabbit connected?

   _____

8. Who went bankrupt in 1923?

   _____

9. Where did Disney go to try to pitch his *Alice's Wonderland* film?

   _____

10. How much money did Disney have when he set off for California?

   _____

121   JACKIE ROBINSON: BARRIER BREAKER (PART ONE)

Read the article about baseball great Jackie Robinson, and then answer the ten questions that follow it. The paragraphs are numbered for easy reference. Where a choice is given, write the answer code for the correct answer in the blank. Use a separate sheet of paper for questions 9 and 10.

(1) Jack Roosevelt Robinson (January 31, 1919–October 24, 1972) became the first African American Major League Baseball player of the modern era in 1947. The significance of this event in U.S. history is honored by the fact that every Major League team has retired his uniform number, 42.

(2) Born in Cairo, Georgia, Robinson was a football and baseball star at the University of California in Los Angeles, where he played with Kenny Washington, who would become one of the first black players in the National Football League since the early 1930s. Robinson's brother Mack competed in the 1936 Summer Olympics, finishing second in the 100-meter sprint, behind another great African American athlete, Jesse Owens. After UCLA, which is where he met his future wife, Rachel Isum, Jackie Robinson served in the military during World War II, receiving an honorable discharge after being exonerated at a court martial for insubordination. He played baseball for a while for the Kansas City Monarchs in the Negro American League, where he was noticed by a scout working for Branch Rickey.

(3) Rickey was the club president and general manager of the Brooklyn Dodgers and had the secret ambition of attracting the Negro Leagues' top players to his team. Although there was no official ban on blacks in organized baseball, previous attempts at signing black ballplayers had been repeatedly thwarted by league officials and rival clubs, so Rickey operated undercover. His scouts were told that they were seeking players for a new all-black league Rickey was forming; not even the scouts knew his true objective.

(4) Robinson drew national attention when Rickey selected him from a list of promising candidates and signed him. Robinson was assigned to play for the Dodgers' minor league affiliate in Montreal in 1946. Although that season was very trying emotionally for Robinson, it was also a spectacular success. The city treated him with unbridled fan support, a welcome change from the hate-filled harassment he had experienced elsewhere.

(5) Robinson was a somewhat unlikely candidate to be the first black Major Leaguer in sixty years. Not only was he twenty-seven (old to be considered a "prospect"), he also had a fiery temperament. Whereas some observers felt that his future Dodger teammate Roy Campanella might have been a better candidate to face up to the expected abuse, Rickey chose Robinson knowing that the man's outspoken nature would in the long run be more beneficial for their cause than Campanella's relative docility.

(6) Robinson's debut at second base with the Brooklyn Dodgers on April 15, 1947, was one of the most eagerly awaited events in baseball history and one of the most profound in the history of the U.S. civil rights movement.

(7) During that first season, the abuse to which Robinson was subjected pushed him close to losing his patience more than once. Many Dodgers were initially resistant to his presence. A group of Dodger players, mainly from the South and led by Dixie Walker, suggested that they

121 JACKIE ROBINSON: BARRIER BREAKER (PART ONE) *(continued)*

would strike rather than play alongside Robinson, but the mutiny was crushed when Dodger management informed the players that they were welcome to find employment elsewhere. Robinson did have the support of shortstop Pee Wee Reese, who proved to be his closest comrade on the team. The pair became a very effective defensive combination as a result. Pittsburgh Pirate Hank Greenberg, the first major Jewish baseball star, who had experienced anti-Semitic abuse, also gave Robinson encouragement.

(8) During that first season, Robinson was harassed by both players and fans. The Philadelphia Phillies—encouraged by manager Ben Chapman, a southerner—were particularly abusive. In their April 22 game against the Dodgers, they jeered him continually, shouted racial epithets from the bench, and urged him to "go back to the jungle." Rickey would later recall that "Chapman did more than anybody to unite the Dodgers. When he poured out that string of unconscionable abuse, he solidified and united thirty men." Baseball Commissioner Albert "Happy" Chandler admonished the Phillies but asked Robinson to pose for photographs with Chapman as a conciliatory gesture; Robinson refused.

1. _____ Which paragraph discusses Branch Rickey's bold and secretive idea?
   (a) paragraph 1 (b) paragraph 2 (c) paragraph 3 (d) paragraph 4

2. _____ Which paragraph described how Canada welcomed Robinson?
   (a) paragraph 1 (b) paragraph 2 (c) paragraph 3 (d) paragraph 4

3. _____ Which paragraph traces Robinson's early athletic career?
   (a) paragraph 1 (b) paragraph 2 (c) paragraph 3 (d) paragraph 4

4. _____ Which paragraph speaks of history in the making?
   (a) paragraph 1 (b) paragraph 2 (c) paragraph 3 (d) paragraph 4

5. _____ Which paragraph focuses on Robinson's teammates' reactions?
   (a) paragraph 1 (b) paragraph 2 (c) paragraph 7 (d) paragraph 8

6. _____ Which paragraph tells why Rickey selected Robinson?
   (a) paragraph 5 (b) paragraph 6 (c) paragraph 7 (d) paragraph 8

7. _____ Which paragraph covers opposing managers' tactics?
   (a) paragraph 5 (b) paragraph 6 (c) paragraph 7 (d) paragraph 8

8. _____ Which paragraph describes Robinson's debut as a Major League player?
   (a) paragraph 5 (b) paragraph 6 (c) paragraph 7 (d) paragraph 8

9. Do you think that you could do what Jackie Robinson did? Why?

10. Did Branch Rickey ultimately do the right thing in signing Jackie Robinson? Why?

122   JACKIE ROBINSON: BARRIER BREAKER (PART TWO)

Here is the second part of the story of Jackie Robinson, the first African American Major League Baseball player of the modern era. He was inducted into the Baseball Hall of Fame in 1962. Read this part of Robinson's story. Then answer the ten questions that follow by writing the letter corresponding to the correct answer in the blank next to the number. The paragraphs are numbered for easy reference.

(1) During Robinson's rookie season, he earned the Major League minimum salary of $5,000. He played in 151 games, batted .297, and was the league leader in stolen bases with twenty-nine.

(2) Robinson was awarded the Rookie of the Year award in 1947 and the Most Valuable Player award for the National League in 1949. He not only contributed to Brooklyn pennants in both years, but his determination and hustle kept the Dodgers in pennant races in 1950 and 1951 when they might otherwise have been eliminated much sooner.

(3) Robinson's Major League career was fairly short. He did not enter the majors until he was twenty-eight, and he retired by the time he was thirty-seven. But in his prime, he was respected and feared by every opposing team in the league. By the time of his retirement, he was disillusioned with the Dodgers and in particular with Walter O'Malley, who had forced Branch Rickey out as general manager, and with manager Walter Alston.

(4) Robinson was an exceptionally talented and disciplined hitter, with a career average of .317 and substantially more walks than strikeouts. He played several defensive positions extremely well and was the most aggressive and successful base runner of his era. Both his talent and his physical presence disrupted the concentration of pitchers, catchers, and middle infielders. Robinson's overall skill was such that he is often cited as one of the very best players of his time. He is also frequently claimed to be one of the smartest baseball players ever, a claim that is well supported by his plate discipline and defensive prowess. Robinson was regarded as a fierce competitor in the truest sense: he never gave up on a game if his team was losing, to the point that he would try everything to avoid being the last man out for his side.

(5) Robinson retired from the game on January 5, 1957. He had wanted to manage or coach in the Major League but received no offers. He became a vice president for the Chock Full O' Nuts Corporation instead and served on the board of the National Association for the Advancement of Colored People (NAACP) until 1967 (at which time he resigned, protesting the lack of younger voices in the movement). In 1960, he involved himself in the presidential election, meeting with both Richard Nixon and John F. Kennedy and citing their record on civil rights as his reason for supporting Nixon. Nixon did not win the presidency until eight years later, at which time Robinson wrote that he regretted the endorsement.

(6) Crippled by the effects of diabetes later in his life and distraught by the death of his eldest son, Jackie Jr., at the age of twenty-four, Jackie Robinson died in Stamford, Connecticut, on October 24, 1972 and was interred in the Cypress Hills Cemetery in Brooklyn, New York.

122 JACKIE ROBINSON: BARRIER BREAKER (PART TWO) *(continued)*

1. _____ Which paragraph details Robinson's life after baseball? **(a)** paragraph 1
(b) paragraph 2 **(c)** paragraph 3 **(d)** paragraph 4 **(e)** paragraph 5 **(f)** paragraph 6

2. _____ Which paragraph focuses on Robinson's exceptional athletic skills? **(a)** paragraph 1
(b) paragraph 2 **(c)** paragraph 3 **(d)** paragraph 4 **(e)** paragraph 5 **(f)** paragraph 6

3. _____ Which paragraph is devoted to Robinson the rookie? **(a)** paragraph 1 **(b)** paragraph 2
(c) paragraph 3 **(d)** paragraph 4 **(e)** paragraph 5 **(f)** paragraph 6

4. _____ Which paragraph documents a brief career that ends in broken loyalties?
(a) paragraph 1 **(b)** paragraph 2 **(c)** paragraph 3 **(d)** paragraph 4 **(e)** paragraph 5
(f) paragraph 6

5. _____ Which paragraph describes Robinson's family problems and death? **(a)** paragraph 1
(b) paragraph 2 **(c)** paragraph 3 **(d)** paragraph 4 **(e)** paragraph 5 **(f)** paragraph 6

6. _____ Which paragraph covers Robinson's early Major League career? **(a)** paragraph 1
(b) paragraph 2 **(c)** paragraph 3 **(d)** paragraph 4 **(e)** paragraph 5 **(f)** paragraph 6

7. _____ What made Robinson leave the NAACP? **(a)** lack of leadership **(b)** lack of funding
(c) lack of involvement of young people **(d)** lack of motivation

8. _____ Walter Alston was a **(a)** U.S. president **(b)** politician **(c)** baseball manager
(d) baseball executive.

9. _____ Branch Rickey was a **(a)** U.S. president **(b)** politician **(c)** baseball manager
(d) baseball executive.

10. _____ Richard Nixon was a **(a)** U.S. president **(b)** football player **(c)** baseball manager
(d) baseball executive.

123 DAVID BECKHAM: SOCCER SENSATION

How well do you read articles about sports heroes? Here is your chance to shine. Read the following information about David Beckham, a famous British soccer player. Then answer the questions on the lines provided.

David Robert Joseph Beckham was born in the Leytonstone area of London, England, on May 2, 1975. Signed by the Manchester United soccer club as a junior player during his teen years, Beckham initially played as a substitute for the Manchester senior team in 1992 and played his first league game for that same team three years later. His very next season began on a memorable note as he scored from his team's own half of the field in the first game of the season versus Wimbledon.

Well known for his bending shots on goal, this athletic midfielder possesses a hard shot that often brings crowds to their feet. Beckham's specialty is long-range free kicks. Awards and other accomplishments have certainly come Beckham's way. Not only did his team win the Premier League titles in both the 1996 and 1997 seasons, but he was also voted the Professional Football Association (FA) Young Player of the Year for the 1996 soccer season.

The goal that established Beckham as a name in soccer was perhaps the one that happened during the World Cup of 1998. There he scored on a tremendous free kick. Unfortunately for Beckham, he was disqualified from the World Cup during the second round after he aimed a kick at Argentina's Diego Simeone. Beckham's action created much trouble for him, his family, his team, and the game of soccer itself. Opposing fans were abusive toward Beckham and his family. During the 1998–1999 season, Beckham's team, Manchester United, captured the European Champions' League, FA Premiership, and FA Cup titles.

In 2001, Beckham's goal helped England enter the World Cup. Shortly thereafter, he broke his foot, yet still played in the tournament. Eventually, England was beaten by Brazil, the World Cup winner that year. At season's end, Beckham came in second to the Portuguese star Luis Figo in the voting for the World Player of the Year award. Beckham's contract was sold to Real Madrid on 2003.

Rated by many as England's greatest soccer player, Beckham has many outstanding skills, including great passing, composure, and determination. These attributes have added to David Beckham's renown.

123 DAVID BECKHAM: SOCCER SENSATION *(continued)*

1. What country was Beckham's birthplace? _____

2. What was Beckham's team in 1992? _____

3. In what year did Beckham score a goal from his own team's half of the field against Wimbledon?

   _____

4. What is Beckham's specialty? _____

5. What individual personal distinction came to Beckham in 1996?

   _____

6. What two memorable actions was Beckham involved in during the 1998 World Cup

   tournament? _____

   _____

7. What was the result of the negative action that Beckham took in the 1998 World Cup

   tournament? _____

   _____

8. Who is Diego Simeone? _____

9. Who is Luis Figo? _____

10. What unfortunate event happened to Beckham before the 2001 World Cup tournament?

    _____

124   ALI VERSUS LISTON

The two prize fights pitting Muhammad Ali against Sonny Liston were among the most anticipated, most watched, and most controversial in boxing history. The following is the story behind the two famous bouts. Read the story, and then answer the questions on the lines provided.

Sonny Liston was the world heavyweight champion, having dethroned Floyd Patterson with a knockout in the first round in 1962 to win the title. Thanks to Liston's impressive winning knock-out record, not many other fighters in his division at that time were willing to fight him. Often described as reclusive and timid, Liston did not like to smile or talk to the press.

By contrast, Muhammad Ali—at the time still known by his birth name, Cassius Clay—was a fast-talking twenty-two-year-old challenger who enjoyed the spotlight; he had won the gold medal at the 1960 Rome Olympics, and he had hand speed and a lot of confidence. Nevertheless, he had been knocked out by journeyman Sonny Banks in a previous fight. Few observers or fans believed he could beat Liston, and the oddsmakers pegged him as a 7-to-1 betting underdog.

During training, Ali took to driving a school bus across to the site where Liston was training; he started calling Liston a "big, ugly bear." Liston resented this. Ali told everyone within earshot that he would knock Liston out in eight rounds.

During the physical checkup the day before their first fight, Ali's heartbeat was recorded at 120 pulses per minute. Many thought of this as a sign either that Ali wasn't in proper shape or that he was nervous about fighting Liston.

Their first fight was held on February 25, 1964, in Miami Beach, Florida, where Ali was residing (his trainer, Angelo Dundee, operated a gym nearby). Ali arguably dominated the first two rounds. By the third round, however, Liston seemed reinvigorated, and Ali fought most of the round complaining that he was blind. It has been argued ever since that the attendants in Liston's corner, seeing their fighter being beaten by Ali, might have put petroleum jelly or some other type of ointment on Liston's gloves. Dundee instructed Ali to back away from Liston until he recovered his sight.

Ali had recovered it by the fifth round, and he began to outjab the champion again. Suddenly, between rounds six and seven, Liston complained of shoulder numbness and said he was quitting. Many analysts have suggested that Liston faked the injury to prevent himself from being further embarrassed by Ali; this view remains unproven, as the fight was tied on the judges' scorecards after six rounds. Ali was declared the winner and proclaimed the now famous words, "I shocked the world!"

Because of the strange ending of the first fight, boxing authorities ordered a second match, this time with Ali as the defending world champion and Liston as the challenger. The bout would have been held in November 1964, but Ali fell ill and needed emergency surgery for a strangulated hernia. The fight was rescheduled, to take place in Boston. But the promoters did not have a license to promote fights in Massachusetts, so the venue was moved to a high school gymnasium in tiny Lewiston, Maine, and set for May 25, 1965. Owing to the remote location, only 2,434 fans attended, setting an all-time record for the lowest attendance at a world championship boxing match.

124   ALI VERSUS LISTON *(continued)*

This proved to be one of the most controversial fights in history. Midway through the first round, Liston fell to the canvas in what many observers have argued was not an original knockdown. Referee Jersey Joe Walcott, a former world heavyweight champion himself, seemed to be confused after he sent Ali to a neutral corner and the champion refused, instead posing over Liston and dancing around his fallen rival with his fists up in the air, celebrating the fall. Walcott took twenty seconds to figure out what to do. Nat Fleischer, publisher of *Ring* magazine, finally told Walcott that Liston had spent about twenty seconds on the canvas, and Walcott then stopped the fight, awarding Ali with a first-round knockout.

The Ali–Liston rematch became known as "the ghost punch fight." Most people at ringside did not see the punch that knocked Liston out. Many actually continue to claim that Liston had bet against himself because he owed money to organized crime; therefore, according to the ones who believe that theory, he went to the floor on purpose. Slow-motion replays of the knockout moment, however, show Ali connecting with a quick right to Liston's head the second before Liston fell.

Although Ali is recognized by many boxing experts and fans as the greatest boxer of all time, many others continue to question the results of his two confrontations with Liston.

1. List three reasons why Sonny Liston was the heavy favorite in the first bout against Muhammad Ali (Cassius Clay).

_____

_____

_____

_____

_____

_____

2. What were some of Ali's accomplishments before the first Liston bout?

_____

_____

3. What may have caused Ali's "blindness" in the third round of the first bout?

_____

_____

124 ALI VERSUS LISTON (continued)

4. What did Liston's "shoulder injury" indicate to some boxing fans?

_____

_____

5. What two major problems forced the second Ali–Liston fight to be held in a high school gymnasium?

_____

_____

_____

6. What major reason was cited for why only 2,434 fans showed up for the second Ali–Liston bout?

_____

_____

7. Why was the second bout so controversial?

_____

_____

_____

8. Did Ali actually hit Liston with a punch that sent Liston to the floor in the second fight?

_____

_____

125   LANCE ARMSTRONG: CYCLING CHAMP

One of the world's premiere athletes and the most famous cyclist of all time is Lance Armstrong. He won the prestigious and challenging race known as the Tour de France six years in a row. Read about Armstrong's skills, techniques, and accomplishments in the following paragraphs. Then fill in your answers to the crossword puzzle about Lance Armstrong. The first letter of each answer is provided.

Lance Armstrong (born September 18, 1971) is an American cyclist from Austin, Texas. He is most famous for recovering from testicular cancer and subsequently winning the Tour de France six consecutive times (from 1999 to 2004), more wins than any other cyclist to date (five have won five times). His great success at winning the Tour has resulted in that event's being nicknamed the "Tour de Lance" by some.

Armstrong's achievements have been widely lauded. In 2002, *Sports Illustrated* magazine named Armstrong its Sportsman of the Year. He was also named Associated Press Male Athlete of the Year for both 2002 and 2003, received ESPN's ESPY Award for Best Male Athlete in 2003 and 2004, and won the BBC Sports Personality of the Year Overseas Personality Award in 2003. In April of 2005 he announced that he will retire after the 2005 Tour de France.

Armstrong has triumphed partly because he has made a career of the Tour de France, training in Spain for the year leading up to the Tour and making frequent trips to France to fully analyze and ride key parts of the next Tour course. For example, during his preparation for the 2004 Tour, he rode virtually every stage at least once and rode the Alpe d'Huez climb, site of a key time trial, four times.

His riding style is also distinctive. Pedaling very quickly in a very low gear and reaching a cadence of 120 cycles per minute on flats, he is able to rapidly accelerate away from his main rivals, who tend to use higher gears but pedal more slowly while riding uphill. Miguel Induráin, a Spanish cyclist who is one of Armstrong's rivals, would power a huge gear at a low cadence. Armstrong can maintain incredible speeds even when going up the most daunting climbs of the Tour, and at times even specialist climbers are unable to keep pace with him on a consistent basis. The ability to maintain this high cadence for such long distances is based on his extremely high lactic acid threshold, allowing him to work at a high intensity without building up lactic acid levels that force lesser athletes to back off. Much of his training is based on raising this level and in learning exactly where the limit is.

Unlike most gifted climbers, however, Armstrong is also exceptional in the individual time trial and is as good as, if not better than, those physically more suited to the discipline, such as German rival Jan Ullrich. Also, unlike many of the past Tour winners, Armstrong is very aggressive during the mountainous stages, preferring to take the lead and attack spectacularly. Although these attacks usually come toward the end of stages, he is capable of opening immense leads over his rivals and leaving the rest of the field scattered behind him down the mountainside.

125 LANCE ARMSTRONG: CYCLING CHAMP (continued)

Armstrong's success in recent years has also been due to his U.S. Postal Service cycling team. The team is custom-built solely to help Armstrong win. Armstrong has gained crucial time in past years in the team time trial, but the team really comes into its own on the mountain stages. One team member will set a fast pace by riding at the front of the main group. As he tires, he will drop off and another member of the team will continue. Because the pace is so fast, only the strongest riders are able to keep up, and hence the main group will dwindle, leaving only Armstrong and his main contenders. Armstrong will not have used much energy due to his strength, but the rivals will have used a lot in just keeping up with the pace set by the U.S. Postal team. This helps prevent anyone from attacking while Armstrong can just ride away. This commonly used tactic has enabled Armstrong to dominate on many of the mountain stages.

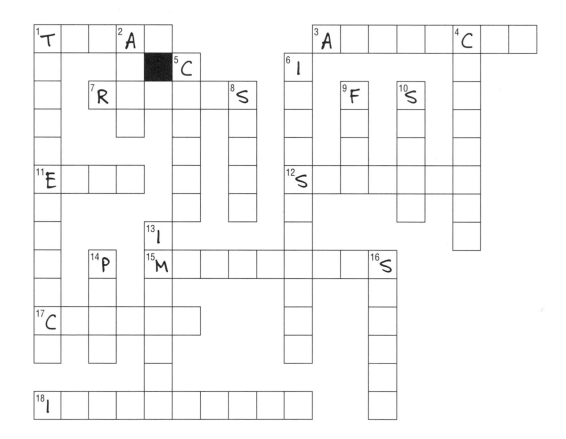

125   LANCE ARMSTRONG: CYCLING CHAMP *(continued)*

Across

1. Armstrong's home state

3. Armstrong's nationality

7. competitors

11. Other cyclists compete in many cycling events to _____ a living.

12. Armstrong is a member of the U.S. Postal _____ cycling team.

15. Armstrong is especially strong in stages that run through _____.

17. Armstrong can reach 120 _____ per minute on flat land.

18. Armstrong can maintain _____ speeds even when he is pedaling up in the mountains.

Down

1. name of the world's most famous bicycle race

2. Armstrong has a high tolerance for lactic _____.

4. Specialist _____ cannot keep up with Armstrong on a consistent basis.

5. disease from which Armstrong recovered

6. Armstrong was awarded Sportsman of the Year from *Sports* _____ magazine.

8. Each portion of the Tour de France is known as a _____.

9. Armstrong rode the Alpe d'Huez _____ times in training.

10. where Armstrong trains for the year leading up to the Tour de France

13. Armstrong opens up _____ leads over his competitors.

14. Armstrong can maintain a fast _____ for long periods of time.

16. The other racers are usually _____ out behind Armstrong.

126   BARRY BONDS: BASEBALL'S BOOMER

Few Major League Baseball players have played the game as well as Barry Bonds. His record-setting 73 home runs excited fans around the globe during the 2001 baseball season. Read his story, and then respond to the questions that follow it by writing the letter corresponding to the correct answer in the blank.

The son of former all-star Bobby Bonds, Barry Bonds graduated from San Mateo, California's Serra High School in 1982, where he excelled in baseball, basketball, and football. Although he was originally drafted in 1982 by the San Francisco Giants, Bonds chose to go to college before pursuing professional baseball. He played college baseball at Arizona State University. After graduating, Bonds began his Major League career in 1986 with the Pittsburgh Pirates. In 1993, he returned home to California to join the San Francisco Giants.

Teammate Shawon Dunston, speaking of Bonds in the June 5, 2000, issue of *Sports Illustrated*, said, "He's not going to hit 70 homers, but he believes he can. That's frightening." The very next year, Bonds set the single season home run record, hitting 73 (breaking the record of 70, set by Mark McGwire in 1998). Some analysts consider Bonds's 2001 season among the greatest hitting seasons in baseball history; in addition to the home run record, Bonds set single-season marks for bases on balls (177, breaking the previous record of 170, set by Babe Ruth in 1923) and slugging percentage with .863 (exceeding the mark of .847 set by Ruth in 1920). Bonds also tied the National League record for most extra base hits in a season (107, first accomplished by Chuck Klein in 1930). In 2002, all eyes were on Bonds as opposing pitchers refused to give him as many balls to hit. As a result, a repeat of 73 homers was impossible, but he still won the National League batting title with a .370 average, set a Major League record with a .582 on-base percentage (breaking Ted Williams's record of .551, set in 1941), and broke his own record for walks, with 198.

Bonds has been voted the National League's Most Valuable Player six times, in 1990, 1992, 1993, 2001, 2002, and 2003. He is the first player in Major League Baseball history to be voted Most Valuable Player in three consecutive years, and no other player has won the award more than three times. He was second in the voting for that award twice: in 1991, behind Terry Pendleton of the Atlanta Braves, and in 2000, when teammate Jeff Kent won it. During the 2002 season, Bonds became the fourth man to hit 600 career home runs and ended the season with 613. He also hit .370 to win his first batting title (making him the oldest player to win a batting title for the first time in a career), and he drew 198 walks, beating his own record—feats that saw him unanimously voted the 2002 MVP.

Bonds has won eight Gold Glove awards as an outfielder, the third most ever for that position. He has been named to twelve National League All-Star teams, in 1990, 1992–1998, 2000–2003.

As noted, his father, Bobby Bonds, was a professional baseball player. Baseball Hall of Famer Willie Mays is his godfather. Another Baseball Hall of Famer, Reggie Jackson, is his cousin.

Bonds became the first ever 400–400 player (achieving 400 home runs and 400 stolen bases) on August 23, 1998, when he hit home run number 400 off Florida's Kirt Ojala. He stole his 400th base on July 26, 1997, against the Pittsburgh Pirates. On June 23, 2003, Bonds recorded

Reading Comprehension in Biography and Current Affairs

126 BARRY BONDS: BASEBALL'S BOOMER *(continued)*

his 500th stolen base in the eleventh inning of a game against the Los Angeles Dodgers. Bonds later scored the winning run. By chance, his ailing father Bobby was in attendance that night. With 633 career home runs at the time, Bonds became the first 500–500 player in baseball history, already the only member of the 400–400 club. In addition, in 1996, Bonds became the second of the three current members of the so-called 40–40 club: 40 home runs and 40 stolen bases in one season. The other two members are Jose Canseco and Alex Rodriguez.

On April 12, 2004, Bonds hit his 660th home run, tying him with his godfather Willie Mays for third on the all-time career home run list, in a game against the Milwaukee Brewers. A man named Larry Ellison caught the home run and returned it to Bonds. The slugger hit his 661st home run the next day, April 13, placing him third behind Babe Ruth (714) and Hank Aaron (755). Ellison again caught number 661 but kept it for himself, with Barry's blessing. (Ellison was in a kayak in McCovey Cove, an arm of San Francisco Bay that lies behind the right-field stands at SBC Park, so this wasn't quite the amazing coincidence it appears at first glance.)

On July 4, 2004, Bonds passed Rickey Henderson to take the lead in career walks, with his 2,191st walk.

1. _____ Babe Ruth, Ted Williams, and Barry Bonds are recognized as the greatest all-time
   (a) fielders **(b)** interviewees **(c)** showmen **(d)** hitters.

2. _____ How many sports did Bonds play in high school? **(a)** one **(b)** two **(c)** three **(d)** four

3. _____ Bonds has played for how many Major League teams? **(a)** one **(b)** two **(c)** three **(d)** four

4. _____ Which of these Major League records does Bonds *not* hold?
   (a) on-base percentage **(b)** walks **(c)** home runs **(d)** triples

5. _____ No Major League player has ever won the MVP award more than how many times?
   (a) one **(b)** two **(c)** three **(d)** four

6. _____ How many Major Leaguers have hit over 600 home runs in their career?
   (a) one **(b)** two **(c)** three **(d)** four

7. _____ Whose record for bases on balls did Bonds break?
   (a) Jeff Kent **(b)** Babe Ruth **(c)** Bobby Bonds **(d)** Ted Williams

8. _____ What distinction do Alex Rodriguez, Jose Canseco, and Barry Bonds hold? **(a)** All have hit over 500 home runs. **(b)** All have stolen 40 bases and hit 40 home runs in a single season. **(c)** All have played all nine positions during a single game. **(d)** All have played for the San Francisco Giants.

9. _____ What did Larry Ellison do? **(a)** caught Bonds's 660th home run **(b)** caught Bonds's 661st home run **(c)** steered a kayak **(d)** all of these

10. _____ Whose stolen base record did Bonds break in 2004?
    (a) Ricky Henderson **(b)** Maury Wills **(c)** Willie Mays **(d)** Mark McGwire

127 SIR ELTON JOHN: A MUSICAL LEGEND

Here is a brief look at the musical career of Elton John, a talented and world-famous singer, composer, and musician. Read the following paragraphs, and then match the items in Column A with those in Column B. Write the answer letter in Column B in the blank next to the number in Column A. Copy the answer letters, in order, onto the line below the columns. Your answers will spell out the name of Elton John's 1972 hit followed by the middle initial of his current (adopted) name.

Sir Elton John was born Reginald Dwight on March 25, 1947, in Pinner, Middlesex, England. He was educated at Pinner County Grammar School and the Royal Academy of Music, to which he won a scholarship at the age of 11.

Working in a band called Bluesology throughout the mid to late 1960s, Dwight changed his name in homage to his fellow "Bluesologists," the saxophonist Elton Dean and singer Long John Baldry. He scored his first international hit in 1970 with his second album, which included one of his still most popular compositions, "Your Song." His success can partly be attributed to his collaboration with lyricist Bernie Taupin, who has provided the words to John's music for most of his career.

John went on to become one of the most successful recording artists of the 1970s, with globally successful singles including "Crocodile Rock," "Saturday Night's Alright (for Fighting)," "Goodbye Yellow Brick Road," and "Bennie and the Jets." His biggest 1980s hits included "I Guess That's Why They Call It the Blues," "I'm Still Standing," and a 1986 live rendition of "Candle in the Wind," which he recorded with the Melbourne Symphony Orchestra. The song, a tribute to Marilyn Monroe, was originally included on his *Goodbye Yellow Brick Road* album in 1973. Twenty-four years later, he updated the lyrics of "Candle in the Wind" in a special version mourning the death of Diana, Princess of Wales, which became the biggest-selling single of all time.

He has also done work both for and in films. In 1971, he wrote original songs for the movie *Friends.* In 1975, he appeared as the Pinball Wizard in the movie version of the Who's rock opera *Tommy.* Then in 1994, he and Tim Rice wrote the songs for the Disney animated film *The Lion King* (the two subsequently won an Academy Award for Best Original Song for "Can You Feel the Love Tonight?"). Rice was reportedly astonished by the rapidity with which John was able to set his words to music. In 1999, John wrote the score for *The Muse* and a year later composed songs for another animated film, *The Road to El Dorado.*

In each of thirty consecutive years, from 1970 through 1999, John had at least one single reach the top forty of *Billboard* magazine's Hot 100 record chart—a feat unmatched by any other recording artist in the United States or the United Kingdom. He was knighted by Queen Elizabeth II for his major contributions to music.

Reading Comprehension in Biography and Current Affairs

127   SIR ELTON JOHN: A MUSICAL LEGEND *(continued)*

In 2003, he hit number one in the United Kingdom with a rerelease of the single "Are You Ready for Love?" which had been only a minor hit when first released in 1979. In 2004, John expanded his theater repertoire by composing songs for the musical adaptation of *Billy Elliot*. In December of that year, he was a recipient of the Kennedy Center Honors for a lifetime of contribution to entertainment.

Sir Elton John continues to release new material to commercial success and tours extensively, despite being fitted with a pacemaker. His face-to-face tours with fellow pianist Billy Joel have been a fan favorite throughout the world since the mid-1990s.

Column A

1. ____ *Tommy*
2. ____ Bernie Taupin
3. ____ Elton Dean
4. ____ "Candle in the Wind"
5. ____ "Can You Feel the Love Tonight?"
6. ____ *Goodbye Yellow Brick Road*
7. ____ Billy Joel
8. ____ *Billboard*
9. ____ Tim Rice
10. ____ Pinball Wizard

Column B

a. magazine that charts songs

c. a saxophone player

e. song from *The Lion King*

h. movie role played by Elton John

k. a tribute to Marilyn Monroe and later to Diana, Princess of Wales

m. a pianist who has toured with Elton John

n. collaborator who was stunned by how quickly Elton John can write music

o. lyricist for John's songs

r. a rock opera

t. album that introduced "Candle in the Wind"

The ten letters are _____ .

The 1972 hit is _____ . Elton John's middle initial is ____ .

128 QUOTATIONS ABOUT LIFE

Here are ten quotations about various aspects of life. Read each one. Then on the back of this page or on a separate sheet of paper, paraphrase all ten of these quotations. Be ready to tell why you agree or disagree with each statement. Enjoy the exchange of ideas with your classmates.

1. "Life is what happens to you while you're busy making other plans."—John Lennon

2. "The life which is unexamined is not worth living."—Socrates

3. "The goal of life is living in agreement with nature."—Zeno

4. "When people talk, listen completely. Most people never listen."—Ernest Hemingway

5. "The worst loneliness is not to be comfortable with yourself."—Mark Twain

6. "Shallow men believe in luck. Strong men believe in cause and effect."—Ralph Waldo Emerson

7. "Man's best possession is a sympathetic wife."—Euripedes

8. "Creditors have better memories than debtors."—Benjamin Franklin

9. "I have always found that mercy bears richer fruits than strict justice."—Abraham Lincoln

10. "Be not ashamed of mistakes and thus make them crimes."—Confucius

129   THE WORLD OF WORK

Listed on the next page are twenty-five careers that you might eventually pursue. For now, simply match each person in Column A with the job description in Column B. In the magic square, write the answer number from Column B next to the corresponding letter code from Column A. Four answers have already been done for you. If your answers are correct, the rows, the columns, and the two diagonals will each add up to the same magic number. Let's get to work!

A = 10	B =	C =	D =	E = 11
F =	G =	H =	I =	J =
K =	L =	M = 19	N =	O =
P =	Q =	R =	S =	T =
U =	V = 16	W =	X =	Y =

Magic Number: _____

129   THE WORLD OF WORK (continued)

Column A

- A. janitor
- B. anesthesiologist
- C. temporary office worker
- D. chauffeur
- E. interior designer
- F. auditor
- G. assembler
- H. graphic designer
- I. EMT
- J. automotive mechanic
- K. receptionist
- L. paralegal
- M. marketing assistant
- N. disc jockey
- O. constable
- P. dietitian
- Q. city planner
- R. audiologist
- S. dental hygienist
- T. landlord
- U. school superintendent
- V. real estate agent
- W. stockman
- X. optician
- Y. actuary

Column B

1. greets people at the entrance to an office or business
2. evaluates hearing defects and the rehabilitation of people who have such defects
3. working with statistics, calculates risks and premiums for life insurance clients
4. administers a drug or a gas before surgery
5. assists patients who are in emergency medical situations
6. designs visual artistic representations
7. keeps the peace in a town or village
8. arranges or assists in urban development
9. prepares and dispenses eyeglasses
10. keeps buildings clean
11. designs interiors of houses, apartments, and offices
12. puts vehicle parts together
13. plays records (or CDs) on the radio or at an event
14. specializes in planning meals or diets
15. owns or raises livestock; maintains store's inventory
16. buys and sells dwellings and other buildings
17. drives a private automobile for somebody else
18. checks on the accuracy of financial accounts
19. helps position and sell goods
20. rents out land, homes, and the like
21. assists in the health and maintenance of a patient's teeth
22. supervises and manages a school district
23. does clerical work on a nonpermanent basis
24. repairs and maintains cars and trucks
25. aids lawyers but does not practice law

Name: _____ Date: _____ Period: _____

130   THE DEATH PENALTY

The death penalty has been a controversial issue for many years. Some people favor it; other people think it is wrong. Read the article below. Then read the twelve statements that follow it. On the line next to each statement, write Y (for yes) if the statement supports the death penalty or N (for no) if the statement does not support the death penalty.

Key Arguments Against the Death Penalty

The death penalty can encourage police misconduct, as in the incident described in the documentary film *The Thin Blue Line.* In the late 1970s, an innocent man named Randall Adams was framed by the Dallas County police department in Texas for a notorious murder of a police officer because they knew that the more likely suspect, David Harris, was still a minor and thus ineligible for the death penalty, so they made Adams serve as a scapegoat for their vengeance.

The death penalty is not a deterrent because anyone who would be deterred by the death penalty would be equally deterred by the prospect of life in prison, and people who are not deterred by that prospect won't be stopped by any punishment.

The death penalty does not deter murder because most murders are either "crimes of passion," committed in the heat of the moment, or are planned by people who don't think they'll get caught. (This argument could in fact be used for any penalty.)

Some people argue that the death penalty brutalizes society by sending out the message that killing people is the right thing to do in some circumstances.

Statistics show that the death penalty either makes no difference in the number of murders committed or actually causes them to increase.

With mandatory appeals and enhanced procedural and evidentiary requirements for capital cases in the United States, the cost of a death penalty case far exceeds (usually by a factor of ten) the cost of a trial and life imprisonment.

Executed "terrorists" may be turned into "martyrs."

The death penalty denies redemption, in a nonreligious sense. Some people hold that the judicial system should have the role of educating and rehabilitating individuals found guilty of crimes. Someone who has been executed has no opportunity for becoming educated and made a better person.

Key Arguments in Support of the Death Penalty

People committing the most heinous crimes (usually murder, in Western countries that practice the death penalty) have forfeited the right to life.

Government is not an individual and is given far more powers.

The death penalty shows the greatest respect for the inviolability of the ordinary person who is victimized by a criminal.

It exposes fewer innocent persons to harm than alternative penalties, as many ex-prisoners commit new crimes.

130 THE DEATH PENALTY *(continued)*

It provides closure for many victims of horrible crimes and their families.

It recognizes humanity's natural sense of justice.

It is less cruel than prolonged sentences of imprisonment, especially under the conditions that would be popularly demanded for heinous criminals.

It is explicitly allowed in constitutions and other documents of basic law.

Having the death penalty as an option provides leverage for the prosecutor to negotiate for important testimony and information.

It shows how seriously society regards the most serious crimes.

It enjoys democratic support of the people.

It may deter violent crime and murder. (Most advocates do not hold, however, that this is a primary reason for supporting the death penalty.)

1. _____ Government is given far more powers than an individual.

2. _____ The death penalty is less cruel than prolonged sentences of imprisonment.

3. _____ Individuals who have committed the most heinous crimes have forfeited the right to life.

4. _____ The death penalty brutalizes society, sending out the message that killing people is the right thing to do in some circumstances.

5. _____ Executed "terrorists" may become "martyrs."

6. _____ The death penalty does not deter murderers.

7. _____ The cost of the death penalty far exceeds the cost of a trial and life imprisonment.

8. _____ The death penalty provides closure for many victims of horrible crimes and their families.

9. _____ The death penalty recognizes humanity's natural sense of justice.

10. _____ Statistics show that the death penalty makes no difference in the number of murders.

11. _____ The death penalty denies redemption and rehabilitation.

12. _____ The death penalty shows the greatest respect for the inviolability of the ordinary person who is victimized by a criminal.

Name: _____ Date: _____ Period: _____

131 SEAFORD, LONG ISLAND, NEW YORK

Let us learn about a small town called Seaford. You will be asked to read many facts about the town. After you complete your reading, answer the ten questions by writing the letter corresponding to the correct answer in the blank next to the number.

Seaford is a town located in Nassau County, New York, located at 40°40'7" N, 73°29'33" W. According to the United States Census Bureau, the town has a total area of 2.6 square miles. Only 0.38% of its surface is water. The 2000 census revealed that there are 15,791 people, 5,257 households, and 4,200 families in the town. The population density is 6,072.9 per square mile. There are 5,358 housing units, at an average density of 2,060.6 per square mile. Racially, the town is 96.80 percent white, 0.31 percent African American, 0.06 percent Native American, 1.68 percent Asian, 0.02 percent Pacific Islander, 0.54 percent from other races, and 0.59 percent from two or more races. Some 3.71 percent of the population is Hispanic of any race.

Of the 5,257 households, 37.2 percent have children under the age of eighteen living with them, 68.4 percent consist of married couples living together, 8.6 percent have a female householder with no husband present, and 20.1 percent are nonfamilies. Households consisting of a single individual account for 16.3 percent of all households, and 8.3 of them have someone living alone who is sixty-five years of age or older. The average household size is 3.00 persons, and the average family size is 3.38 persons.

The town's residents span the entire range from young to old, with 25.2 percent under the age of eighteen, 6.9 percent from eighteen to twenty-four, 30.2 percent from twenty-five to forty-four, 23.9 percent from forty-five to sixty-four, and 13.7 percent who are sixty-five years of age or older. The median age is thirty-eight years. For every 100 females, there are 95.5 males. For every 100 females age eighteen and over, there are 93.0 males.

The median income for a household in the town is $78,572, and the median income for a family is $85,751. Males have a median income of $60,092, versus $39,083 for females. The per capita income for the town is $29,244. Some 3.6 percent of the population and 2.8 percent of families fall below the poverty line. Of the people living in poverty, 2.9 percent are under the age of eighteen and 3.9 percent are sixty-five or older.

131   SEAFORD, LONG ISLAND, NEW YORK *(continued)*

1. _____ Which is associated with the town's location?
   (a) 83 percent **(b)** 5,257 **(c)** 40º40'7" N, 73º29'33" W **(d)** 85,751

2. _____ Nearly how many people lived in Seaford at the end of the twentieth century?
   (a) 78,000 **(b)** 16,000 **(c)** 60,000 **(d)** 30,000

3. _____ Most of Seaford's population is **(a)** white **(b)** Hispanic **(c)** African American **(d)** Asian.

4. _____ There are more females than males in Seaford. Is this statement **(a)** true or **(b)** false?

5. _____ Which Seaford residents earn more per year, **(a)** the males or **(b)** the females?

6. _____ What is the topic of the final paragraph? **(a)** population **(b)** geography **(c)** homes
   (d) finances

7. _____ What is the topic of the next-to-last paragraph? **(a)** household finances
   (b) religions **(c)** population makeup **(d)** people and their wages

8. _____ Which is not cited in the article? **(a)** location **(b)** population **(c)** financial aspects
   (d) religious beliefs

9. _____ What is the average number of people living in a house in Seaford?
   (a) 3.38 **(b)** 3 **(c)** 3.71 **(d)** 2.3

10. _____ What percentage of the surface area of Seaford is water?
    (a) less than 1 percent **(b)** 38 percent **(c)** about 4 percent **(d)** none of these

132 FASHION

What we wear tells something about us. Why people wear certain types of clothing is explored in this article about fashion. Who sets the tone for what is cool to wear? That, too, is discussed below. Read the article; then, using the words from the word bank, fill in the missing word in each sentence. Write the words neatly in the blanks—it's the fashionable thing to do!

Fashion, by definition, changes constantly. The change may proceed more rapidly than in most other fields of human activity (language, thought, and so on). For some observers, modern fast-paced change in fashion embodies many of the negative aspects of capitalism: it results in waste and encourages people, as consumers, to buy things unnecessarily. Other people, however, especially young people, enjoy the diversity that changing fashion can provide, regarding the constant change as a way to satisfy their desire to experience "new" and "interesting" things. Note too, though, that fashion can change to enforce uniformity, as when so-called Mao suits became the national uniform of Mainland China.

Materially affluent societies can offer a variety of fashions in clothes or accessories to choose from. At the same time, there remains an equal or larger range designated (at least currently) "out of fashion." (These or similar fashions may cyclically come back into fashion in due course, and remain in fashion again for a while.)

Practically every aspect of appearance that can be changed has been changed at some time. In the past, new discoveries and lesser-known parts of the world could provide an impetus to change fashions based on the exotic: Europe in the eighteenth or nineteenth centuries, for example, might favor things Turkish at one time, things Chinese at another, and things Japanese at a third. The global village has reduced the options of exotic novelty in more recent times.

Fashion houses and their associated fashion designers, as well as high-status consumers (including celebrities), appear to have some role in determining the rates and directions of fashion change.

Fashion can suggest or signal status in a social group. Groups with high cultural status like to keep in fashion to display their position; people who do not keep in fashion within a so-called style tribe can risk shunning (this is a form of peer pressure). Because keeping in fashion often requires considerable amounts of money, fashion can be used to show off wealth. Adherence to fashion trends can thus serve as an index of social affluence and an indicator of social mobility.

Fashion can help attract a partner. In addition to showing certain features of a person's personality that appeal to prospective mates, keeping up with fashion can advertise a person's status to such candidates.

"Fashion sense" consists of the ability to tell what clothing and accessories look good and what ones don't. Since the entire notion of fashion depends on subjectivity, so does the question of who possesses fashion sense. Some people style themselves as "fashion consultants" and charge clients to help the latter choose what to wear.

Fashion can operate differently, depending on gender, or it can promote homogeneity, as in unisex styles.

---

132 FASHION *(continued)*

affluent	partner
capitalism	subjectivity
consultants	uniformity
diversity	unisex
high-status	wealth

1. For some observers, modern fast-paced change in fashion embodies many of the negative aspects of _____.

2. Other people, however, especially young people, enjoy the _____ that changing fashion can provide.

3. Fashion can change to enforce _____, as when so-called Mao suits became the national uniform of Mainland China.

4. Materially _____ societies can offer a variety of fashions in clothes or accessories to choose from.

5. Fashion houses and their associated fashion designers, as well as _____ consumers (including celebrities), appear to have some role in determining the rates and directions of fashion change.

6. Because keeping in fashion often requires considerable amounts of money, fashion can be used to show off _____.

7. Fashion can help attract a _____.

8. Since the entire notion of fashion depends on _____, so does the question of who possesses fashion sense.

9. Some people style themselves as "fashion _____" and charge clients to help the latter choose what to wear.

10. Fashion can operate differently, depending on gender, or it can promote homogeneity, as in _____ styles.

133   VIDEO GAMES AND THEIR CRITICS

If you like playing video games, that's fine. But there are people who have problems with video games. They complain about the violence, cruelty, and crime featured in video games. Read the article and see if you agree or disagree with the critics' opinions. After completing the article, match the beginnings of the sentences in Column A with the ends in Column B that make the most sense. Write the three-letter answer code in the corresponding blank in Column A. When you are done, copy the thirty letters, in order, onto the line beneath the columns. If your answers are correct, they will spell out the name of a man who is a critic of video games and his home state.

From time to time, video games have been criticized by parents' groups, psychologists, politicians, and some religious organizations for allegedly glorifying violence, cruelty, and crime and exposing children to this violence. It is particularly disturbing to some adults that some video games allow children to act out crimes (for example, the *Grand Theft Auto* series) and reward them for doing so. Some studies have shown that children who watch violent television shows and play violent video games have a tendency to act more aggressively on the playground, and some people are concerned that this aggression may predict violent behavior when the children grow to adulthood. These concerns have led to voluntary rating systems adopted by the industry that are aimed at providing guidance to parents about the types of games their children are playing (or are begging to play).

Critics of movies, television, and books as a group look down on video games as an inferior form of entertainment. This is probably because of the observation that most video games have very little plot and even less character development, which may or may not be true. A frequent counterargument is that this is like complaining that a game of football does not contain much plot or character development and that although video games include a narrative, they are really about acting in and against a virtual world, which is not primarily based on passively seeing and hearing. Another point of view compares video games to the movies, which during the silent era were also considered mere entertainment.

133 VIDEO GAMES AND THEIR CRITICS *(continued)*

Column A

1. _____ *Grand Theft Auto*
2. _____ Kids who watch violent television shows
3. _____ Childhood aggression
4. _____ Rating systems
5. _____ Some critics of video games feel that
6. _____ Some decry the fact that most video games
7. _____ The plotline of a story is its
8. _____ Some people who do not object to video games
9. _____ Because video games include interaction by its users,
10. _____ Psychologists and parents

Column B

ato. act more aggressively on the playground.

cti. they are not a passive activity.

cut. are among the critics of video games.

ebe. video games are an inferior form of entertainment.

eli. have been created to provide guidance to parents about video games.

nco. narrative.

nne. compare them to the silent movies of the past.

rjo. can be a predictor of adult violent behavior.

rma. have little plot or character development.

sen. is a video game series that allows children to act out crimes.

The thirty letters are _____.

One critic of video games is _____

_____

of _____.

134 SKATEBOARDING

Let's get rolling with this activity about the popular activity known as skateboarding. Even if you know a great deal about skateboarding, you might learn a little more today after reading this article. If you are somewhat unfamiliar with skateboarding, you will enjoy learning about this fast-moving sport. Read the article. Then answer the questions. Where you are given a choice (items 1–5), fill in the letter code for the correct answer in the blank. In the other questions, fill in the missing word from the word bank. Each word is used only once. The paragraphs are numbered for easy reference. Roll on!

(1) Skateboarding has its origins in surfing and was originally called "sidewalk surfing." Now, with wakeboarding replacing much waterskiing and snowboarding replacing much skiing, skateboarding is becoming increasingly popular.

(2) In the 1970s, skateboarding was a sidewalk "sport" with surfboard-shaped boards designed more for the California look than for function. Narrow trucks kept the wheels close together and made the board somewhat unstable. As boards and trucks widened, terrain skating became more feasible. Originally, drainage ditches and empty swimming pools were used as skating surfaces, but soon skaters began to build their own terrain, the ramp. In the beginning, the ramp was a quarter pipe that you would skate up to and try to reach the top edge. A big improvement came with the halfpipe. Though there are skateboard parks with extremely complex 3-D terrains, the halfpipe is still the core of upper level skateboarding. Ski resorts have them for snowboarders, and the pipes for skateboarders are also commonly used for in-line skaters and BMX bicycles.

(3) Around the same time as skateboard parks and ramp riding were evolving, the skateboard itself began to change. Street riding originally consisted of basically two-dimensional tricks—riding on only the front wheels (a nose wheelie), spinning like an ice skater on the back wheels (a 360), high-jumping over a bar, long-jumping from one board to another (often over fearless teenagers lying on their backs), slalom, and so on. Around 1978 or so, street riding became transformed by the invention of the ollie or no-hands aerial, the first modern skateboarding trick, by Alan Ollie Gelfand. The ollie involves flying off the ground (or flat surface or wall) on the board without holding on to the board and then landing back on the board. It involves using the feet to press against the board in various complicated combinations, depending on the trick to be performed. No longer is the trick to fly from one place to another. On the way, the board can twist and flip, and so can the rider, ultimately to be united before hitting ground. The development of these complex tricks went from the street to the vertical tops of the halfpipes (and other terrains).

(4) Very skillful skateboarders often become famous through sponsorships and endorsements. Examples include Tony Hawk (who has a series of video games in his name), Bob Burnquist, Rodney Mullen, Steve Caballero, and Josh Kalis (who has appeared in numerous television advertisements for DC Shoes). Hawk has recently appeared on MTV music video awards programs.

134   SKATEBOARDING *(continued)*

(5) All this has been inspired by an object that was never designed to lock into grinds, flip in the air, or do the tricks performed by today's elite skateboarders. Throwing themselves down large staircases and boarding on handrails only ups the ante for today's skateboarders, who differ greatly from their counterparts a mere decade ago not only in terms of tricks and consistency but also in terms of style.

1. _____ Which paragraph traces early developments and improvements in skateboarding?
   (a) paragraph 1 (b) paragraph 2 (c) paragraph 3 (d) paragraph 4 (e) paragraph 5

2. _____ Which paragraph describes skateboarding techniques and maneuvers?
   (a) paragraph 1 (b) paragraph 2 (c) paragraph 3 (d) paragraph 4 (e) paragraph 5

3. _____ Which paragraph covers the current state of skateboarding?
   (a) paragraph 1 (b) paragraph 2 (c) paragraph 3 (d) paragraph 4 (e) paragraph 5

4. _____ Which paragraph discusses skateboarding's origins and current popularity?
   (a) paragraph 1 (b) paragraph 2 (c) paragraph 3 (d) paragraph 4 (e) paragraph 5

5. _____ Which paragraph focuses on popular skateboarders?
   (a) paragraph 1 (b) paragraph 2 (c) paragraph 3 (d) paragraph 4 (e) paragraph 5

drainage	ollie	sponsorships	wakeboarding
elite	ramps	style	
nose	sidewalk	terrain	

6. In the 1970s, skateboarding was a _____ sport.

7. For many water enthusiasts, _____ has replaced waterskiing.

8. The first modern skateboarding track was the _____ or no-hands aerial.

9. Very skillful skateboarders have become famous through _____ and endorsements.

10. Today's skateboarders differ from those of the past in terms of tricks, consistency, and _____.

11. One of the first terrains built by skateboarders themselves was called the _____.

12. As boards and trucks widened, _____ skating became more feasible.

13. Riding on only the front wheels of a skateboard is called a _____ wheelie.

14. The finest skateboarders are referred to as _____ skateboarders.

15. _____ ditches and empty swimming pools were used as skating surfaces by the early skateboarders.

135   HIP-HOP

Where did hip-hop originate? What accounts for its popularity? How is hip-hop similar to folk music? This article will answer these and other questions that you may have about hip-hop. Read the article; then answer the questions that follow it on a separate sheet of paper. Hip-hop to it!

The roots of hip-hop are in West African and African American music. The griots of West Africa are a group of traveling singers and poets whose musical style is reminiscent of hip-hop. True hip-hop arose during the 1970s when block parties became common in various ethnic neighborhoods of New York City, especially the Bronx. Block parties were usually accompanied by music, especially funk and soul music. The early DJs at block parties began isolating the percussion breaks from hit songs, realizing that these were the most danceable and entertaining parts; this technique was then common in Jamaican "dub music" and had spread via the substantial Jamaican immigrant community in New York City, especially through the efforts of the "godfather of hip-hop," DJ Kool Herc. Dub had arisen in Jamaica through the influence of American sailors and radio stations playing R&B. Large sound systems were set up to accommodate poor Jamaicans who couldn't afford to buy records, and dub developed at the sound systems' sites.

Explaining the rise of hip-hop is complex. Perhaps the most important factor was that it required little expense to purchase the equipment (as the Beck song goes, it takes only "two turntables and a microphone"). Virtually anyone could MC along with the popular beats of the day (since the original rhymes were simple and unoriginal) and then perform at block parties. There was no expectation of recording, thus making hip-hop a form of folk music. MCs could be creative, pairing nonsense rhymes and teasing friends and enemies alike in front of crowds (this teasing was similar to the Jamaican practice of "toasting" at blues parties).

Another reason for hip-hop's rise was the decline of disco, funk, and rock in the mid to late 1970s. Disco arose among the black community and gay males in America and quickly spread to Europe. Once disco broke into the mainstream in the United States and was thus appropriated by the masses, its original fans and many other listeners rejected it as prepackaged and soulless. Inner-city black young people were rejecting disco and discofied rock, soul, and funk (which was virtually everything on the radio at the time). If disco had anything redeemable for urban audiences, however, it was the strong, danceable beats, and hip-hop emerged to take advantage of the beats while providing a musical outlet for the masses that hated disco. Disco-inflected music (though comparatively little actual disco) was one of the most popular sources of beats in the first ten or twelve years of hip-hop's existence. In Washington, D.C., gogo also emerged as a reaction against disco and eventually blended with hip-hop during the early 1980s; electronic music did the same, developing as house music in Chicago and techno music in Detroit.

135   HIP-HOP *(continued)*

Along with the low expense and the diminished appeal of other forms of popular music, social and political events further accelerated the rise of hip-hop. In 1959, an expressway was built through the heart of the Bronx, displacing many of the middle-class white communities and causing widespread unemployment among the remaining blacks as stores and factories fled the area. By the 1970s, poverty was rampant. When a 15,000+ apartment building was built at the northern edge of the Bronx in 1968, the last of the middle-class fled, and the area's black and Latino gangs began to grow in power. This provided the seedbed in which hip-hop would grow.

1. What three major reasons contributed to hip-hop's popularity?

2. In what way or ways was hip-hop a form of folk music?

3. How could MCs be creative at block parties?

4. What MC activity was similar to the Jamaican activity of toasting?

5. What two reasons does the article cite for disco's decline?

6. What two aspects of disco did urban populations enjoy?

7. Name the cities in which house music, techno, and gogo evolved.

8. Cite three effects of the building of the expressway through the Bronx in 1959.

9. What is DJ Kool Herc's nickname?

10. Who are the griots?

136   ETHICS IN PHOTOJOURNALISM

Does a news photographer usually give an objective picture of what he or she sees? If you answered no, how does the photographer distort what is photographed? Why might the photographer want to show something other than what actually happened? Read the following article about ethics—the principles of proper conduct—in photojournalism. Then answer the questions that follow it by writing your responses in the blanks. You might want to discuss the article's content with your classmates.

Journalism is the collecting, editing, and presenting of news material for publication or broadcast. Photojournalism is a particular form of journalism that uses still and moving images to tell a story.

Because the message an image conveys can be affected by the photographer's choice of things like focal length, angle of view, lighting, and cropping, an ethical photojournalist attempts to present an accurate, objective viewpoint by relying on the same values, principles, and loyalties that any journalist stands by.

The proper practice of photojournalism requires a balance of several conflicting ethical philosophies when deciding what to shoot and how to edit. A utilitarian view of the photojournalist's mission would say that he or she benefits the community by providing a record of the day's events. When that mission involves the capture and distribution of images that disturb those who view them, however, it may conflict with the Golden Rule view that would ask, "Would I want someone to take that picture of me?"

These conflicts can be resolved by realizing that seeing a picture of a drowning man in the local newspaper may upset the victim's family, but the level of awareness raised by that picture may have numerous positive outcomes for many other people. Often these conflicts can be mitigated by an editor who is able to find satisfactory middle ground in deciding whether or not to use an image, such as printing the image smaller on an inside page or presenting footage later in a broadcast.

The emergence of digital photography and whole new realms of opportunity for the manipulation, reproduction, and transmission of images has complicated many of the issues involved.

136 ETHICS IN PHOTOJOURNALISM *(continued)*

For items 1–6, write T if the statement is true and F if the statement is false.

1. _____ Photojournalism can include both still and moving images to tell a story.

2. _____ An ethical journalist should not attempt to present an accurate, objective viewpoint.

3. _____ A utilitarian view of a journalist's mission would say that the photographer benefits the community by providing a record of what occurred that day.

4. _____ The Golden Rule says to do unto others as you would have them do unto you.

5. _____ An editor can print a smaller picture of a catastrophe in an attempt to lessen the negative effects on the victims' family members.

6. _____ Digital photography has made the job of the ethical journalist even more complicated.

7. _____ Complete this analogy: "Article" is to "publication" as "film" is to
   (a) "print" **(b)** "broadcast" **(c)** "editing" **(d)** "image."

For the remaining items, write Y (for yes) if you agree with the statement and N (for no) if you disagree. (There are no right or wrong answers.)

8. _____ Do you think that graphic depictions of automobile accidents should be published on a newspaper's front page?

9. _____ Do you think that newspapers should be barred from placing graphic depictions of crime victims' injuries on the front page out of respect for the victims' families?

10. _____ Would you like to become a photojournalist?

137   THE 2004 TSUNAMI

A tsunami is a very large ocean wave, often 20 to 60 feet high, caused by an underwater earthquake or volcanic eruption, and as you can imagine, being hit by such a wall of water can have devastating effects. How people deal with the aftermath of a tsunami is both interesting and awesome. Read the following article, and then answer the questions that follow it. Write your answers in the blanks.

On December 26, 2004, an earthquake along the edge of the Indian Ocean, off the northwestern coast of the Indonesian island of Sumatra, spawned a tsunami that wreaked havoc in nearly every country located on or in the Indian Ocean. Hit particularly hard were Indonesia, Thailand, Sri Lanka, and India. More than 280,000 people were killed, tens of thousands more were injured, and over one million were made homeless.

The tsunami exacted a heavy toll on coastal communities in the region. In India and Thailand, governments and volunteer organizations were able to mobilize resources, responding as quickly as possible under the circumstances. India also provided assistance to neighboring countries. The people and governments in Sri Lanka and Indonesia were overwhelmed by the enormity of the catastrophe. Rescuers could not reach those in inaccessible areas.

The first tasks of the governments and humanitarian aid agencies were to bury the massive numbers of dead and prevent an epidemic of communicable diseases. The World Health Organization warned that the number of deaths from preventable diseases such as cholera, diphtheria, dysentery, and typhoid could rival the death toll from the disaster itself. These diseases are spread primarily through the bodily wastes of the living as a result of the loss of sanitary facilities, the use of makeshift facilities by large numbers of people, and the lack of clean water.

Many of the usual sources of water were tainted by saltwater, knocked out by the force of the tsunami, or contaminated with bodies of dead people or livestock, making it necessary to bring water purification equipment or potable water into the affected regions on a massive scale and on short notice. Other high priorities were the delivery of medical supplies and personnel to overwhelmed hospitals and clinics, providing tent shelters and clothing to people who lost their homes and belongings, and supplying food, especially baby food. The safe and respectful disposal of corpses was another major concern for survivors.

Governments, humanitarian organizations, and individuals around the world scrambled to offer aid and technical support. The World Bank initially estimated the amount of aid needed at $5 billion. In the wake of the disaster, Australia, India, Japan, and the United States formed a coalition to coordinate aid efforts to streamline immediate assistance; the following month, the coalition transferred responsibility to the United Nations.

137   THE 2004 TSUNAMI *(continued)*

1. A tsunami can be caused by either _____

   _____.

2. The December 26, 2004, earthquake occurred in the _____
   Ocean.

3. Which word in the first paragraph means "gave rise to" or "caused"?

   _____

4. The number of people made homeless by the tsunami was more than

   _____.

5. The first tasks of the governments and humanitarian agencies were to

   _____

   _____.

6. Which is not a disease mentioned in this article?
   (a) measles **(b)** cholera **(c)** dysentery **(d)** typhoid

7. Which word in the article means "drinkable"? _____

8. Supplying what type of food was a high priority?
   (a) meat **(b)** breakfast cereal **(c)** baby food **(d)** canned vegetables

9. The World Bank initially estimated the amount of aid needed to be about

   _____.

10. Which organization assumed responsibility for coordinating efforts to provide assistance?

    _____

138   PYRAMID SCHEMES

A pyramid scheme is a business model that involves the exchange of money primarily for enrolling other people into the scheme, without any product or service being delivered. Pyramid schemes have been in existence for at least a century. The method of conducting business known as multi-level marketing, as well as matrix schemes, often closely resembles pyramid schemes.

Read this article about pyramid schemes. Then answer the questions that follow it by writing the letter corresponding to the correct answer in the blank next to the question number.

Pyramid schemes come in many variations. The earliest schemes involved a chain letter distributed with a list of five to ten names and addresses on it. The recipient was told to send a specified small sum of money (typically $1 to $5) to the first person on the list. The recipient was then to remove this first person from the list, move all of the remaining names up one place, and add his or her own name and perhaps additional names to the bottom of the list. Then the person was to copy the letter with its new list of names and pass it along to others. As the procedure was repeated, eventually the person's name would arrive at the top of the list, and the person would receive money sent by others.

Success in this scheme rested solely on the exponential growth of new members. Hence the name "pyramid," conveying the increasing population needed at each successive level. Unfortunately, simple analysis will reveal that within a few iterations, the entire global population would need to subscribe in order for all of the members to earn any income. This is impossible, and the vast majority of people who participate in these schemes simply lose their money.

Although pyramid schemes have been declared illegal, they still persist in many forms. Whereas schemes involving the blatant exchange of money have generally disappeared, many schemes persist that purportedly "sell" a product to mask the primary intention of simply enrolling new members. One debatable example is Quixtar, a reincarnation of Amway; the Federal Trade Commission determined in 1979 that Amway was not an illegal pyramid scheme, and Quixtar is structured very similarly. The distinguishing feature of these schemes is the fact that the product being sold has little to no intrinsic value of its own. Examples include "products" such as brochures, cassette tapes, or systems that merely explain to the purchaser how to enroll new members or the purchasing of name and address lists of future prospects. The costs for these "products" can range up into the hundreds or thousands of dollars. A common Internet version involves the sale of documents titled "How to Make $1 Million on the Internet" and the like.

Numerous pyramid schemes selling intrinsically worthless products market themselves as "multilevel marketing" (MLM) programs. This is unfortunate, because there are, in fact, a number of perfectly legitimate businesses that use the MLM business model.

The key tipoffs of a pyramid scheme are the following:

- An excited sales pitch
- Vaguely phrased promises of limitless income potential

138   PYRAMID SCHEMES (continued)

- No product or a product being sold at a price ridiculously in excess of its real market value
- An income stream that chiefly depends on the commissions earned by enrolling new members
- A tendency for only the early investors or joiners to make any real income

The key distinction between these schemes and legitimate MLM businesses is that in the latter cases, a meaningful income can be earned solely from the sales of the associated product or service. Although these MLM businesses also offer commissions for recruiting new members, this is not essential to successful operation of the business by any individual member.

1. _____ The essay's opening paragraph (a) introduces the pyramid scheme and at least one other business model (b) provides examples of pyramid schemes (c) tells the pros and cons of the pyramid scheme (d) all of these.

2. _____ To get the most money, a member of the pyramid scheme would prefer to be (a) on the bottom of the pyramid (b) in the middle of the pyramid (c) at the top of the pyramid.

3. _____ In a pyramid with five names on it, what would have to happen for Joanna, the person on the bottom of the pyramid, to receive any money? (a) She would have to stay at the bottom. (b) She would have to move up two spaces. (c) She would have to move up three spaces. (d) She would have to move up four spaces.

4. _____ The second paragraph (a) explains the many problems of the pyramid scheme (b) explains how a pyramid scheme works (c) illustrates the positive aspects of the pyramid scheme (d) all of these.

5. _____ The vast majority of participants in a pyramid scheme make back at least five times the number of dollars that they put in it. Is this statement (a) true or (b) false?

6. _____ The main purpose of today's pyramid schemes is (a) to ensure that all the people on the pyramid earn as much money as they can (b) to enroll new members (c) both *a* and *b* (d) neither *a* nor *b*.

7. _____ Quixtar is cited as an example of a scheme that (a) makes many people rich (b) offers useful products to potential buyers (c) offers products that have little or no intrinsic value (d) has gone bankrupt.

8. _____ Logically and practically speaking, if all the people on earth enrolled in a pyramid scheme, why would they not receive any money from it? (a) The last layer of people to enroll would not have others to recruit. (b) The government would hear about it and shut it down. (c) Since all the people of the world do not speak the same language, they would not be able to communicate with one another. (d) All of these.

138 PYRAMID SCHEMES (continued)

9. Have you ever been asked to participate in a pyramid scheme? Did you participate or not? Give your reasons why you would or would not participate.

_____

_____

_____

_____

_____

_____

_____

_____

_____

_____

_____

10. If you had the final decision, would you allow pyramid schemes or make them illegal? Why?

_____

_____

_____

_____

_____

_____

_____

_____

_____

_____

_____

139   THE RIGHT CHOICE

Read this story about Jose, a marvelous high school soccer player. Then answer the questions that follow it. Write the letter of the correct answer in the blank next to the question number.

The members of the soccer team selected Jose, a senior, to be their captain for the upcoming season. The choice seemed very appropriate, for Jose had been on the varsity team for the past four years. What's more, he had never missed a practice and had never been late to one either. Last season, he was the leading scorer in this very competitive league and was voted Team Most Valuable Player, League Most Valuable Player, and All-State.

Coach Hugbert, after informing the team that Jose was chosen as the team's captain, said, "In all of my thirty years as the coach of the Plandome High soccer and basketball teams, I have been fortunate enough to coach some great high school players. Jose is among this fine group. He has the drive, the work ethic, and the will to win that make him a champion. I am ecstatic that you guys have made Jose our team's captain. I could not think of a finer selection. I am extremely happy that Jose's teammates have selected him as their leader."

That fall season, Jose did all that was expected of him—and more. He led the team to the state finals, where Plandome defeated Refton Academy in double overtime. The Academy players and fans were baiting Jose throughout the game, trying to unnerve him and get him off his game. Their efforts were unsuccessful. He was too mature and too focused to allow these hecklers to get the better of him. At the game's conclusion, Jose was given the Harry T. Young Award as the game's outstanding player. Two months later, Jose had to choose from among more than forty scholarship offers to various colleges and universities. Next week, he will announce his decision before a crowd of more than four hundred students and residents at an assembly held in the Plandome High auditorium.

Reading Comprehension in Biography and Current Affairs

139 THE RIGHT CHOICE *(continued)*

1. _____ Jose's senior year on the Plandome High School varsity soccer team was his
   (a) third **(b)** fourth **(c)** fifth season on the team.

2. _____ Who selected Jose as captain of the soccer team?
   (a) his coach **(b)** the school principal **(c)** his teammates

3. _____ One would assume that Coach Hugbert must be at least how many years old?
   (a) fifty **(b)** sixty **(c)** seventy

4. _____ *Ecstatic* means **(a)** happy **(b)** moderately happy **(c)** very happy.

5. _____ The Refton Academy players and fans displayed good sportsmanship during the game
   against Plandome High School. Is this statement **(a)** true or **(b)** false?

6. _____ Who apparently counted the votes for selecting the Plandome High School soccer team
   captain? **(a)** Coach Hugbert **(b)** Jose **(c)** Jose's teammates

7. _____ A *heckler* is someone who is **(a)** rude **(b)** considerate **(c)** friendly.

8. _____ "Their efforts" in the final paragraph refers to whom? **(a)** the Refton Academy
   coaches **(b)** the Refton Academy players and fans **(c)** the Plandome High School
   players

9. _____ Jose's high school team played in a challenging soccer league. Is this statement
   (a) true or **(b)** false?

10. _____ Coach Hugbert has coached high school **(a)** soccer and baseball teams **(b)** basketball
    and lacrosse teams **(c)** basketball and soccer teams.

Section Seven

READING COMPREHENSION IN LANGUAGE ARTS CLASSES

The first three of the twenty-one activities in this section review this subject's terminology. The remainder feature excerpts and examples in various literary genres, including a look at character (Activity 143), an advice column (144), a biography (145), a novel (146), a speech (147), a fable (148), a play (149), a diary (150), a journal entry (151), and several sonnets and poems (156 through 160). The work of William Shakespeare is featured in Activities 152 through 155.

All of these activities are designed to strengthen your students' language arts skills. The questions focus on paraphrasing, word and idea interpretation, characters' motivations, imagery, diction, syntax, figurative devices, and the overall purpose of words.

Name: _____ Date: _____ Period: _____

140 LITERARY TERMS

All twenty-five answers in this activity are literary terms. Match each term in Column A with its definition in Column B. Write the number of the corresponding definition in the appropriate box. Five answers have been provided. If your answers are correct, the rows, the columns, and two diagonals will each add up to the same magic number. Have fun!

A = 1	B =	C =	D =	E =
F =	G =	H = 11	I =	J =
K =	L =	M =	N = 17	O =
P =	Q = 16	R =	S =	T =
U =	V =	W =	X =	Y = 20

Magic Number: _____

Column A

  A. protagonist

  B. monologue

  C. oxymoron

  D. sonnet

  E. genre

  F. idiom

  G. dramatic irony

  H. conflict

  I. personification

  J. epic

  K. alliteration

  L. hyperbole

  M. ode

  N. cliché

  O. simile

  P. rhyme

  Q. infer

Column B

  1. the main character

  2. a Japanese poem with three lines and seventeen syllables

  3. the lesson of a literary work

  4. exaggeration

  5. giving human qualities to inhuman things

  6. the end of the literary work

  7. the coincidence of words with final syllables that sound alike

  8. a lyric poem characterized by lofty feeling and elaborate form, addressed to a person or thing

  9. a long narrative poem about the deeds of a hero or heroes

  10. a long speech by a single speaker

  11. two or more forces in opposition

  12. kind or type of literary work, such as novel, play, or poem

140   LITERARY TERMS *(continued)*

Column A

R. comparison

S. dialogue

T. moral

U. foil

V. metaphor

W. haiku

X. conclusion

Y. onomatopoeia

Column B

13. the comparison of two seemingly unlike persons or things

14. conversation involving two or more people; passages of talk within a play

15. the repetition of the initial consonant sound in a word

16. draw a conclusion

17. an overused expression

18. an expression (such as "You are driving me up the wall") that is not to be taken literally

19. two words used together that seem contradictory, such as "sweet sorrow" or "roaring silence"

20. the creation or use of words that sound like what they mean, such as *roar* or *boom*

21. comparison of two seemingly unlike things using *like* or *as*

22. the situation created when the audience knows something that the characters in the work do not

23. a fourteen-line poem with a rigid rhyme scheme

24. a character in a literary work who sets off the main character

25. pointing out similarities and differences

141   WHERE HAVE ALL THE VOWELS GONE? (FINE ARTS)

Painting, sculpture, music, dance, and architecture make up the field known as the fine arts. Identify these twenty words from the fine arts. Only the consonants are given; the vowels have flown the coop! The remaining letters appear in the order in which they appear in the word itself. If the first letter is capitalized, that is the first letter in the word. The number in parentheses indicates the total number of letters in the complete word. Write the complete word in the blank. Have fun!

1. _____ Msc (5)

2. _____ Prtrt (8)

3. _____ nstrmnt (10)

4. _____ Tn (4)

5. _____ Pntng (8)

6. _____ Pctr (7)

7. _____ Brsh (5)

8. _____ Lndscp (9)

9. _____ Mldy (6)

10. _____ rchtct (9)

11. _____ Sngr (6)

12. _____ Flm (4)

13. _____ Bllt (6)

14. _____ Dnc (5)

15. _____ Mvs (6)

16. _____ Bllrn (9)

17. _____ Chrgrphr (13)

18. _____ Dlg (8)

19. _____ sl (5)

20. _____ pr (5)

142   WHERE HAVE ALL THE VOWELS GONE? (ENGLISH)

Twenty terms that you will hear in your English class are listed below. Unfortunately, the vowels have skipped out and have left the consonants to fend for themselves. The remaining letters are in the order in which they appear in the complete word. If the first letter is capitalized, that is the first letter in the word. The number in parentheses indicates how many letters are in the complete word. Write the complete word in the blank. Good luck!

1. _____ Nvl (5)

2. _____ Bgrphy (9)

3. _____ Ply (4)

4. _____ Drm (5)

5. _____ Scn (5)

6. _____ Cnflct (8)

7. _____ ssy (5)

8. _____ Chrctr (9)

9. _____ pc (4)

10. _____ Pm (4)

11. _____ Hk (5)

12. _____ Snnt (6)

13. _____ Blld (6)

14. _____ rny (5)

15. _____ Nrrtr (8)

16. _____ Gnr (5)

17. _____ xymrn (8)

18. _____ dm (5)

19. _____ Prsnfctn (15)

20. _____ Sml (6)

143   WHAT IS CHARACTER?

Here are seven quotes that deal with character. The author of each quote is identified in parentheses. On the lines below each quote, paraphrase the quote. Then, on the back of this page or on a separate sheet of paper, using any one of these quotes, write a fictional or real incident that illustrates that quote. Share your paraphrases and illustrative stories with your classmates.

1. "The true test of character is not how much we know how to do, but how we behave when we don't know what to do." (John Holt)

    _____

    _____

    _____

    _____

2. "The measure of a man's real character is what he would do if he knew he would never be found out." (Thomas B. Macaulay)

    _____

    _____

    _____

    _____

3. "When the character of a man is not clear to you, look at his friends." (Japanese proverb)

    _____

    _____

    _____

    _____

143   WHAT IS CHARACTER? *(continued)*

4. "Character cannot be developed in ease and quiet. Only through experience of trial and suffering can the soul be strengthened, ambition inspired, and success achieved." (Helen Keller)

_____

_____

_____

_____

_____

5. "Nearly all men can stand adversity, but if you want to test a man's character, give him power." (Abraham Lincoln)

_____

_____

_____

_____

_____

6. "The farther behind I leave the past, the closer I am to forging my own character." (Isabelle Eberhardt)

_____

_____

_____

_____

_____

7. A person reveals his character by nothing so clearly as the joke he resents." (Georg Christoph Lichtenberg)

_____

_____

_____

_____

_____

144   THE ADVICE COLUMN

Assume that this is a letter sent to a newspaper advice columnist. Read it carefully. Then, on a separate sheet of paper, write a reply responding directly to the issues raised in the letter. Share your reply with your classmates. Discuss the advice that you and your classmates gave to the writer.

Dear Advice Columnist,

Recently, two of my friends have begun to do things that I do not think that they have done before. Now that we are in the tenth grade, these friends do not seem to care about a lot of things that they used to think were important.

To start with, they have begun to cut classes more and more frequently. At first, they would both skip a class every other week. Cutting at least one class a day is not unusual for them these days. Though their teachers turn in cut slips on them, our school's principal, vice principal, and dean do not punish them very severely, making it attractive for the two to cut with little or no penalty.

Another problem is that I see them caring less and less about doing well in school. In addition to cutting class, they are also failing at least two of their courses. Both had been A and B students until a few months ago. Now they do very little homework and are not bothered by the prospect of attending summer school.

Last, their behaviors outside the school setting are deteriorating, showing that they care little about their former values. They are into bad habits involving alcohol, tobacco, and possibly even stronger drugs. Why they find these activities so attractive, I do not pretend to know.

I was hoping that you could help me help them. They are both essentially good people who at the moment seem to have lost their way.

Thomasita Reiagudo
Thomasita Reiagudo

145   J. K. ROWLING: HARRY POTTER'S CREATOR

Talk about a major change in one's life! J. K. Rowling rose from humble beginnings to accumulate great wealth through her writing. Her Harry Potter books have been a smashing success around the world, and movies based on these books have set records at the box office. And the series isn't over yet, so neither is the story of J. K. Rowling. After reading her biography, examine the statements that follow it, and write in each blank T if the statement is true or F if the statement is false. Now on to a really good story!

Joanne K. Rowling (born July 31, 1965) is the author of the internationally famous series of children's fantasy stories concerning the exploits of the boy wizard Harry Potter. She was born in Chipping Sodbury, South Gloucestershire, England. She had always been known by her first name, but the publisher who agreed to release the first Harry Potter book was afraid that an obviously female name on the cover would scare away the target readers, boys and young men, and so convinced her to use just initials.

As of 2004, Rowling was one of only five self-made female billionaires in the world and the first person in history to achieve that status by writing books. She is the wealthiest woman in the United Kingdom, well ahead of even Queen Elizabeth II.

Rowling had written two novels for adults—neither of which she tried to publish—before she had the idea for Harry Potter, which came to her during a four-hour train trip. By the time she reached her destination, she said, she had the characters and a good part of the plot for *Harry Potter and the Philosopher's Stone* in her head. She started writing the first Harry Potter book in 1990 during her lunch hours and continued working on the manuscript while teaching English as a second language in Portugal. Rowling returned to Britain three years later and moved to Edinburgh, Scotland. Now unemployed, divorced, and trying to support her young daughter, Rowling finally did complete *Harry Potter and the Philosopher's Stone* (renamed *Harry Potter and the Sorcerer's Stone* for the U.S. edition). Numerous publishers rejected the manuscript before one took an interest, but as soon the book was published in 1997, it became a huge success. Rowling has since written several equally successful sequels. The sales of these books brought her a financial windfall, and in 2001 she used the proceeds to buy a luxurious nineteenth-century mansion on the banks of the River Tay in Perthshire, central Scotland, where she married her second husband, Dr. Neil Murray, on December 26, 2001.

Soon after the fourth Potter book was published, she published two booklets for Comic Relief—purportedly Harry Potter's schoolbooks—the royalties on which go to charity. She has given large amounts of money and support to many charitable causes over the world, especially research and treatment of multiple sclerosis, from which her mother died in 1990.

145   J. K. ROWLING: HARRY POTTER'S CREATOR *(continued)*

The Harry Potter series is expected to run to seven volumes, one for each year Harry spends in school. Five of these have already been published. The fifth book, titled *Harry Potter and the Order of the Phoenix,* was delayed by an unsuccessful plagiarism suit directed against Rowling. She took some time off from writing at this point because she felt her workload had become too heavy. Rowling admitted that at one point she had considered breaking her arm to get out of writing because the pressure on her was too much. After forcing her publisher to extend her deadline, she enjoyed three years of quiet writing. The fifth book was released on June 21, 2003.

Toward the end of that year, Rowling was approached by the television producer Russell T. Davies to contribute an episode to the famous British television science-fiction series *Doctor Who.* Although she was "amused by the suggestion," she turned down the offer, as it would have taken time away from her work on the next book in the Potter series, *Harry Potter and the Half-Blood Prince.*

1. _____ J. K. Rowling's first name is Joan.

2. _____ Rowling is the third person in history to become a billionaire by writing books.

3. _____ Rowling came up with the idea for the first Harry Potter book on a train.

4. _____ Rowling owns a mansion in Scotland.

5. _____ Rowling is a charitable and generous woman.

6. _____ Rowling broke her arm so that she would not have to write any additional Harry Potter books.

7. _____ She enjoyed three years of quiet writing after several years of stressful work on the Harry Potter series.

8. _____ The Harry Potter series is expected to run to nine volumes.

9. _____ Rowling turned down an opportunity to write for a British science-fiction series.

10. _____ Rowling has never felt pressure during her writing of the Harry Potter series.

146   FRANKENSTEIN: THE MAN AND THE MONSTER

Mary Shelley started writing the novel *Frankenstein* in 1815, when she was eighteen years old. It was published three years later. What an achievement! The story of a monster and his creator, Victor Frankenstein, has fascinated readers ever since. (Note that in the novel, the monster is given no name; he is referred to as "the creature" and "Frankenstein's monster," and Victor Frankenstein often calls him "the fiend.") Read the following summary of the story. Then fill in the crossword puzzle; all twenty-one answers are related to *Frankenstein*. The first letter of each has been provided. Have a fiendishly good time!

The novel *Frankenstein* opens with Captain Walton in a ship sailing north of the Arctic Circle. Walton's ship becomes icebound, and as he contemplates his isolation and paralysis, he spots (perhaps) a figure walking across the ice. This is Victor Frankenstein. Walton's narrative is a frame that allows Victor's story to be told. At the same time, Walton's predicament is symbolically appropriate for Victor's tale of displaced passion and brutalism.

Curious and intelligent from a young age, Victor leaves his beloved family in Geneva, Switzerland, to study science in Germany. In a moment of inspiration, Victor discovers the means by which inanimate matter can be imbued with life. (At the time the book was written, scientists had a very imperfect understanding of the difference between living and dead matter.) With great drive and fervor, he sets about constructing a creature—intended as a companion, perhaps— from various materials, including cadavers.

He intends the creature to be beautiful, but when the creature awakens, the creator is disgusted by its yellow eyes, rough stitching, and large size. Victor finds this revolting, and although the creature expresses no hostility toward him (in fact, it grins at him), Victor runs out of the room in terror, whereupon the creature disappears. Overwork causes Victor to take ill for several months. After recovering, he receives a letter from home informing him of the murder of his youngest brother, William. He departs for Switzerland at once. Near Geneva, Victor sees the creature and is convinced it killed William. Upon arriving home, he finds Justine, the family's maid, framed for the murder. She is convicted and executed. To recover from the ordeal, Victor goes hiking into the mountains. He meets his creation atop a glacier.

The creature is strikingly eloquent and describes his feelings of confusion, then rejection and hate. He explains how he learns how to talk by studying a family through a crack in the wall. He performs in secret many kind deeds for this family, but in the end, they drive him away when they see his appearance. He gets the same response from any human who sees him. The creature confesses that it was indeed he who killed William and framed Justine and that he did so out of revenge. But now the creature wants only one thing: he begs Victor to create a female companion for him.

146 FRANKENSTEIN: THE MAN AND THE MONSTER *(continued)*

At first Victor agrees, but later he tears up the half-made companion in disgust. In retribution, the creature kills Henry, Victor's best friend. On Victor's wedding night, the creature kills his wife. Victor now becomes the hunter: he pursues the creature into the arctic ice, though in vain—near exhaustion, he is stranded when an iceberg breaks away, carrying him out into the ocean. At that moment, Captain Walton's ship arrives, and he is rescued.

Walton assumes the narration again, describing a temporary recovery in Victor's health, allowing him to relate his extraordinary story. However, Victor's health soon fails, and he dies. The creature boards the ship and finds Victor dead and greatly laments what he has done to his maker. He vows to commit suicide and leaves.

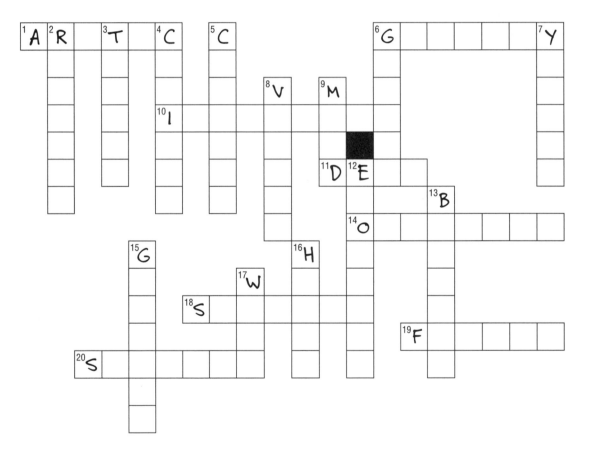

146 FRANKENSTEIN: THE MAN AND THE MONSTER (continued)

Across

1. Walton's ship was north of the _____ Circle.

6. country where Victor studied science

10. not living

11. condition in which the creature found his creator on the ship

14. what caused Victor to become ill

18. the subject Victor studied

19. The monster wanted a _____ for companionship.

20. The monster vows to commit _____.

Down

2. The creature killed out of _____.

3. Victor ran out of the room in _____.

4. the kind of person Victor was

5. a dead body

6. Swiss city where the Frankenstein family lived

7. color of the creature's eyes

8. the creator's first name

9. Justine was the family's _____.

12. The creature was _____ and well spoken.

13. William was Victor's _____ .

15. where Victor and his monster meet for the last time

16. Victor's best friend

17. The monster killed his creator's _____.

147   A GRADUATION SPEECH

Read the high school graduation speech below. Then on the lines provided answer the questions about the speech. Discuss your answers with your classmates.

Hillboro classmates, members of the board of education, teachers, parents, and friends:

We are gathered here this afternoon to celebrate and to reflect. These past thirteen years have given all of us many memories—some happy and some sad. We started together as kindergartners and now leave as graduates ready to take on the world. Some of us will go into the workforce; some will go into the military; others will go to college. Yet even though all of us will soon go our separate ways and have different stories to tell in the years ahead, remember that we will always have each other and the experiences that we have shared.

Last night I looked at our yearbook, the history of our lives here in Hillboro. I laughed; I cried; I remembered; I wondered. How will we remember what we have done in this school, in this town? Though your story *is* my story, your story is also *not* my story. Each of us is somewhat the same and somewhat different. Each of us saw many of the same people, places, and things. Yet how did you see them? More important, how will you remember them? Will the next forty or more years change how you remember these past thirteen years? Perhaps.

Think of the good times. Try to put the bad times in perspective. They have helped us grow and prepared us for the challenges of the future.

Today, the graduation speeches will be delivered, the diplomas will be presented, and then the school orchestra will play our school song—one last time for us. Then our class will march up those two aisles and exit from those two doors for the last time as a class. And as you walk up the aisles and out the doors, I ask all of you to think about what you were just a few years ago, what you are today, and what you hope to be in the years ahead.

Finally, I ask you to leave a part of yourself here as you leave Hillboro. I also ask you to take a part of yourself beyond Hillboro's boundaries and leave your mark on the world. Make Hillboro proud of what you will do in whatever path life takes you. Your parents, teachers, and classmates have believed in you and continue to believe in you. Make them—and Hillboro—proud. Do well, be well, and be proud.

147   A GRADUATION SPEECH *(continued)*

1. What aspects of the speech do you like? Why?

   _____

   _____

   _____

   _____

   _____

2. What aspects of the speech could be improved? How would you improve them?

   _____

   _____

   _____

   _____

   _____

3. What are some of the author's purposes in this speech? Cite specifics to support your answer?

   _____

   _____

   _____

   _____

   _____

4. How does the speaker motivate the graduates?

   _____

   _____

   _____

   _____

   _____

5. What are some words that would describe the tone or mood of the speech? Cite specifics from the speech to support your answer.

   _____

   _____

   _____

   _____

   _____

148   THE BOY WHO CRIED WOLF

"The Boy Who Cried Wolf" is a fable written by the Greek fabulist, Aesop, at least 2,600 years ago. A fable is a story that illustrates a moral or lesson. The characters in fables are often animals. The following story incorporates animals, but the main character is a boy who learns a valuable lesson.

Read the fable, and then complete the magic square. Your job is to figure out which word from Column A is missing from each sentence in Column B. Write the correct word from Column A in the corresponding sentence in Column B. Then write the number of the correct answer in Column B in the appropriate box. Three answers are provided already. If your answers are correct, the rows, the columns, and the two diagonals will each add up to the same magic number. Have a howling good time!

Once upon a time there was a shepherd boy, who was sitting on the hillside watching the village sheep. However, he was bored, so he decided to play a trick on the villagers. He screamed at the top of his voice, "Wolf! Wolf! The wolf is chasing the sheep!"

The villagers came running up the hill as fast as they could to help him. But when they arrived, they couldn't see a wolf. The boy laughed his head off when he saw their angry faces. "Don't cry 'wolf' when there is no wolf!" admonished the villagers. And off they went back down the hill.

Nevertheless, the boy, who thought this was a great game, decided to do the same thing again a couple of days later. He cried out, "Wolf! Wolf! The wolf is chasing the sheep!" To his delight, he watched the villagers come running up the hill to help him. When the villagers saw that there was no wolf, they said, in a very stern voice, "Don't cry 'wolf' when there is no wolf!" But the boy just smiled and watched them go grumbling down the hill again.

The next day, he saw a real wolf, which was prowling about his flock. Frightened, the boy leaped to his feet and screamed as loudly as he could, "Wolf! Wolf!" The villagers heard him calling for help, but they thought it was just another one of his tricks, so they ignored him.

In the evening, everyone wondered why the shepherd boy hadn't returned to the village with their sheep, so they went up the hill to look for him. They found him weeping, but they couldn't see their sheep. They asked the boy why he was crying and where their sheep were. He told them, "There really was a wolf here! The sheep have run away! I cried out 'Wolf!' but nobody came to help me!"

An old man tried to comfort the boy as they walked back to the village. "We'll help you look for the lost sheep in the morning," he said, putting his arm around the boy.

The moral of the story is that *nobody believes a liar, even when he is telling the truth.*

148   THE BOY WHO CRIED WOLF (continued)

A = 11	B =	C =	D =
E =	F =	G =	H = 9
I =	J =	K =	L =
M =	N = 12	O =	P =

Magic Number: _____

Column A

A. wondered

B. grumbling

C. prowling

D. shepherd

E. leaped

F. decided

G. help

H. chasing

I. tricks

J. stern

K. angry

L. delight

M. comfort

N. game

O. weeping

P. moral

Column B

1. They found him _____, but they couldn't see their sheep.

2. Once upon a time there was a _____ boy, who was sitting on the hillside watching the village sheep.

3. When the villagers saw that there was no wolf, they said, in a very _____ voice, "Don't cry 'wolf' when there is no wolf!"

4. Frightened, he _____ to his feet and screamed as loudly as he could, "Wolf! Wolf!"

5. The villagers heard him calling for help, but they thought it was just another one of his _____, and so they ignored him.

6. However, he was bored, so he _____ to play a trick on the villagers.

7. The _____ of the story is that *nobody believes a liar, even when he is telling the truth.*

8. The next day, he saw a real wolf, which was _____ about his flock.

9. He screamed at the top of his voice, "Wolf! Wolf! The wolf is _____ the sheep!"

10. The boy laughed his head off when he saw their _____ faces.

11. In the evening, everyone _____ why the shepherd boy hadn't returned to the village with their sheep, so they went up the hill to look for him.

148   THE BOY WHO CRIED WOLF *(continued)*

Column B

12. Nevertheless, the boy, who thought this was a great _____, decided to do the same thing again a couple of days later.

13. But the boy just smiled and watched them go _____ down the hill again.

14. An old man tried to _____ the boy as they walked back to the village.

15. He said, "There really was a wolf here! The sheep have run away! I cried 'Wolf!' but nobody came to _____ me!"

16. To his _____, he watched the villagers come running up the hill to help him.

Reading Comprehension in Language Arts Classes

Name: _____ Date: _____ Period: _____

149   *A DOLL'S HOUSE*

The following scene is from the 1876 play *A Doll's House,* written by the Norwegian playwright Henrik Ibsen. The play, which deals with the relationships between men and women, specifically that between Nora Helmer and her husband, Torvald, was quite controversial for its time. In this scene below, Nora is visited by a friend, Christine Linde. Read the scene—several times if you must. Then answer the questions that follow it by writing the two-letter code for the correct answer in the blank next to the question number. Copy those twenty letters, in order, onto the line beneath the last question. If your answers are correct, they will spell out a five-word phrase from this scene.

Maid: A lady's called, madam. A stranger.
Nora: Well, ask her to come in.
Maid: And the doctor's here too, sir.
Helmer: Has he gone to my room?
Maid: Yes, sir.
Mrs. Linde: Good evening, Nora.
Nora: Good evening—
Mrs. Linde: I don't suppose you recognize me.
Nora: No, I'm afraid I—Yes, wait a minute—surely—Why, Christine! Is it really you?
Mrs. Linde: Yes, it's me.
Nora: Christine! And I didn't recognize you! But how could I—? How you've changed, Christine!
Mrs. Linde: Yes, I know. It's been nine years—nearly ten—
Nora: Is it so long? Yes, it must be. Oh, these last eight years have been such a happy time for me! So you've come to town? All that way in winter! How brave of you!
Mrs. Linde: I arrived by the steamer this morning.
Nora: Yes, of course—to enjoy yourself over Christmas. Oh, how splendid! We'll have to celebrate! But take off your coat. You're not cold, are you? There! Now let's sit down here by the stove and be comfortable. No, you take the armchair. I'll sit here in the rocking-chair. Yes, now you look like your old self. It was just at first that—you've got a little paler, though, Christine. And perhaps a bit thinner.
Mrs. Linde: And older, Nora. Much, much older.
Nora: Yes, perhaps a little older. Just a tiny bit. Not much. Oh, but how thoughtless of me to sit here and chatter away like this! Dear, sweet Christine, can you forgive me?
Mrs. Linde: What do you mean, Nora?
Nora: Poor Christine, you've become a widow.
Mrs. Linde: Yes. Three years ago.
Nora: I know, I know—I read it in the papers. Oh, Christine, I meant to write to you so often, honestly. But I always put it off, and something else always cropped up.

149 *A DOLL'S HOUSE* (continued)

Mrs. Linde: I understand, Nora dear.

Nora: No, Christine, it was beastly of me. Oh, my poor darling, what you've gone through! And he didn't leave you anything?

Mrs. Linde: No.

Nora: No children, either?

Mrs. Linde: No.

Nora: Nothing at all, then?

Mrs. Linde: Not even a feeling of loss or sorrow.

Nora: But, Christine, how is that possible?

Mrs. Linde: Oh, these things happen, Nora.

Nora: All alone. How dreadful that must be for you. I've three lovely children. I'm afraid you can't see them now, because they're out with nanny. But you must tell me everything—

Mrs. Linde: No, no, no. I want to hear about you.

Nora: No, you start. I'm not going to be selfish today, I'm just going to think about you. Oh, but there's one thing I must tell you. Have you heard of the wonderful luck we've just had?

Mrs. Linde: No. What?

Nora: Would you believe it—my husband's just been made manager of the bank!

Mrs. Linde: Your husband? Oh, how lucky—!

Nora: Yes, isn't it? Being a lawyer is so uncertain, you know, especially if one isn't prepared to touch any case that isn't—well—quite nice. And of course Torvald's been very firm about that—and I'm absolutely with him. Oh, you can imagine how happy we are! He's joining the bank in the New Year, and he'll be getting a big salary, and lots of percentages too. From now on we'll be able to live quite differently—we'll be able to do whatever we want. Oh, Christine, it's such a relief! I feel so happy! Well, I mean, it's lovely to have heaps of money and not to have to worry about anything. Don't you think?

Mrs. Linde: It must be lovely to have enough to cover one's needs, anyway.

Nora: Not just our needs! We're going to have heaps and heaps of money!

149 *A DOLL'S HOUSE* (continued)

1. _____ Torvald has been promoted to what position?
   (la) nanny **(be)** lawyer **(he)** bank manager **(ad)** funeral director

2. _____ Which character seems to have had a difficult time of it during the past decade?
   (st) Nora **(ri)** the maid **(ko)** Torvald **(ap)** Christine

3. _____ How did Nora find out that Christine's husband had died? **(as)** from the maid
   (sa) in the newspapers **(es)** at a local town meeting **(se)** from Christine's children

4. _____ Which character seems selfish by his or her words and actions?
   (ee) the maid **(nd)** Nora **(oo)** Helmer **(su)** Christine

5. _____ How many children did Christine and her husband have?
   (he) none **(lo)** one **(ve)** two **(rs)** three

6. _____ Which line indicates that Nora and her husband have had financial difficulties in the
   past? **(ap)** "It's such a relief." **(ce)** "But I always put it off." **(lt)** "Not even a feeling of
   loss or sorrow." **(vi)** "And of course Torvald's been firm about that."

7. _____ Why does Nora not introduce her children to Christine? **(ut)** They are upstairs
   sleeping. **(he)** They did not want to meet Christine. **(so)** They are not home at the
   moment. **(tu)** They are being punished.

8. _____ What character does not have a speaking role in this excerpt?
   (gr) the maid **(fm)** the doctor **(ol)** Christine **(ye)** Nora

9. _____ Christine and Nora had not seen each other for nearly
   (mo) three years **(nn)** twenty years **(do)** several months **(on)** a decade.

10. _____ According to Nora, Christine has become **(tt)** taller **(ss)** younger looking
    (ey) paler **(ry)** angry.

The twenty letters are _____ .

The five-word phrase from this scene is " _____

_____ ."

150   PEPYS'S DIARY

Samuel Pepys (pronounced "peeps") was born on Fleet Street in London in 1633. His claim to fame is his diary, a series of entries, originally written in shorthand, that recorded what was happening in England during the entire decade of the 1660s. He also recorded details of his professional and personal life. Pepys died in 1703.

Below is Pepys's entry for August 8, 1665. Read it over several times, and then answer the questions that follow it by writing the code letter for the correct answer in each blank. If your answers are correct, these letters will spell out a ten-letter word.

[August 8, 1665]. Up and to the office, where all the morning we sat. At noon I home to dinner alone, and after dinner Bagwell's wife waited at the door, and went with me to my office. . . . So parted, and I to Sir W. Batten's, and there sat the most of the afternoon talking and drinking too much with my Lord Bruncker, Sir G. Smith, G. Cocke and others very merry. I drunk a little mixed, but yet more than I should do. So to my office a little, and then to the Duke of Albemarle's about some business. The streets mighty empty all the way, now even in London, which is a sad sight. And to Westminster Hall, where talking, hearing very sad stories from Mrs. Mumford; among others, of Mrs. Michell's son's family. And poor Will, that used to sell us ale at the Hall-door, his wife and three children died, all, I think, in a day. So home through the City again, wishing I may have taken no ill in going; but I will go, I think, no more thither. Late at the office, and then home to supper, having taken a pullet home with me, and then to bed. The news of De Kuyter's coming home is certain; and told to the great disadvantage of our fleete, and the praise of De Kuyter; but it cannot be helped, nor do I know what to say to it.

150 PEPYS'S DIARY *(continued)*

1. _____ Pepys and his colleagues sat all morning in the **(a)** alley **(b)** church **(c)** office **(d)** none of these.

2. _____ With whom did the diarist eat lunch? **(m)** Shakespeare **(n)** the king **(o)** himself **(p)** none of these

3. _____ Lord Bruncker and the diarist spent most of the afternoon **(n)** drinking **(o)** bowling **(p)** playing checkers **(q)** reading.

4. _____ The diarist saw the Duke of Albemarle about some **(p)** land **(q)** machine **(r)** friends **(s)** business.

5. _____ In the diarist's entry, the streets of London this day are **(a)** paved with gold **(b)** wet **(c)** empty **(d)** dark.

6. _____ Whose wife and three children died?
   (i) Will's **(j)** Mrs. Mumford's **(k)** the king's **(l)** Shakespeare's

7. _____ Will sold **(e)** ale **(f)** chicken **(g)** pasta **(h)** fish.

8. _____ What did the diarist bring home with him?
   (m) a bed **(n)** a pullet **(o)** a newspaper **(p)** all of these

9. _____ Who is returning near the entry's conclusion?
   (c) De Kuyter **(d)** the king of France **(e)** the wife of the prince **(f)** the librarian

10. _____ The modern-day spelling of *fleete* is **(e)** *fleet* **(f)** *flyte* **(g)** *fleat* **(g)** none of these.

151 OLD TIMES

In 1826, the American writer John Winthrop wrote the following sentence in his journal. Read the sentence several times, and then answer the questions below it. Write the letter corresponding to the correct answer in the blank next to each question number.

> There was great hope that the late general assembly would have had some good effect in pacifying the troubles and dissensions of religion; but it fell otherwise. . . .

1. _____ *Late* in this quote means **(a)** not on time **(b)** recent **(c)** deceased **(d)** none of these.

2. _____ The verb form of the noun *assembly* is **(a)** assemblage **(b)** resemble **(c)** assemble **(d)** none of these.

3. _____ In this context, *effect* means **(a)** conflict **(b)** result **(c)** causes **(d)** none of these.

4. _____ *Pacifying* means **(a)** causing **(b)** belittling **(c)** determining **(d)** none of these.

5. _____ *Dissensions* are **(a)** differences **(b)** sounds **(c)** unions **(d)** violent actions.

6. _____ *Fell* is the past tense of a verb meaning **(a)** disagree **(b)** agree **(c)** steal **(d)** happen.

7. _____ *Otherwise* in this quotation means **(a)** in a similar way **(b)** differently **(c)** comparatively **(d)** sometimes.

8. _____ The quotation's tone is **(a)** positive **(b)** negative **(c)** both positive and negative **(d)** neither positive nor negative.

9. _____ The tense of the quotation is **(a)** future **(b)** present **(c)** past **(d)** all of these.

10. _____ What is the purpose of the word *but* in this quotation? **(a)** It serves as a transition. **(b)** It sets up a comparison. **(c)** It is a simile. **(d)** All of these.

Name: _____ Date: _____ Period: _____

152   MAKING SENSE OF *MACBETH*

The following is the famous from William Shakespeare's tragedy *Macbeth* (Act 5, Scene 5, Lines 22–31). The lines are spoken by Macbeth, the king of Scotland, upon learning that his wife, Lady Macbeth, has died. Read it carefully; then, on the lines provided or on a separate sheet of paper, answer the questions that follow it.

> Tomorrow and tomorrow and tomorrow
> Creeps in this petty pace from day to day
> To the last syllable of recorded time.
> And all our yesterdays have lighted fools
> The way to dusty death. Out, out, brief candle!
> Life's but a walking shadow, a poor player
> That struts and frets his hour upon the stage
> And then is heard no more. It is a tale
> Told by an idiot, full of sound and fury,
> Signifying nothing.

1. What effect does Shakespeare intend by repeating the word *tomorrow* in the first line of the excerpt?

   _____

   _____

   _____

   _____

2. What is the effect of having the first sentence run to three full lines?

   _____

   _____

   _____

   _____

3. Paraphrase the lines "And all our yesterdays have lighted fools / The way to dusty death."

   _____

   _____

   _____

   _____

152 MAKING SENSE OF *MACBETH* (continued)

4. Shakespeare makes good use of metaphors, comparing seemingly unlike things, in these lines of poetry. Name the four metaphors.

   _____

   _____

   _____

   _____

5. What tone is given by these four metaphors and the adjectives and verbs associated with them?

   _____

   _____

   _____

6. Why does Shakespeare use an exclamation point after the word *candle* in line 5?

   _____

   _____

   _____

   _____

7. What opinion about life does the end of the excerpt give the reader?

   _____

   _____

   _____

8. Write a two-sentence summary of these excerpted lines.

   _____

   _____

   _____

   _____

   _____

153   *ROMEO AND JULIET*

Shakespeare's play *Romeo and Juliet* begins with a fourteen-line prologue. The speaker explains to the audience that the story concerns two warring families in Verona, Italy, and that the feud ends in a manner that neither side could have wanted or expected. Read the following summary of the play. Below it, ten events are listed. Place the first group of five events in chronological order by numbering them from 1 to 5, and put the second group of five events in order by numbering them from 6 to 10.

The action starts with a typical street brawl between the two families, the Montagues (Romeo's family) and the Capulets (Juliet's family) started by their servants and put down by the Prince of Verona. He fines the heads of both families and declares severe penalties, including death, for those who disturb the peace again and then leaves.

Paris, a nobleman and the prince's relative, talks to old Capulet about marrying Capulet's daughter, Juliet. Capulet asks him to attract the attention of Juliet during a ball that the family is to hold the next day. Meanwhile, Juliet's mother tries to persuade her young daughter to accept Paris's wooing during the upcoming ball. Juliet does not want to, but she does so because her mother asked her to.

Romeo, the son of Montague, is infatuated with Rosaline, a relative of the Capulets. Hearing that she will appear at the ball at the Capulets, he decides to visit the Capulets' house masked with his cousin Benvolio and friend Mercutio, who want him to forget about Rosaline and find another woman, since Rosaline does not return Romeo's love.

At the ball, Romeo falls instead for Juliet, who is around fourteen years old. He stays behind, risking his life by remaining on Capulet property, to catch another glimpse of Juliet at her room, and in the famous balcony scene, the two eloquently declare their love for each other. The young lovers decide to marry without informing their parents, who would undoubtedly disallow it due to the planned union between Paris and Juliet.

With the help of Juliet's nurse and the Franciscan priest Friar Lawrence, the two are wed, without their parents' permission, days later. Friar Lawrence performs the ceremony, hoping to bring the two families to peace with each other through their union.

Things take a darker turn in the next act. Tybalt, a bloodthirsty Capulet and Juliet's cousin, decides to seek out Romeo for appearing in the Capulets' house uninvited. Romeo refuses to fight him because he is now part of the family, but Mercutio accepts the duel on his behalf. In the ensuing fight, Mercutio is fatally wounded by Tybalt, and Romeo, in anger, kills Tybalt. Although under the Prince of Verona's prior proclamation Romeo would be subject to the death penalty, the prince reduces Romeo's punishment to exile in light of the fact that Tybalt initiated the duel. Romeo flees to Mantua.

153 *ROMEO AND JULIET* (continued)

Juliet is extremely grieved when she hears this, and when she realizes that her father, still unaware that she has wed Romeo, will force her to go through with the marriage to Paris, she seeks the help of Friar Lawrence once more. Friar Lawrence, an expert in herbal medicines and potions, gives Juliet a potion and a plan: the potion will put her in a deathlike coma for two days; she is to take it before her wedding day, and when she is found "dead," she will be laid in the family crypt. Meanwhile, the friar will send a messenger to inform Romeo so that he can rejoin her when she awakens. The two can then leave for Mantua and live happily ever after.

Juliet takes the potion, and things proceed as planned. Unfortunately, the friar's messenger is unable to reach Romeo due to Mantua's being under quarantine, and Romeo learns of Juliet's supposed death through a family servant. Grief-stricken, he buys some strong poison, returns to Verona in secret, and proceeds to the Capulets' crypt, determined to join Juliet in death. After killing Paris, who has come to mourn privately for his lost love, Romeo drinks the poison after seeing Juliet one last time. Seconds later, Juliet awakens and sees Romeo dead. Juliet cannot imagine a rewarding life without Romeo, and so she stabs herself fatally with his dagger. The two lovers lie dead by each other's side, madly in love and devoted until the last breath of life.

The two families meet at the tomb with the prince, and Friar Lawrence, who has hurried to the crypt but is too late to prevent the tragedy, reveals to them the love and secret marriage of Romeo and Juliet. The feuding families are reconciled by their children's deaths, as explained in the prologue.

Group One

_____ Friar Lawrence gives Juliet a potion to fake her death.

_____ Mercutio is fatally wounded by Tybalt.

_____ Romeo and Juliet are married.

_____ Romeo falls for Juliet at the ball.

_____ Romeo is infatuated with Rosaline.

Group Two

_____ Friar Lawrence sends a messenger to tell Romeo of his plans regarding Romeo and Juliet.

_____ Juliet awakens from the potion and sees Romeo dead.

_____ Juliet takes the potion.

_____ Romeo kills Paris.

_____ The feuding families are reconciled by their children's deaths.

154   PROLOGUE TO *ROMEO AND JULIET*

The following fourteen-line poem is the prologue or opening to *Romeo and Juliet,* one of William Shakespeare's most popular plays. Here Shakespeare informs the audience of the story's background and some of the events that will happen in the play. He also admonishes his audience to be attentive throughout the performance.

Read the prologue. Then answer the questions that follow it. Write the two-letter code for the correct response in the blank next to each question number. Then copy those twenty letters, in order, onto the line below the final question. If your answers are correct, the letters will spell out the names of three other plays by William Shakespeare.

> Two households, both alike in dignity,
> In fair Verona, where we lay our scene,
> From ancient grudge break to new mutiny,
> Where civil blood makes civil hands unclean.
> From forth the fatal loins of these two foes
> A pair of star-cross'd lovers take their life;
> Whole misadventured piteous overthrows
> Do with their death bury their parents' strife.
> The fearful passage of their death-mark'd love,
> And the continuance of their parents' rage,
> Which, but their children's end, nought could remove,
> Is now the two hours' traffic of our stage;
> The which if you with patient ears attend,
> What here shall miss, our toil shall strive to mend.

154   PROLOGUE TO *ROMEO AND JULIET* (continued)

1. _____ The two households are "alike in dignity." *Dignity* means
(**po**) poverty (**ma**) esteem (**ri**) wealth (**ho**) friendship.

2. _____ The play's setting is (**te**) England (**rt**) Stratford-upon-Avon (**cb**) Verona (**el**) Scotland.

3. _____ Which words indicate that the families have been fighting for a number of years?
(**et**) "ancient grudge" (**st**) "civil hands" (**un**) "patient ears" (**gh**) "Two households"

4. _____ Which term refers to the couple, Romeo and Juliet? (**oo**) "parents' rage"
(**ch**) "ancient grudge" (**ar**) "two hours' traffic" (**ho**) "star-cross'd lovers"

5. _____ Where do we learn that people will die in the play?
(**he**) "civil blood" (**er**) "continuance of their parents' rage"
(**th**) "lovers take their life" (**ss**) "with patient ears"

6. _____ What effect will the deaths referred to in question 5 have?
(**el**) The parents will stop their feud. (**re**) The children will be reincarnated.
(**rd**) It will have no effect. (**ff**) The town officials will have nothing to do with either family.

7. _____ How many minutes are we told that the play will take to perform?
(**rt**) 60 (**co**) 80 (**lo**) 120 (**rr**) 200

8. _____ What line is a word of caution to the audience? (**ha**) "The which if you with patient ears attend" (**hi**) "Where civil blood makes civil blood unclean" (**nn**) "A pair of star-cross'd lovers take their life" (**lo**) "And the continuance of their parents' rage"

9. _____ The word *nought* means (**we**) all (**sa**) some (**ky**) understanding (**ml**) nothing.

10. _____ What are the only two consecutive lines that rhyme? (**et**) the last two lines
(**re**) the first two lines (**er**) All the lines rhyme. (**at**) None of the lines rhyme.

The twenty letters are _____.

The names of three other Shakespearean plays are _____,

_____, and _____.

155   SHAKING THINGS UP WITH SHAKESPEARE

One of the most famous playwrights and poets in the English language is the Englishman William Shakespeare (April 23, 1564–April 23, 1616). His words and images have been quoted for hundreds of years, and his works have been translated into many different languages and transcend many different cultures.

Today is your day to work with Shakespeare's words. Read his "Sonnet 29" below. Then write your answers to the ten questions that deal with the sonnet on the lines provided. Discuss your answers with your classmates.

Sonnet 29
When, in disgrace with Fortune and men's eyes,
I all alone beweep my outcast state,
And trouble deaf heaven with my bootless cries,
And look upon myself and curse my fate,
Wishing me like to one more rich in hope,   5
Featured like him, like him with friends possessed,
Desiring this man's art and that man's scope,
With what I most enjoy contented least;
Yet in these thoughts myself almost despising,
Haply I think on thee, and then my state   10
(Like to the lark at break of day arising
From sullen earth) sings hymns at heaven's gate;
For thy sweet love remembered such wealth brings
That then I scorn to change my state with kings.

---

1. What is the tone or mood of the sonnet's first eight lines?

   _____

2 Give at least three specific examples to support your answer to question 1.

   _____

   _____

   _____

   _____

3. What word signifies a change or transition in tone or mood?

   _____

155   SHAKING THINGS UP WITH SHAKESPEARE *(continued)*

4. Poets often use *similes*—comparisons between two persons or things using the word *like* or *as.* What two things does Shakespeare use in the simile found in lines 10–12?

   _____

   _____

5. Poets also use *personification,* a literary device that gives human qualities to nonhuman things. What example of personification does Shakespeare use in line 3?

   _____

6. Sound often contributes to sense or measuring in poems. "All alone" in line 2 helps the reader feel the poet's downcast and lonely state. The word *curse* in line 4 is a harsh word that displays the poet's unhappy state. Cite two additional examples of how sounds contribute to sense in this sonnet.

   _____

   _____

7. Paraphrase the sonnet's last line.

   _____

   _____

8. What accounts for the poet's change of mood?

   _____

   _____

9. A poet uses repetition for emphasis. Cite two examples of that in this sonnet.

   _____

   _____

   _____

10. Shakespeare's sonnets often have ten syllables per line. Can you find any lines in this sonnet that do not have ten syllables? If so, which are they?

   _____

Name: _____ Date: _____ Period: _____

156   ELIZABETH BARRETT BROWNING'S "SONNET 43"

A sonnet is a fourteen-line poem that generally has a predictable rhyme pattern and a specific number of beats per line. Elizabeth Barrett Browning wrote the following sonnet in 1845 or 1846. It is one of the most quoted poems in the English language. Read the fourteen lines of the poem, and then answer the questions that follow it. Write the two-letter answer codes in the appropriate blanks. Then copy the twenty answer letters, in order, onto the line below item 10. If your answers are correct, they will spell out four names that are closely related to the name Elizabeth.

> How do I love thee? Let me count the ways.
> I love thee to the depth and breadth and height
> My soul can reach, when feeling out of sight
> For the ends of Being and ideal Grace.
> I love thee to the level of everyday's   5
> Most quiet need, by sun and candle-light.
> I love thee freely, as men strive for Right;
> I love thee purely, as they turn from Praise.
> I love thee with the passion put to use
> In my old griefs, and with my childhood's faith.   10
> I love thee with a love I seemed to lose
> With my lost saints,—I love thee with the breath,
> Smiles, tears, of all my life!—and, if God choose,
> I shall but love thee better after death.

156 ELIZABETH BARRETT BROWNING'S "SONNET 43" (continued)

1. _____ What lines rhyme with line 1? **(be)** 4 and 5 **(li)** 8 and 14 **(ma)** 12 and 13 **(re)** 2 and 9

2. _____ One would assume by this poem serving as an example of a typical sonnet that a sonnet
(xi) has no rhyme **(tt)** has fourteen lines **(gg)** talks about earthly major problems
(ll) is generally written without any reference to the author in the poem.

3. _____ The author repeats "I love thee" **(yb)** for emphasis **(he)** out of boredom
(ee) out of laziness **(nn)** because the rhyme scheme requires repetition.

4. _____ Where does the speaker feel that her love is stronger?
(io) on earth **(es)** in the afterlife

5. _____ The phrase "to the depth and breadth and height" is intended to
(sa) baffle the reader **(sl)** show the extent of the speaker's love
(po) compare the speaker's love to heaven's beauty **(ed)** all of these.

6. _____ The phrase "by sun and candle-light" (line 6) is a reference to
(ut) heaven and hell **(ty)** earth and hell **(gh)** heaven and earth **(ib)** night and day.

7. _____ Time's passage is exemplified through which of these?
(hu) line 2 **(ed)** line 5 **(by)** line 10 **(ky)** line 12

8. _____ Which line includes an example of the sense of sight?
(be) line 6 **(fr)** line 7 **(we)** line 12 **(nd)** line 13

9. _____ Most of the sonnet's lines have how many syllables?
(ik) nine **(ss)** ten **(ne)** eight **(ee)** eleven

10. _____ A synonym for the word *shall* (line 14) is **(oo)** *grant* **(et)** *forbid* **(dd)** *cannot* **(ie)** *will*.

The twenty consecutive letters are _____.

The four names related to Elizabeth are _____, _____,

_____, and _____.

157   BRADSTREET'S EPITAPHS

An epitaph is the writing on a deceased person's tombstone. The following two poems, written by America's first female poet, Anne Bradstreet (1612–1672), are epitaphs she composed for her parents. Read both poems carefully, and then answer the questions regarding comprehension and Bradstreet's style on the lines provided or on a separate sheet of paper.

Her Mother's Epitaph

Here lies
A worthy matron of unspotted life,
A loving mother and obedient wife,
A friendly neighbor, pitiful to poor,
Whom oft she fed, and clothed with her store;   5
To servants wisely aweful, but yet kind,
And as they did, so they reward did find:
A true instructor of her family,
The which she ordered with dexterity,
The public meetings ever did frequent,   10
And in her closest constant hours she spent;
Religious in all her words and ways,
Preparing still for death, till end of days:
Of all her children, children lived to see,
Then dying, left a blessed memory.   15

Her Father's Epitaph

Within this tomb a patriot lies
That was both pious, just and wise,
To truth a shield, to right a wall,
To sectaries* a whip and maul,
A magazine of history,   5
A prizer of good company
In manners pleasant and severe
The good him loved, the bad did fear,
And when his time with years was spent
In some rejoiced, more did lament.   10

---

*dissenters, religious nonconformists

---

157   BRADSTREET'S EPITAPHS (continued)

On "Her Mother's Epitaph"

1. Define the following words (line number is in parentheses):

   matron (2) _____

   pitiful (4) _____

   oft (5) _____

   dexterity (9) _____

2. What line indicates that Bradstreet's mother led a pure life? _____

3. Name at least two roles, other than mother, that Bradstreet's mother played in life. Indicate the line in which each is mentioned.

   _____

   _____

4. What type of system did her mother use to get the most out of her servants? Indicate the line or lines that tell you this.

   _____

5. Was she a responsible member of her local community? Indicate the line or lines that tell you this.

   _____

6. Was she religious? Indicate the line or lines that tell you this.

   _____

7. What was the gift that the mother left for her children? Indicate the line or lines that tell you this.

   _____

8. Select five adjectives that describe her mother in a positive way. Indicate the line on which each adjective appears.

   _____

   _____

   _____

157   BRADSTREET'S EPITAPHS (continued)

On "Her Father's Epitaph"

9. Define the following words. (Line number is in parentheses.)

patriot (1) _____

pious (2) _____

maul (4) _____

magazine (5) _____

prizer (6) _____

lament (10) _____

10. List at least three values that Bradstreet's father had. Indicate the line or lines that tell you this.

   _____

   _____

   _____

11. What line indicates that her father was a source of valuable information about events?

   _____

12. Did he treat all people the same? Indicate the line or lines that tell you this.

   _____

   _____

13. Who or what are the "good" and the "bad" in line 8?

   _____

   _____

14. Paraphrase the epitaph's last two lines.

   _____

   _____

15. Which epitaph do you prefer? Why?

   _____

   _____

158   SITTING THERE

The following eleven-line poem was written by the poet as he sat on a park bench near the water. Read the poem several times; once you think you have a good understanding of what it says, answer the questions on the lines provided.

The sun reflects, like a flame across the river.
Haze creeps over Jersey's apartments and buildings.
Sailboats bob in the water's gentle waves.
Joggers compete with cyclists and skaters along the gravel path.
Dogs skillfully maneuver the grasses and bushes.   5
Couples hand in hand stroll the shoreline.
Older people chat and reminisce on the wooden benches.
The tugboats churn their way upstream.
A homeless man rummages the garbage for what he can use.
Jersey beckons across the way.   10
Another early Saturday evening along the Hudson.

1. Which lines contain nature images? _____

2. Which line contains a simile? _____

3. Which lines contain personification? _____

4. Which verb in the poem means "move jerkily up and down"? _____

5. Which verb means "physically move through something"? _____

6. Which verb means "think about the past"? _____

7. Which verb means "stir up"? _____

8. Which verb means "search through by moving the contents around"?

   _____

9. Which direction is the poet facing? _____

10. What is the "Hudson"? _____

11. What is the poet's purpose in the poem? _____

159   WHEATLEY'S WAY

Phillis Wheatley was born in Africa in 1753 or 1754. When she was eight years old, she was kidnapped and brought to Boston, Massachusetts. There, in 1761, John Wheatley bought her as a personal servant for his wife, Susanna. John and Susanna gave Phillis their last name, Wheatley, which was the custom of the time. An intelligent youngster, Phillis learned English, Latin, ancient history, mythology, and classical literature quite quickly. She took to writing poetry and was very good at this craft.

Read Wheatley's poem, "On Being Brought from Africa to America." Then answer the questions on the lines provided.

> ### *On Being Brought from Africa to America*
> 'Twas mercy brought me from my Pagan land,
> Taught my benighted soul to understand
> That there's a God, that there's a Saviour too:
> Once I redemption neither sought nor knew,
> Some view our sable race with scornful eye,   5
> "Their colour is a diabolic die."
> Remember, Christians, Negroes, black as Cain,
> May be refin'd, and join th' angelic train.

1. Which word in line 1 means "having no religion"? _____

2. Which word in line 2 means "obscured," "uninformed," or "not intelligent"?
   _____

3. What continent is referred to as a "Pagan land"? _____

4. What word in line 5 means "black"? _____

5. Which word in line 5 means "dishonorable" or "not worthy of respect"?
   _____

6. Which word in this poem means "satanic" or "devil-like"? _____

7. Which biblical figure is mentioned in this poem? _____

8. Which word in line 1 is personified? _____

9. Is the overall tone of this poem optimistic, pessimistic, or neutral?
   _____

10. Cite three religious references in the poem: _____
    _____.

160 POET WILLIAM WORDSWORTH

William Wordsworth was a British poet who was born in 1780 and died in 1850. The following lines from his poetry contrast two different time periods in this life. Read the lines, and then answer the questions that follow them. Write the answer code for each question in the blank next to the question number. When you are done, discuss the poem with your classmates.

There was a time when meadow, grove, and stream,
The earth, and every common sight,
To me did seem
Apparelled in celestial light,
The glory and the freshness of a dream.   5
It is not now as it hath been of yore;—
Turn wheresoe'er I may,
By night or day.
The things which I have seen I now can see no more.

The Rainbow comes and goes,   10
And lovely is the Rose,
The Moon doth with delight
Look round her when the heavens are bare,
Waters on a starry night
Are beautiful and fair;   15
The sunshine is a glorious birth;
But yet I know, where'er I go,
That there hath past away a glory from the earth.

Reading Comprehension in Language Arts Classes

160   POET WILLIAM WORDSWORTH *(continued)*

1. _____ The word *apparelled* in line 4 means **(a)** dressed **(b)** outlived **(c)** depressed
   (d) thought.

2. _____ Which line marks a transition between the past and the present?
   (a) line 5 **(b)** line 6 **(c)** line 7 **(d)** line 8

3. _____ Which two lines rhyme?
   (a) lines 1 and 6 **(b)** lines 5 and 7 **(c)** lines 2 and 4 **(d)** lines 3 and 8

4. _____ Which of the following is given human qualities?
   (a) dream (line 5) **(b)** night (line 8) **(c)** Rose (line 11) **(d)** Moon (line 12)

5. _____ Which lines are more pessimistic (looking on the negative side of life) than optimistic
   (looking on the bright side of life)?
   (a) lines 12 and 13 **(b)** lines 9 and 18 **(c)** lines 1–4 **(d)** lines 14 and 15

6. _____ The poem's message is primarily that **(a)** nature is scary **(b)** humans have destroyed
   much of nature **(c)** things do not always remain the same **(d)** rainbows can be deceiving.

7. _____ Each section of a poem is called **(a)** a paragraph **(b)** an essay **(c)** a simile
   (d) a stanza.

8. _____ The apostrophe in the contracted words found in lines 7 and 17 takes the place of
   what letter? **(a)** *l* **(b)** *m* **(c)** *v* **(d)** *t*

9. _____ Which line indicates the lack of stars?
   (a) line 13 **(b)** line 4 **(c)** line 14 **(d)** line 18

10. _____ Which two lines indicate newness?
    (a) lines 2 and 4 **(b)** lines 5 and 16 **(c)** lines 9 and 18 **(d)** lines 3 and 14

ANSWER KEY

1 HOW QUICK ARE YOU?

1. B	6. C	11. A	16. A	21. D
2. A	7. A	12. D	17. B	22. A
3. D	8. B	13. D	18. D	23. D
4. D	9. C	14. C	19. C	24. B
5. C	10. B	15. C	20. B	25. B

2 SOUNDING LIKE WHICH OTHER?

Group One	Group Two	Group Three
A. 2	A. 3	A. 2
B. 3	B. 1	B. 2
C. 2	C. 2	C. 3
D. 2	D. 3	D. 2
E. 3	E. 3	E. 3
Total: 12	Total: 12	Total: 12

3 WHAT A DIFFERENCE ONE LETTER MAKES!

1. pond	6. frame	11. irked	16. others
2. beast	7. thyme	12. thread	17. spurt
3. jelly	8. billow	13. report	18. gist
4. tried	9. viper	14. changes	19. Dell
5. window	10. seminar	15. grime	20. needed

4 ONE LETTER DOES IT

1. o (loose)	7. b (babble)	14. p (wrapping)
2. m (committees)	8. i (This)	15. a (bazaar)
3. e (gruesome)	9. s (mysteries)	16. n (announcements)
4. l (Halloween)	10. c (recommendation)	17. c (occasion)
5. e (deceive)	11. u (vacuum)	18. a (spectacular)
6. t (congratulate)	12. i (negligence)	19. k (picnicking)
	13. t (writing)	20. e (essential)

The three words are OMELET, BISCUIT, and PANCAKE.

5 LOOKING FOR POLES

1. n	6. t	11. m	16. t	21. s
2. o	7. o	12. a	17. i	22. h
3. r	8. t	13. g	18. c	23. i
4. t	9. e	14. n	19. f	24. n
5. h	10. m	15. e	20. i	25. g

There are four poles: the NORTH, TOTEM, MAGNETIC, and FISHING poles!

6 SPELLING CAN BE MUCH FUN

1. s	5. l	9. c	13. e	17. h
2. p	6. i	10. a	14. m	18. f
3. e	7. n	11. n	15. u	19. u
4. l	8. g	12. b	16. c	20. n

The sentence is SPELLING CAN BE MUCH FUN.

7 USAMNERBLC HET URNIENDELD WRDO

1. never	6. rusty	11. advance
2. bushels	7. complete	12. sneaked
3. snowstorm	8. rumbled, hissed	13. agile
4. dismal	9. glance	14. lesson
5. revolver	10. Think	15. idly

8 MISSING LETTERS

1. The little boy was quietly walking down the street.

2. No man is an island.

3. A new program will air tonight at seven o'clock.

4. My family loves to talk about politics at the dinner table.

5. Her oldest son is very tall.

6. The latest peace treaty will be signed next week.

7. The current problem involves many of these factors.

8. My best friend has three sisters.

9. Despite the fact that he had been arrested twice before, the culprit denied any association with the crime.

10. There are different kinds of penalties for different offenses.

9 SWEET SIXTEEN WITH PLURALS

Group One	Group Two	Group Three	Group Four
A. 3	F. 4	K. 4	P. 2
B. 5	G. 3	L. 4	Q. 4
C. 2	H. 3	M. 1	R. 3
D. 1	I. 2	N. 3	S. 2
E. 5	J. 4	O. 4	T. 5
Total: 16	Total: 16	Total: 16	Total: 16

10 CONQUERING CLAUSES

1. (L) To get into the locked building, we needed to find the custodian who had the keys.

2. (D) If you need help with these math problems, ask Mrs. Jenkins, our teacher, to assist you.

3. (A) After Juanita scored the winning goal, the crowd erupted with loud applause.

4. (F) Having smoked cigarettes for more than fifty years, she developed lung cancer and died last June.

5. (B) Because he misplaced his wallet yesterday, Mr. Borritan spent two hours looking for it today.

6. (I) Here is the flower arrangement that we ordered over the phone last week.

7. (E) If you would like to be a contestant on that television quiz show, you need to send in your application this week.

8. (K) Whenever Monica sits for a math test, she becomes anxious and need to take a deep breath.

9. (G) We quickly perceived that all the seats in the first ten rows were taken.

10. (C) As he crouched to fan the fire, the camper began to hear noises from the nearby woods.

11. (J) If you select the six correct numbers in the lottery, you will win $1 million a year for life.

12. (H) The ticket that the traffic officer handed him carried a fine of $100.

11 FINDING SUCCESS WITH ANALOGIES

A = 11	B = 22	C = 18	D = 9	E = 5
F = 8	G = 4	H = 15	I = 21	J = 17
K = 25	L = 16	M = 7	N = 3	O = 14
P = 2	Q = 13	R = 24	S = 20	T = 6
U = 19	V = 10	W = 1	X = 12	Y = 23

Magic Number: 65

12 REASON IT OUT

1. an	4. yq	7. io	10. ec	13. en
2. al	5. ue	8. ns	11. ha	14. gi
3. og	6. st	9. ar	12. ll	15. ng

The thirty letters spell out ANALOGY QUESTIONS ARE CHALLENGING.

13 PERFECTING PREFIXES (PART ONE)

A = 4	B = 15	C = 10	D = 5
E = 6	F = 9	G = 16	H = 3
I = 13	J = 2	K = 7	L = 12
M = 11	N = 8	O = 1	P = 14

Magic Number: 34

14 PERFECTING PREFIXES (PART TWO)

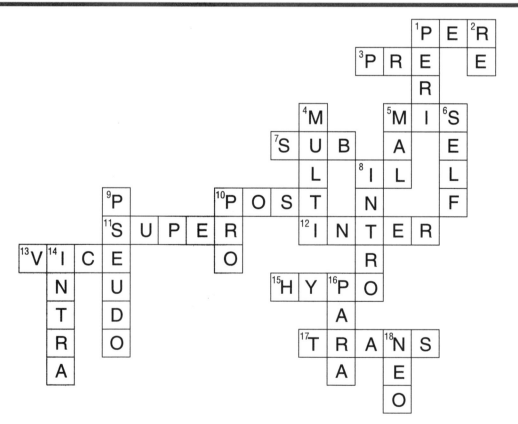

15 NUMBER AND SIZE PREFIXES

A = 12	B = 13	C = 1	D = 8
E = 6	F = 3	G = 15	H = 10
I = 7	J = 2	K = 14	L = 11
M = 9	N = 16	O = 4	P = 5

Magic Number: 34

16 COUNTING WITH PREFIXES

1. one	4. eight	7. four	10. four	13. one
2. ten	5. three	8. one	11. two	14. ten
3. three	6. five	9. six	12. seventh	15. one

17 BY THE NUMBERS

1. at	4. io	7. es	10. wo	13. he
2. te	5. nl	8. om	11. so	14. ig
3. nt	6. on	9. et	12. me	15. ht

The four words are ATTENTION, LONESOME, TWOSOME, and HEIGHT. (The numbers in them are underlined.)

18 FLYING HIGH

1. pa	4. sp	7. ww	10. ov	13. le
2. rr	5. ar	8. re	11. ee	14. ha
3. ot	6. ro	9. nd	12. ag	15. wk

The six birds are the PARROT, the SPARROW, the WREN, the DOVE, the EAGLE, and the HAWK.

19 LET'S PARTY

1. de	5. sr	9. ca	13. pe
2. mo	6. ep	10. ns	14. nd
3. cr	7. ub	11. in	15. en
4. at	8. li	12. de	16. ts

The three words associated with parties are DEMOCRATS, REPUBLICANS, and INDEPENDENTS.

20 ALL IN THE FAMILY

1. he	4. oo	7. kp	10. ba	13. df
2. rd	5. dp	8. ri	11. nd	14. lo
3. br	6. ac	9. de	12. po	15. ck

The groups are the HERD, the BROOD, the PACK, the PRIDE, the BAND, the POD, and the FLOCK.

21 PUNCTUATE IT

1. co	4. er	7. as	10. he	13. ic
2. mm	5. io	8. hh	11. ns	14. ol
3. ap	6. dd	9. yp	12. em	15. on

The five "punctuate it" tools are the COMMA, the PERIOD, the DASH, the HYPHEN, and the SEMICOLON.

22 AROUND THE WORLD

1. nai	4. got	7. del	10. lcu	13. saw
2. rob	5. áph	8. phi	11. tta	14. cit
3. ibo	6. ila	9. aca	12. war	15. ies

The five names are NAIROBI (Kenya), BOGOTÁ (Colombia), PHILADELPHIA (United States), CALCUTTA (India), and WARSAW (Poland). All are CITIES.

23 ROLLIN' ON THE RIVER

1. fe	4. ac	7. ip	10. hy	13. ek
2. rr	5. ht	8. di	11. ca	14. ay
3. yy	6. sh	9. ng	12. no	15. ak

The six things that are "rollin' on the river" are a FERRY, a YACHT, a SHIP, a DINGHY, a CANOE, and a KAYAK.

24 TO AND FRO

1. at	4. ro	7. er	10. ic	13. [1]fr
2. on	5. mt	8. [2]fr	11. to	14. os
3. ef	6. ow	9. ol	12. ll	15. ty

The six *to* and *fro* words are A<u>TONE</u>, <u>FROM</u>, <u>TOWER</u>, <u>FROL</u>IC, <u>TOLL</u>, and <u>FROST</u>Y. (The words in them are underlined.)

25 OUT IN THE WOODS

1. bi	4. lm	7. es	10. pe	13. ca
2. rc	5. cy	8. so	11. ar	14. mo
3. he	6. pr	9. ak	12. sy	15. re

The six types of things you might find out in the woods are BIRCH, ELM, CYPRESS, OAK, PEAR, and SYCAMORE (trees).

26 RUNNING RAMPANT WITH ROOTS (PART ONE)

A = 6	B = 2	C = 13	D = 24	E = 20
F = 14	G = 25	H = 16	I = 7	J = 3
K = 17	L = 8	M = 4	N = 15	O = 21
P = 5	Q = 11	R = 22	S = 18	T = 9
U = 23	V = 19	W = 10	X = 1	Y = 12

Magic Number: 65

27 RUNNING RAMPANT WITH ROOTS (PART TWO)

believe (cred)	equal (equi)	pleasing (grat)	tooth (dent)
bend (flex)	faith, trust (fid)	run (cur)	trick (fall)
blood (hemo)	hard, lasting (dur)	say, speak (dic)	wheel, circular (cycl)
break (fract)	heavy, weighty (grav)	skin (derm)	write, written (graph)
different (hetero)	lead (duc)	sleep (dorm)	
earth (geo)	marriage (gam)	step, go (grad)	
end (fin)	people (dem)	strong (fort)	

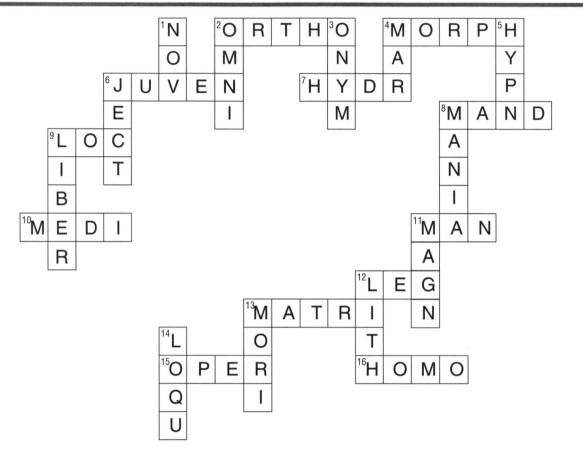

29 RUNNING RAMPANT WITH ROOTS (PART FOUR)

A = 2	B = 15	C = 17	D = 23	E = 8
F = 10	G = 22	H = 1	I = 20	J = 12
K = 21	L = 19	M = 13	N = 7	O = 5
P = 14	Q = 6	R = 25	S = 4	T = 16
U = 18	V = 3	W = 9	X = 11	Y = 24

Magic Number: 65

30 SETTLING IN WITH SUFFIXES (PART ONE)

A = 13	B = 3	C = 6	D = 12
E = 8	F = 10	G = 15	H = 1
I = 11	J = 5	K = 4	L = 14
M = 2	N = 16	O = 9	P = 7

Magic Number: 34

31 SETTLING IN WITH SUFFIXES (PART TWO)

A = 2	B = 3	C = 15	D = 14
E = 13	F = 16	G = 4	H = 1
I = 8	J = 5	K = 9	L = 12
M = 11	N = 10	O = 6	P = 7

Magic Number: 34

32 PUTTING WORDS TOGETHER

1. f	5. t	9. a	13. e	17. o
2. i	6. s	10. c	14. n	18. w
3. g	7. q	11. k	15. d	19. b
4. h	8. u	12. m	16. r	20. y

The six-letter word is FIGHTS.

The five-letter word is QUACK.

The four-letter word is MEND.

The three-letter word is ROW.

The two-letter word is BY.

33 IDIOMATICALLY SPEAKING (PART ONE)

A = 12	B = 13	C = 1	D = 8
E = 6	F = 3	G = 15	H = 10
I = 7	J = 2	K = 14	L = 11
M = 9	N = 16	O = 4	P = 5

Magic Number: 34

34 IDIOMATICALLY SPEAKING (PART TWO)

A = 1	B = 15	C = 8	D = 10
E = 4	F = 14	G = 5	H = 11
I = 13	J = 3	K = 12	L = 6
M = 16	N = 2	O = 9	P = 7

Magic Number: 34

35 A FEATHER IN YOUR CAP

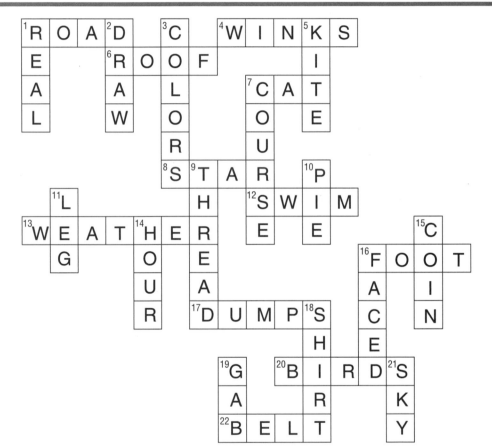

36 EXPRESSING YOURSELF

1. on
2. ce
3. in
4. ab
5. lu
6. em
7. oo
8. nb
9. ut
10. te
11. rs
12. om
13. eo
14. ne
15. up

The two expressions are ONCE IN A BLUE MOON (not very often) and BUTTER SOMEONE UP (flatter someone).

37   ACCORDING TO FORBES

1. to	4. ur	7. ma	10. su	13. sh
2. me	5. et	8. nm	11. re	14. [2]ea
3. as	6. he	9. [1]ea	12. hi	15. rt

The quote from Malcolm Forbes is "To measure the man, measure his heart."

38   POSITIVELY—OR NEGATIVELY—SPEAKING

Positive	Negative
1. d	2. d
4. e	3. i
6. t	5. a
7. e	8. b
10. r	9. o
13. m	11. l
14. i	12. i
17. n	15. c
18. e	16. a
20. d	19. l

The answers for the positive adjectives spell DETERMINED.

The answers for the negative adjectives spell DIABOLICAL.

39   FOR THE BIRDS

1. l	5. w	9. h	13. d	17. g
2. a	6. r	10. a	14. o	18. u
3. r	7. e	11. w	15. v	19. l
4. k	8. n	12. k	16. e	20. l

The names of the five birds are LARK, WREN, HAWK, DOVE, and GULL.

40 CONSTRUCTING FIFTEEN WORDS

1. disgrace
2. unfortunately
3. nevertheless
4. fundamental
5. international

6. insanity
7. replacement
8. malnourished
9. daydreaming
10. carelessness

11. console
12. dominate
13. championship
14. whatsoever
15. quarterback

41 WHERE WORDS COME FROM

A = 4	B = 15	C = 10	D = 5
E = 6	F = 9	G = 16	H = 3
I = 13	J = 2	K = 7	L = 12
M = 11	N = 8	O = 1	P = 14

Magic Number: 34

42 AMERICANISMS

1. u
2. n
3. d

4. e
5. r
6. p

7. r
8. i
9. v

10. i
11. l
12. e

13. g
14. e
15. d

The word introduced into the English language in 1896 is UNDERPRIVILEGED.

43 MULTIPLE MEANINGS

1. iron
2. perform
3. capital

4. index
5. project
6. body

7. receive
8. bottom
9. rose

10. curl
11. proof
12. digest

44 THE HIDDEN TITLE

1. a
2. r
3. a

4. i
5. s
6. i

7. n
8. i
9. n

10. t
11. h
12. e

13. s
14. u
15. n

The name of the play is *A RAISIN IN THE SUN*.

45   MATCHING THE WORDS

A = 4	B = 6	C = 11	D = 13
E = 9	F = 15	G = 2	H = 8
I = 14	J = 12	K = 5	L = 3
M = 7	N = 1	O = 16	P = 10

Magic Number: 34

46   MUSIC TO YOUR EARS

1. ob	4. ar	7. or	10. ui	13. ru
2. oe	5. in	8. ga	11. ta	14. mp
3. cl	6. et	9. ng	12. rt	15. et

The five things that can bring music to your ears **are the** OBOE, the CLARINET, the ORGAN, the GUITAR, and the TRUMPET.

47   WISE WORDS IN OTHER WORDS

1. lov	4. ^{2}ndt	7. one	10. ^{1}ndt	13. tfo
2. eis	5. ime	8. yti	11. ide	14. rno
3. bli	6. ism	9. mea	12. wai	15. man

The three adages are LOVE IS BLIND, TIME IS **MONEY**, and TIME AND TIDE WAIT FOR NO MAN.

48   CEASE TO ERR

A = 2	B = 15	C = 17	D = 23	E = 8
F = 10	G = 22	H = 1	I = 20	J = 12
K = 21	L = 19	M = 13	N = 7	O = 5
P = 14	Q = 6	R = 25	S = 4	T = 16
U = 18	V = 3	W = 9	X = 11	Y = 24

Magic Number: 65

49   MEET AT THE RIGHT PAIR

A = 11	B = 22	C = 18	D = 9	E = 5
F = 8	G = 4	H = 15	I = 21	J = 17
K = 25	L = 16	M = 7	N = 3	O = 14
P = 2	Q = 13	R = 24	S = 20	T = 6
U = 19	V = 10	W = 1	X = 12	Y = 23

Magic Number: 65

50   INTERESTING A READER FROM THE START

These are suggested answers . Students may argue their own answers.

1. C	4. G	7. D	10. E	13. F
2. B	5. C	8. A	11. B	14. D
3. G	6. A	9. E	12. F	

51   UNLOCKING THE IMPORTANT WORDS

Answers will vary.

52   CREATING THE MOOD

Answers will vary.

53   JUST THE FACTS, PLEASE!

1. O	4. F	7. O	10. F	13. F
2. O	5. F	8. O	11. O	14. F
3. F	6. O	9. F	12. O	15. O

The quotation is "Get your facts first, and then you can distort them as much as you please."
—MT (Mark Twain)

54   LOOKING FOR CLUES

1. a	4. c	7. c	10. c	13. a
2. a	5. c	8. c	11. b	14. a
3. b	6. a	9. b	12. b	15. b

55   TONING UP THE TONE

Answers will vary.

56   THE LONG DAY

Answers will vary.

57   TWO BY TWO

1. old, renovation
2. reaction, enthusiastic
3. paunchy, memorable
4. considered, amnesty
5. failed, haunt

6. deposits, geologists
7. grasp, nervously
8. protesters, convince
9. police, mourners
10. tribute, fallen

11. caterpillar, crawled
12. sound, newcomer
13. flight, discontinued
14. rates, bills
15. freely, water

58   WHAT WORDS ARE MISSING?

Possible answers are given here, underlined. Students' answers will vary.

1. Unaware of the storm, the fisherman seemed to enjoy the fishing during the early morning hours.
2. Eager and restless, the third-grade students hurried out of their classroom to enjoy recess.
3. A bit anxious awaiting the doctor's arrival, the patient thought about the possible results of his blood tests.
4. As we sit here looking out at the sea, we remember that we are very lucky.
5. Remind the children to enjoy themselves during the fireworks later this evening.
6. Ronnie sipped the coffee that his wife had made for him earlier that night.
7. The host comes into the main hall ready to greet the visitors.
8. Smith is a lawyer who got rich by manipulating many of his clients.
9. Criticized as cranky and impatient, the candidate is certainly not as strong as many people would think.
10. Juanita, who will attend the meeting, is studying the report.
11. Some of the members spoke before the audience at last night's meeting.
12. Judging from your background, I would agree that you are a good candidate.

59   MONEY, MONEY, MONEY

1. sailors, deck
2. teacher, specific
3. opinionated, view
4. cheetahs, elephants
5. kangaroo, baby

6. strong, granite
7. burrowed, dirt
8. often, scary
9. necessarily, only
10. dutifully, camp

11. systematically, components
12. colors, resin
13. avidly, favorite
14. scholarship, job
15. harried, motorist

The three words related to money are STOCKS, BONDS, and CASH.

60   SENTENCE CLUES

1. microwave
2. abandoned
3. stretcher
4. gourmet
5. anxiety

6. wrest
7. commissioned
8. chestnut
9. eventually
10. robust

11. gruesome
12. or
13. imply
14. smuggle
15. nostalgia

61   FILLING THEM IN

1. hours, explosion, extinguish
2. missing, intended, ricocheted
3. colorful, roadway, trotted
4. understand, concepts, aspects
5. botanist, acknowledged, existence
6. shouldered, burden, crisis
7. astute, solved, minutes
8. hair, shrimp, affair

9. problems, mentor, crucial
10. carefully, sliver, knee
11. anxiety, assure, sedated
12. engaged, delicate, wits
13. ramifications, actions, heed
14. character, novel, heroine
15. established, based, year

62   FILLING IN THE BLANKS

1. into
2. reverberating
3. builders
4. satisfied
5. he

6. despite
7. after
8. neither
9. placid
10. befuddled

11. wonderment
12. gratified
13. commander
14. themselves
15. resounding

16. breathtaking
17. numb
18. expertly
19. magician
20. persuasive

63 IMPROVING SENTENCES

1. F	4. S	7. R	10. G	13. M
2. E	5. T	8. O	11. J	14. P
3. A	6. W	9. N	12. U	15. Y

The three five-letter words are FEAST, WRONG, and JUMPY.

64 COMPLETING THE THOUGHTS

Answers will vary.

65 CAUSE AND EFFECT

Students may wish to debate these answers. The sentences not shown here are statements of fact.

1. [Theodore bought a new car] <u>after his old one was totaled in an accident.</u>

4. <u>Because there were only five tickets to the opera,</u> [you and I will be forced to stay home.]

5. <u>Due to inclement weather,</u> [our trip to the park will be postponed until tomorrow.]

6. <u>Having fallen victim to a disease,</u> [this apple tree will have to be cut down and destroyed.]

9. [Vivian had no time to go back to the cafeteria,] <u>for her class was starting in less than a minute.</u>

10. [My sister is always happy] <u>whenever Mom is cooking a steak dinner.</u>

12. <u>The machine's incessant noise</u> [forced us to keep our windows closed.]

13. <u>The wind was blowing so furiously</u> [that the sunbathers were unable to open their umbrellas.]

66 CAUSE AND EFFECT, HISTORICALLY SPEAKING

1. T	3. U	5. A	7. P	9. L
2. R	4. M	6. N	8. O	10. K

The famous names in U.S. history are TRUMAN and POLK, former U.S. presidents.

67 WHAT IS THE NEXT LINE?

1. sta	2. ple	3. rpe	4. npa	5. per	6. bin	7. der

The four items found on a desk are a STAPLER, a PEN, PAPER, and a BINDER.

68 ANTICIPATING WHAT HAPPENS NEXT

Answers will vary.

69 SORTING THINGS OUT

Article 1: (1) se (2) aw (3) at (4) er: seawater

Article 2: (1) di (2) al (3) ec (4) [1]ts: dialects

Article 3: (1) hy (2) dr (3) an (4) [2]ts: hydrants

Article 4: (1) ju (2) gg (3) le (4) rs: jugglers

Article 5: (1) co (2) ng (3) re (4) ss: Congress

70 GIVING DIRECTIONS

1. east and south
2. Queens
3. Nassau and Suffolk
4. Sagtikos Parkway
5. the right fork
6. Southern State Parkway
7. two
8. three
9. tall water tower
10. left

71 FIXING A FLAT

The correct order is 10, 3, 8, 14, 1, 11, 2, 7, 12, 9, 4, 5, 6, 13.

72 CELLULAR PROBLEMS

Answers may vary slightly.

1. She has owned the phone for two weeks.
2. The problems include static, a faulty message function, and the ringer and vibrator.
3. *Inaudible* means "unable to be heard."
4. *Garbled* means "distorted" or "unclear."
5. *Via* means "by way of."
6. The first paragraph introduces the phone situation. The second paragraph addresses the static problem. The third paragraph covers the message function. The fourth discusses the ringer and vibrator problem. The concluding paragraph suggests how the problems might be resolved.
7. Transition words include *When* and *Therefore* in the first paragraph; *First* and *And* in the second; *Another, At other times,* and *Unfortunately* in the third; and *other* in the fourth. (There may be more.)

73   HEARING IT IN CLASS

1. S	6. D	11. E	16. A	21. E
2. T	7. T	12. D	17. T	22. T
3. A	8. A	13. E	18. E	23. E
4. T	9. S	14. S	19. S	24. S
5. E	10. T	15. T	20. D	25. T

The four words are STATED, TASTED, ESTATES, and DETEST.

74   WHERE HAVE ALL THE VOWELS GONE? (MATH)

1. angle	6. equal	11. quotient	16. zero
2. triangle	7. numerator	12. polygon	17. algebra
3. bisect	8. divide	13. sequence	18. number
4. rectangle	9. multiply	14. square	19. digits
5. formula	10. exponent	15. polynomial	20. million

75   ELEMENTARY ALGEBRA COMPREHENSION

1. c	5. c	9. c
2. a	6. d	10. b
3. d	7. a	
4. d	8. c	

76   WORD PROBLEMS

1. Reggie is eight, and Molly is four.
2. 100 acres
3. two quarters, three pennies, and one nickel
4. sixteen games
5. nine minutes
6. twenty weeks
7. twenty fishermen
8. three hundred games
9. eighteen hours
10. b

77   THE LAW OF AVERAGES

1. a	5. b	9. a
2. d	6. b	10. a
3. a	7. a	
4. b	8. a	

78   WHERE HAVE ALL THE VOWELS GONE? (SCIENCE)

1. heart	6. alloy	11. cell	16. element
2. artery	7. convex	12. cardiac	17. molecule
3. reptile	8. oxygen	13. atom	18. gene
4. calorie	9. carnivore	14. biology	19. muscle
5. proton	10. blood	15. energy	20. lung

79   GHOSTS

A = 4	B = 6	C = 11	D = 13
E = 9	F = 15	G = 2	H = 8
I = 14	J = 12	K = 5	L = 3
M = 7	N = 1	O = 16	P = 10

Magic Number: 34

80   VAMPIRES

1. d	5. e	9. d
2. c	6. d	10. c
3. e	7. a	
4. a	8. b	

81 PHOBIAS

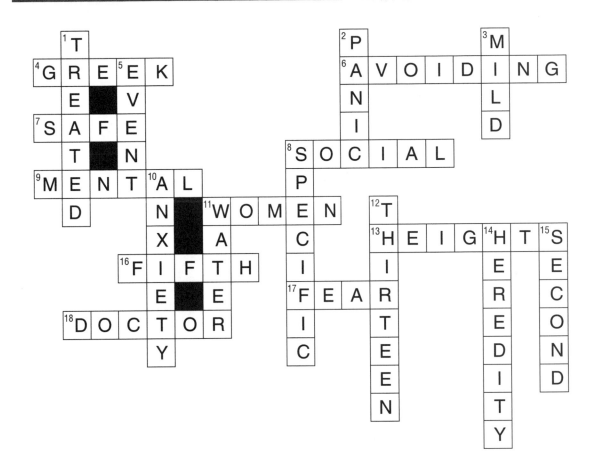

82 ANOREXIA NERVOSA

The true answers are 1, 2, 4, 5, 9, and 10. They spell out PSYCHIATRIST.

The false answers are 3, 6, 7, 8, 11, and 12. They spell out PHYSIOLOGIST.

83 CROCODILES

1. species
2. stalk
3. dangerous
4. careless
5. years

6. fast
7. powerful
8. razor-sharp
9. tearing
10. escaping

11. shut
12. ambush
13. rush
14. predators
15. food

16. appearance
17. top-level
18. environment
19. killing
20. sharks

84 THE TRUTH ABOUT SNAKES

All fifteen statements are true!

85 BATS

1. few
2. bites
3. humans
4. unreasonable

5. teeth
6. felt
7. sequester
8. control

9. analyzed
10. outside

86 SALAMANDERS

1. amphibian
2. slender
3. short
4. long
5. moist

6. habitats
7. forest
8. aquatic
9. lizards
10. scales

11. limbs
12. ponds
13. Northern
14. feet
15. weigh

87 SHARKS

1. olfactory
2. barbels
3. dark
4. smell

5. electrical
6. plankton
7. shallow
8. retreat

9. blood
10. sandpaper

88 RAIN FORESTS

1. b
2. d
3. c
4. a
5. b
6. c
7. a
8. d
9. b
10. c

89 GLOBAL WARMING

1. d
2. b.
3. c.
4. d.
5. a.
6. d.
7. c
8. b
9. a
10. a

90 ECOTOURISM

1. environmental
2. develop gradually
3. twentieth
4. responsible
5. impact

6. involvement
7. vibrant
8. sensitize
9. the United States
10. major

11. irresponsible
12. native
13. Australia
14. controversy
15. harm

91 TORNADOES

1. ap
2. pa
3. re
4. nt
5. te

6. mp
7. er
8. at
9. ur
10. ed

11. if
12. fe
13. re
14. nc
15. es

The three-word phrase associated with tornadoes is APPARENT TEMPERATURE DIFFERENCES.

92 BURNS

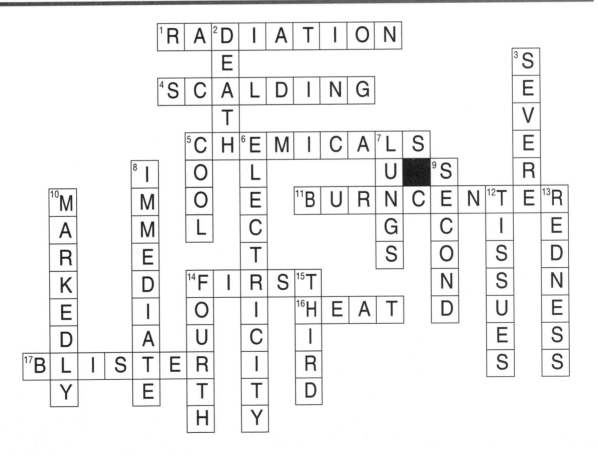

93 CAVING

1. b	3. b	5. b	7. a	9. b
2. c	4. b	6. c	8. a	10. a

94 FRICTION

1. resistive	6. left	11. melt
2. together	7. Static	12. lubricant
3. deformation	8. Kinetic	13. acoustic
4. heat	9. Rolling	14. vibration
5. opposes	10. worn	15. tank

95 THE GOLDEN GATE BRIDGE

A = 4	B = 6	C = 11	D = 13
E = 9	F = 15	G = 2	H = 8
I = 14	J = 12	K = 5	L = 3
M = 7	N = 1	O = 16	P = 10

Magic Number: 34

96 KRAKATOA

A = 7	B = 11	C = 6	D = 10
E = 14	F = 2	G = 15	H = 3
I = 12	J = 8	K = 9	L = 5
M = 1	N = 13	O = 4	P = 16

Magic Number: 34

97 THE TUNGUSKA EVENT

1. eu	3. si	5. pa	7. el	9. ro
2. ra	4. as	6. rs	8. yb	10. ke

The words are EURASIA, SPARSELY, and BROKE.

98   THE MILGRAM EXPERIMENT

All the statements are true!

99   THE FUTURE OF THE CRASH TEST DUMMY

1. b	3. b	5. b	7. c	9. c
2. d	4. a	6. d	8. d	10. a

100   IVAN PAVLOV

1. saliva	5. whistles	9. English	13. food
2. ear	6. Russian	10. bell	14. reflex
3. Nobel	7. mistranslated	11. eye	15. psychology
4. Moscow	8. stimuli	12. dogs	16. Watson

101   WHERE HAVE ALL THE VOWELS GONE? (SOCIAL STUDIES)

1. plateau	6. Congress	11. preamble	16. govern
2. recall	7. island	12. Constitution	17. leader
3. amendment	8. monopoly	13. vote	18. monarchy
4. president	9. recession	14. republic	19. foreign
5. Senate	10. democracy	15. empire	20. economy

102   COMPARING LINCOLN AND KENNEDY

1. Johnson	6. one hundred
2. the validity of their election	7. one hundred
3. Kennedy	8. the head
4. Friday	9. three
5. South	10. a theater

103   LINCOLN'S GETTYSBURG ADDRESS

1. b	3. b	5. c	7. a	9. c
2. c	4. a	6. b	8. b	10. b

104   CIVIL DISOBEDIENCE

1. a	3. c	5. d	7. a	9. a
2. a	4. b	6. c	8. d	10. a

105   GANDHI'S RULES FOR CIVIL DISOBEDIENCE

1. T	3. T	5. T	7. T	9. F
2. F	4. T	6. T	8. T	10. T

106   AMELIA EARHART, LOST FOREVER (PART ONE)

1. T	3. T	5. T	7. T	9. F
2. F	4. F	6. T	8. T	10. F

107   AMELIA EARHART, LOST FOREVER (PART TWO)

1. F	3. T	5. T	7. F	9. T
2. T	4. F	6. T	8. F	10. T

108   JOHN F . KENNEDY'S INAUGURAL ADDRESS (PART ONE)

1. b	3. b	5. b	7. b	9. b
2. a	4. a	6. c	8. c	10. c

109   JOHN F . KENNEDY'S INAUGURAL ADDRESS (PART TWO)

1. c	3. c	5. a	7. a	9. a
2. c	4. b	6. d	8. d	10. b

110   JOHN F . KENNEDY'S INAUGURAL ADDRESS (PART THREE)

1. d	3. c	5. c	7. a	9. c
2. c	4. b	6. d	8. b	10. b

111　THE BLACK DEATH

1. fle

2. asp

3. ois

4. one

5. dwe

6. lls

7. rat

8. sre

9. fug

10. ees

Four things responsible for the spread of the Black Death were FLEAS, POISONED WELLS, RATS, and REFUGEES.

112　THE TOWER OF LONDON

1. T

2. T

3. F

4. T

5. T

6. F

7. F

8. F

9. T

10. T

11. F

12. T

13. T

14. T

15. F

113　GLADIATORS: ANCIENT WARRIORS (PART ONE)

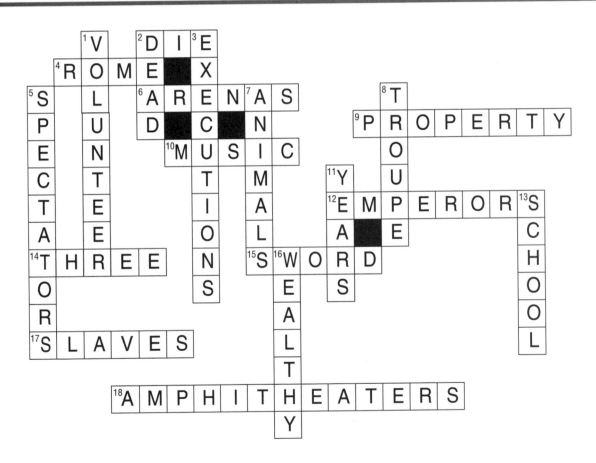

114 GLADIATORS: ANCIENT WARRIORS (PART TWO)

The wording of answers will vary.

1. They were matched one against another. A sponsor or audience could request various combinations.

2. They would point their thumbs in a certain way.

3. He could retire to train other fighters. He was also given a wooden sword as a memento.

4. Socially, they ranked lower than slaves, yet some successful gladiators were treated as celebrities.

5. Many were attracted by the chance to earn money.

6. It acknowledged their slave status and the worst public consideration.

7. No.

8. He pitted female gladiators against dwarfs.

9. Gladiators were deported from Rome and other cities during social disturbances because people feared they might organize and rebel.

10. The final contest took place just over sixteen centuries ago.

115 LEARNING ABOUT MEXICO

1. E	4. A	7. A	10. A or D	13. E
2. E	5. C	8. C	11. A or B	14. B
3. D	6. A	9. D	12. A	15. A

116 ALL ABOUT FRANCE

1. symbol	6. mountains	11. alliance
2. mob	7. economy	12. republic
3. conflict	8. holiday	13. palace
4. topography	9. guillotine	14. capital
5. empire	10. account	15. bankruptcy

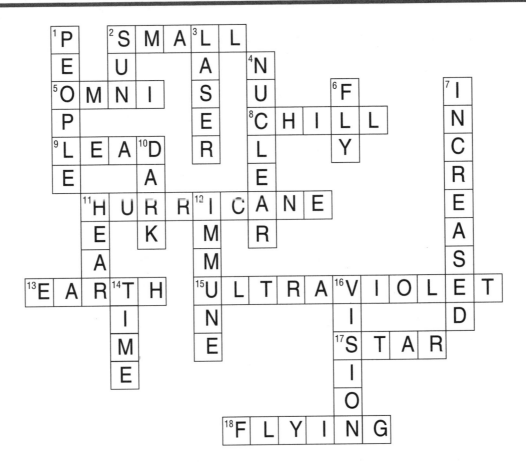

118 RED ADAIR: FIREFIGHTER EXTRAORDINAIRE

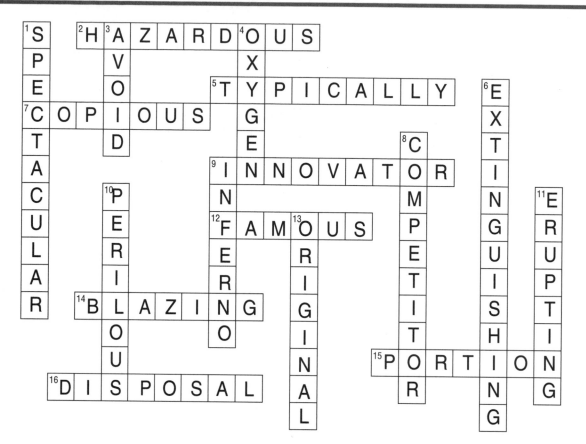

119 HARRY HOUDINI: SUPREME ESCAPE ARTIST

1. ma
2. gi
3. ci
4. an
5. ha

6. nd
7. cu
8. ff
9. sc
10. hi

11. ne
12. se
13. wa
14. te
15. rt

16. or
17. tu
18. re
19. ce
20. ll

The three terms associated with Houdini are MAGICIAN, HANDCUFFS, and CHINESE WATER TORTURE CELL.

120 WALT DISNEY: MORE THAN A CARTOONIST

The wording of answers may vary.

1. film maker, political cartoonist

2. He was not happy with the animated ads that the company he worked for, the Kansas City Film Ad Company, assigned him.

3. They focused on local problems and criticized the local government.

4. live action, animation

5. They were not financially successful.

6. Koko the Clown

7. A live-action character interacted with animal characters in both of these.

8. Disney's team that had created *Alice's Wonderland* went bankrupt.

9. Hollywood

10. $40

121   JACKIE ROBINSON: BARRIER BREAKER (PART ONE)

1. c	5. c	9. Answers will vary.
2. d	6. a	10. Answers will vary.
3. b	7. d	
4. a	8. b	

122   JACKIE ROBINSON: BARRIER BREAKER (PART TWO)

1. e	3. a	5. f	7. c	9. d
2. d	4. c	6. b	8. c	10. a

123   DAVID BECKHAM: SOCCER SENSATION

The wording of answers may vary.

1. England

2. Manchester United

3. 1996

4. long-range free kicks

5. Professional Football Association Young Player of the Year award

6. Beckham scored on a tremendous free kick. He was also disqualified for aiming a kick at Diego Simeone.

7. His disqualifying kick brought Beckham, his family, and his team much trouble and gave the game of soccer a bad name.

8. the player whom Beckham aimed a kick at in the 1998 World Cup

9. World Player of the Year award winner in 2001

10. He broke his foot.

The wording of answers may vary.

1. Liston was the reigning heavyweight champion. He had an impressive winning knockout record. Many other fighters were unwilling to fight him. Ali had lost to Sonny Banks in a previous fight. Liston was a 7-to-1 favorite to win the bout. Ali's pulse rate was 120 beats per minute, a sign that he could have been in bad shape or he was nervous about fighting Liston.

2. Ali had won the gold medal at the 1960 Rome Olympics. He had great hand speed and a lot of confidence.

3. Some people believe that Liston's gloves had petroleum jelly or some other type of ointment on them.

4. Some people think that he did not want to be further embarrassed by Ali.

5. Ali needed surgery before the bout. The fight promoters did not have a license to stage a boxing match in Massachusetts, the original venue.

6. Its location was hard for fans to get to.

7. Some people thought that Liston faked being knocked down by Ali in this "ghost punch fight." Some suspected that Liston threw the fight in order to pay back money that he owed.

8. Yes, the replay shows that he did.

125 LANCE ARMSTRONG: CYCLING CHAMP

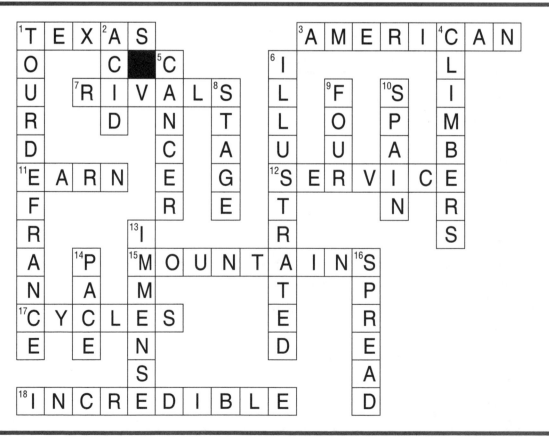

126 BARRY BONDS: BASEBALL'S BOOMER

1. d	3. b	5. c	7. b	9. d
2. c	4. d	6. d	8. b	10. a

127 SIR ELTON JOHN: A MUSICAL LEGEND

1. r	3. c	5. e	7. m	9. n
2. o	4. k	6. t	8. a	10. h

The 1972 hit is "Rocket Man." John's middle initial is H (for Hercules).

128 QUOTATIONS ABOUT LIFE

Answers will vary.

129 THE WORLD OF WORK

A = 10	B = 4	C = 23	D = 17	E = 11
F = 18	G = 12	H = 6	I = 5	J = 24
K = 1	L = 25	M = 19	N = 13	O = 7
P = 14	Q = 8	R = 2	S = 21	T = 20
U = 22	V = 16	W = 15	X = 9	Y = 3

Magic Number: 65

130 THE DEATH PENALTY

1. Y	4. N	7. N	10. N
2. Y	5. N	8. Y	11. N
3. Y	6. N	9. Y	12. Y

131 SEAFORD, LONG ISLAND, NEW YORK

1. c	3. a	5. a	7. c	9. b
2. b	4. a	6. d	8. d	10. a

132 FASHION

1. capitalism
2. diversity
3. uniformity
4. high-status
5. affluent
6. wealth
7. partner
8. subjectivity
9. consultants
10. unisex

133 VIDEO GAMES AND THEIR CRITICS

1. sen
2. ato
3. rjo
4. eli
5. ebe
6. rma
7. nco
8. nne
9. cti
10. cut

One critic of video games is SENATOR JOE LIEBERMAN of CONNECTICUT.

134 SKATEBOARDING

1. b
2. c
3. e
4. a
5. d
6. sidewalk
7. wakeboarding
8. ollie
9. sponsorships
10. style
11. ramp
12. terrain
13. nose
14. elite
15. Drainage

135 HIP-HOP

The wording of answers will vary.

1. Little expense to purchase equipment was necessary; the popularity of disco, funk, and rock music declined in the mid to late 1970s; and social and political events accelerated hip-hop's rise.

2. There was no expectation of recording.

3. They could pair nonsense rhymes. They could tease friends and enemies.

4. teasing

5. It was prepackaged and soulless.

6. The urban audiences enjoyed the danceable beats. Disco also provided a musical outlet.

7. House music arose in Chicago, techno in Detroit, and gogo in Washington, D.C.

8. (Any three will do.) Middle-class white communities left the area. Widespread unemployment among blacks occurred. Stores and factories left the area. Black and Latino gangs grew in power.

9. He is known as the "godfather of hip-hop."

10. Griots are traveling singers and poets in Africa.

136   ETHICS IN PHOTOJOURNALISM

1. T   4. T   7. b
2. F   5. T   8–10. Answers will vary.
3. T   6. T

137   THE 2004 TSUNAMI

1. an underwater earthquake; a volcanic   6. a
   eruption   7. potable
2. Indian   8. c
3. spawned   9. $5 billion
4. one million   10. United Nations
5. bury the dead; prevent an epidemic

138   PYRAMID SCHEMES

1. a   5. b   9. Answers will vary.
2. c   6. b   10. Answers will vary.
3. d   7. c
4. b   8. a

139   THE RIGHT CHOICE

1. c   3. a   5. b   7. a   9. a
2. c   4. c   6. a   8. b   10. c

140   LITERARY TERMS

A = 1	B = 10	C = 19	D = 23	E = 12
F = 18	G = 22	H = 11	I = 5	J = 9
K = 15	L = 4	M = 8	N = 17	O = 21
P = 7	Q = 16	R = 25	S = 14	T = 3
U = 24	V = 13	W = 2	X = 6	Y = 20

Magic Number: 65

141 WHERE HAVE ALL THE VOWELS GONE? (FINE ARTS)

1. music	6. picture	11. singer	16. ballerina
2. portrait	7. brush	12. film	17. choreographer
3. instrument	8. landscape	13. ballet	18. dialogue
4. tune (or tone)	9. melody	14. dance	19. easel
5. painting	10. architect	15. movies	20. opera

142 WHERE HAVE ALL THE VOWELS GONE? (ENGLISH)

1. novel	6. conflict	11. haiku	16. genre
2. biography	7. essay	12. sonnet	17. oxymoron
3. play	8. character	13. ballad	18. idiom
4. drama	9. epic	14. irony	19. personification
5. scene	10. poem	15. narrator	20. simile

143 WHAT IS CHARACTER?

Answers will vary.

144 THE ADVICE COLUMN

Answers will vary.

145 J. K. ROWLING: HARRY POTTER'S CREATOR

1. F	5. T	9. T
2. F	6. F	10. F
3. T	7. T	
4. T	8. F	

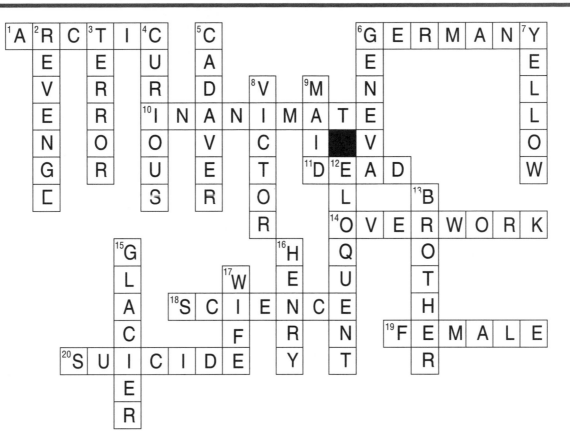

147 A GRADUATION SPEECH

Answers will vary.

148 THE BOY WHO CRIED WOLF

A = 11	B = 13	C = 8	D = 2
E = 4	F = 6	G = 15	H = 9
I = 5	J = 3	K = 10	L = 16
M = 14	N = 12	O = 1	P = 7

Magic Number: 34

149 A DOLL'S HOUSE

1. he	3. sa	5. he	7. so	9. on
2. ap	4. nd	6. ap	8. fm	10. ey

The five-word phrase from this scene is "HEAPS AND HEAPS OF MONEY."

150 PEPYS'S DIARY

1. c	3. n	5. c	7. e	9. c
2. o	4. s	6. i	8. n	10. e

The letters spell out CONSCIENCE.

151 OLD TIMES

1. b	3. b	5. a	7. b	9. c
2. c	4. d	6. d	8. c	10. a

152 MAKING SENSE OF *MACBETH*

These are suggested answers. Students' answers will vary.

1. The repetition conveys a sense of a much longer time than a single *tomorrow* would.
2. It gives the impression of time moving along slowly but relentlessly.
3. "Our past actions have not prevented fools (ourselves) from dying."
4. Brief candle, walking shadow, poor player, tale told by an idiot
5. Negative, demoralized
6. It marks a statement spoken with great emotion.
7. Life is meaningless.
8. Time moves on, and nothing we can do can prevent our dying. Despite the bold things we might do in life, it ultimately amounts to nothing.

153 *ROMEO AND JULIET*

Group One	Group Two
5	6
4	9
3	7
2	8
1	10

154   PROLOGUE TO *ROMEO AND JULIET*

1. ma	3. et	5. th	7. lo	9. ml
2. cb	4. ho	6. el	8. ha	10. et

The names of three other Shakespearean plays are *MACBETH, OTHELLO,* and *HAMLET.*

155   SHAKING THINGS UP WITH SHAKESPEARE

These are possible answers. Students may offer others.

1. depressed, unhappy

2. Words and phrases such as "disgrace with Fortune and men's eyes," "all alone beweep my outcast state," "trouble deaf heaven with my bootless cries," "curse my fate," "wishing me like to one more rich in hope," "deserving this man's art and that man's scope," and "With what I most enjoy contented least."

3. *Yet* (line 9)

4. "My state" is likened to "the lark at break of day arising from sullen earth."

5. "deaf heaven"

6. The harsh *t* sound in "contented least" contributes to the depressing mood.

   Word choices such as "Haply" and "sings hymns at heaven's gate" are uplifting and cheerful.

7. "Then I would hate to exchange my life for the lives that kings live."

8. The mood changes when he thinks about this other person.

9. In lines 3 and 4 the word *and* starts these consecutive sentences. The same is true when *and* is used to show the extent of the poet's condition, as in lines 1, 4, and 7.

10. Lines 3, 9, and 11 have eleven syllables.

156   ELIZABETH BARRETT BROWNING'S "SONNET 43"

1. be	3. yb	5. sl	7. by	9. ss
2. tt	4. es	6. ib	8. be	10. ie

The four names related to Elizabeth are BETTY, BESS, LIBBY, and BESSIE (all nicknames for Elizabeth).

157   BRADSTREET'S EPITAPHS

The following are suggested answers. Students' answers may vary.

1. *matron:* married woman; *pitiful:* full of pity; *oft:* often; *dexterity:* skill

2. Line 2

3. Bradstreet's mother was also a "worthy matron" (line 2), an "obedient wife" (3), a "friendly neighbor" (4), a master of servants (6–7), a "true instructor of the family" (8), and a good citizen (10).

4. The mother used a reward system (line 7).

5. Yes (line10)

6. Yes (lines 11–12)

7. In addition to her being a very positive role model with many outstanding attributes, the mother left her children a "blessed memory" (line 15).

8. The adjectives include *worthy* (line 2), *unspotted* (2), *loving* (3), *obedient* (3), *friendly* (4), *true* (8), and *religious* (12).

9. *patriot:* supporter of one's country; *pious:* religious, virtuous; *maul:* a heavy hammer; *magazine:* storehouse; *prizer:* person who cherishes something; *lament:* feel sorrow

10. Bradstreet's father was a patriot (line 1), was pious, just, and wise (2), held truth and what was right as important concepts (3), was knowledgeable about history (5), enjoyed good company (6), was loved by good people (8), and was missed after he died (10).

11. Line 5

12. No, he did not treat all the same. He was not kind to religious nonconformists (line 4). He could be pleasant or severe (7). When he died, some people were happy, and some were sad (9–10).

13. The "good" and the "bad" were the good and bad people that the father dealt with during this lifetime.

14. "When he died, some people rejoiced but more people were sadden by his death."

15. Answers will vary.

158   SITTING THERE

1. lines 1, 2, 3, 5, 6, 8, and 9

2. line 1

3. lines 2 and 10

4. *bob*

5. *maneuver*

6. *reminisce*

7. *churn*

8. *rummage*

9. east

10. a river

11. Answers will vary.

159 WHEATLEY'S WAY

1. Pagan
2. benighted
3. Africa
4. sable
5. scornful

6. diabolical
7. Cain
8. mercy
9. optimistic
10. God, Saviour, Christians

160 POET WILLIAM WORDSWORTH

1. a	3. c	5. b	7. d	9. a
2. b	4. d	6. c	8. c	10. b

The Vocabulary Teacher's Book of Lists

Edward B. Fry, Ph.D.

Paper   ISBN: 0-7879-7101-4
www.josseybass.com

"Edward Fry has the uncanny ability to take a complex concept—in this case vocabulary—and present it in a form useful to students and teachers."

—Allen Berger, Heckert Professor of Reading and Writing, Miami University

Replete with lists of words, books, teaching strategies, and many other useful tidbits of information related to language and literacy, this book picks up where Dr. Fry's best-selling *Reading Teacher's Book of Lists* leaves off. Its primary focus is on vocabulary improvement for reading and writing.

It contains a comprehensive section on roots and word origins; extensive lists of words used in science, psychology, and literature; and an entire chapter on vocabulary teaching methods and options for curriculum content. Other chapters include spelling, homophones, exonyms, affixes, and specialized subject area terms.

The Vocabulary Teacher's Book of Lists has a special focus on commonly misused words as well as those words that are homophones, homographs, and homonyms—words that are especially troublesome to students at multiple grade levels. This volume provides long lists of these difficult words and each is included in a sentence context.

With a wide variety of levels and lengths, some lists may be appropriate for individual students as extra credit, other lists will help ESL students to master English, and yet other students will use these lists to prepare for college entrance exams.

"Teachers who want to mix test-prep with life-success-prep will welcome *The Vocabulary Teacher's Book of Lists* as an easy-to-use resource for lively lessons. They'll enjoy the wry humor of Dr. Edward Fry's teaching suggestions as he marries word work to wordplay."

—Lee Mountain, professor, curriculum and instruction,
College of Education, University of Houston

Edward B. Fry, Ph.D., is professor emeritus of education at Rutgers University, where for 24 years, he was director of the Reading Center. He is known internationally for his Readability Graph and is the author of many books including co-author of *The Reading Teacher's Book of Lists,* now in its fourth edition from Jossey-Bass.

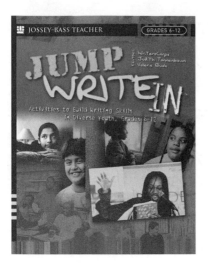

Jump Write In! Creative Writing Exercises for Diverse Communities, Grades 6–12

WritersCorps, edited by Judith Tannenbaum and Valerie Chow Bush

Paper   ISBN: 0-7879-7777-2
www.josseybass.com

Teachers often feel they must choose between using standards-based lessons and offering activities that engage their students' creativity and encourage personal expression. In *Jump Write In!*, however, the experienced teachers from WritersCorps offer numerous exercises that build key standards-based writing skills and also reach out in a meaningful way to all students, particularly at-risk youth.

Through poetry, personal narrative, and essays, students from diverse ethnic, educational, and economic backgrounds will improve their writing skills by accessing their personal voices. Perfect for a moment of improvisation or inspiration, these easy-to-use and field-tested activities can transform any lesson into an opportunity to involve a hard-to-reach student through creative writing.

Each chapter includes

- Dozens of exercises accompanied by teacher notes and suggestions
- Links to standards for each activity
- Examples of student work
- Suggestions for further reading

WritersCorps is an independent program based in San Francisco whose mission is to help children and teens of all ethnic and economic backgrounds improve their literacy and communication skills through creative expression. Founded in 1994 with funding from the National Endowment of the Arts, WritersCorps has helped over 10,000 students. This important achievement was recognized recently when the White House named WritersCorps as one of the two most exemplary programs for at-risk youth. WritersCorps has ties to similar programs in New York City and Washington, D.C. and connections to influential education figures. The WritersCorps website is www.writerscorps.org.

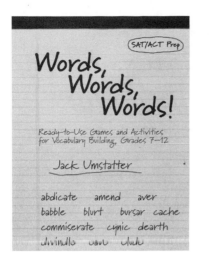

Words, Words, Words: Ready-to-Use Games and Activities for Vocabulary Building, Grades 7–12

Jack Umstatter

Paper   ISBN: 0-7879-7116-2
www.josseybass.com

"*Words, Words, Words* is a student- and teacher-friendly book that incorporates key vocabulary skills in a structured, interesting format. Thematic units, helpful hints, and enjoyable, motivational exercises make this a standout. Umstatter's latest is a great vocabulary book with a sense of humor!"

—Marylou McCullough, director of humanities, West Islip Public School
and former high school English teacher

"Jack Umstatter has created a book filled with meaningful language arts activities. This book can be used as a foundation for a course, for spot lessons, or for remediation. These lessons will engage students and help make learning fun."

—Tom Hall, high school principal, Harvard, Massachusetts

"Jack Umstatter's uniquely engaging word puzzles are not just vocabulary-builders. They invite students to think seriously about the shades of meaning that are so critical to reading comprehension, critical analysis, and self-expression."

—John Tessitore, award-winning author for young adults,
author of *Muhammad Ali: The World's Champion*

Words, Words, Words provides creative and engaging games and activities that teachers can use to improve their students' vocabulary. Written for use with students in grades 7–12, the book is divided into thirty thematic units and offers four different ready-to-use activities for each group of words. Some of the classroom-tested activities include crossword puzzles, magic squares, jumbles, word finds, concealed quotations, and riddles.

Filled with creative games and activities, this resource will help your students to increase their vocabularies and have fun while they are doing it.

Grammar Grabbers! Ready-to-Use Games & Activities for Improving Basic Writing Skills

Jack Umstatter

Paper   ISBN: 0-13-042592-3
www.josseybass.com

Would you like to make learning grammar more fun for your students? Would you like to have more fun teaching it? *Grammar Grabbers!* is packed with more than 200 creative, involving, ready-to-use activities that give students the tools they need to use grammar more effectively in their writing and make the writing process more enjoyable. These challenging grammar games are all designed to spark and hold students' interest.

The activities are organized into eight sections focusing on the elements of grammar: Parts of Speech; Phrases and Clauses; Sentences; Usage; Mechanics; Grammar's Helpers; Grammar Games; Final Test.

They will help students learn to

- Identify the functions of main and subordinate clauses as well as prepositional and verbal phrases.
- Classify sentences according to structure and purpose.
- Review troublesome usage problems such as double negatives, misplaced modifiers, and incorrect pronouns or verbs.
- Counteract common problems in punctuation.

The activities can be used as introductions, reviews, or homework assignments. They feature a stimulating variety of formats, including crosswords, word finds, concealed quotations, cryptograms, scrambled and hidden words, riddles, magic squares, word generating wheels, jumbles and more, providing a range of options for every classroom occasion.

You'll find the 203 ready-to-use activities in *Grammar Grabbers!* give students in grades 4 and up the tools they need to use grammar more effectively in spoken and written communication. And as your students become more proficient and comfortable with grammar, they will become more eager to write!